ASIAN AMERICAN POLITICAL ACTION

ASIAN AMERICAN

POLITICAL ACTION

Suburban Transformations

James S. Lai

LYNNE
RIENNER
PUBLISHERS

BOULDER
LONDON

Published in the United States of America in 2011 by
Lynne Rienner Publishers, Inc.
1800 30th Street, Boulder, Colorado 80301
www.rienner.com

and in the United Kingdom by
Lynne Rienner Publishers, Inc.
3 Henrietta Street, Covent Garden, London WC2E 8LU

Library of Congress Cataloging-in-Publication Data
Lai, James S.
    Asian American political action : suburban transformations / James S. Lai.
        p.   cm.
    Includes bibliographical references and index.
    ISBN 978-1-58826-724-5 (hardcover : alk. paper)
    1. Asian Americans—Politics and government. 2. Asian Americans—Politics
and government—Case studies. 3. Immigrants—Political activity—United States.
4. Political participation—United States. 5. Suburbs—United States. 6. Suburban
life—United States. 7. United States—Politics and government—1989–
8. United States—Ethnic relations. I. Title.
    E184.A75L35   2011
    320.8089'95073—dc22
                                                                    2010026516

British Cataloguing in Publication Data
A Cataloguing in Publication record for this book
is available from the British Library.

Printed and bound in the United States of America

The paper used in this publication meets the requirements
of the American National Standard for Permanence of
Paper for Printed Library Materials Z39.48-1992.

5 4 3 2 1

To my parents,
Masako and Mingtan Lai,
for instilling in me their passion for politics and
for teaching me the important life lesson of
giving back to one's community

Contents

Illustrations

Tables

Maps

Figures

Acknowledgments

I am deeply indebted to my wife, Florence, who inspires me to strive for my best in every endeavor and to do so with humility, and to my sons, Ethan and Desmond, for sharing their unconditional love and laughter with me as I wrote this book. My brother Mark and his family and my sister-in-law Audrey and her family have also supported me since the beginning of my chosen profession.

Many others have helped me during the four-year process of writing the book, and they must also be acknowledged. If I have accidentally omitted some of these individuals, I offer my sincere apologies. My gratitude goes to all of my wonderful colleagues in the Political Science Department and the Ethnic Studies Program at Santa Clara University and also the Asian Pacific American Caucus for giving me the space, support, and opportunity to complete this project. In particular, I extend heartfelt thanks to my colleagues Andy Aoki, Kim Geron, Oki Takeda, Taeku Lee, Natalie Masuoka, Kathy Rim, Francisco Jiménez, Ramón Chacón, Pauline Nguyen, Janet Flammang, Laura Nichols, Juliana Chang, Eric Hanson, and Peter Minowitz for their personal and professional support. Atom Yee, dean of the College of Arts and Sciences, graciously allowed me to take a year sabbatical during 2007–2008 to conduct field research and awarded me a college travel grant to help fund research outside of California. Vice Provost Don Dodson kindly supported me with funds for indexing the book. Alex Friedman, my former Santa Clara University undergraduate research assistant, did a superb job in providing detailed portraits of Bellevue, Washington, and Montgomery County, Maryland, which made my job a lot easier when I performed fieldwork there. Caroline Reebs, a graduate of the University of Toronto; Sergio Martinez, a graduate of Santa Clara University; and Karen Tjhan, a current Santa Clara University student, provided research support for several sections in the book. Melany Dela Cruz and Oiyan

Poon created most of the maps featured at the beginning of each case study chapter.

I would not be in such a privileged position at Santa Clara University were it not for the support and guidance of my two most important graduate school mentors. Don T. Nakanishi, founder of the field of Asian American politics, who retired as director of the UCLA Asian American Studies Center in 2009 after more than thirty years of dedication and commitment to his many students, continues to inspire in me the vision that scholarly research and community service are not mutually exclusive. Michael B. Preston at the University of Southern California taught me about urban politics and the importance of multiracial coalition building that I apply each day whether it is in classroom teaching, academic program building, or electoral politics.

Two manuscript reviewers offered insightful comments and constructive suggestions for making the book better. Leanne Anderson, Jessica Gribble, Shena Redmond, and Diane Foose at Lynne Rienner Publishers provided me with great editorial suggestions.

Christine Chen, former director of APIAVote, and Daphne Kwok, former director of the Angel Island Foundation, delved into their extensive community networks throughout the country to help me identify various Asian American community and political leaders in the non-California suburbs, many of whose comments appear in these pages. The book is an embodiment of the tremendous efforts by these as well as other inspirational individuals around the nation who are committed to achieving political representation, social justice, and equality for their respective Asian American communities in today's multiracial and multiethnic cities. Without their dedication, vision, and public service, the book would never have materialized. And for this, I am greatly indebted. When people refer to the "Asian American community," the idea is that there is a sense of a national community. I truly felt this belief, time and time again, when meeting and interviewing many of the Asian American leaders in the suburbs represented throughout the book.

Beyond the statistical data, traces of the outward migration are evident on every street corner: Ethnic supermarkets and restaurants are growing in suburban areas, selling assortments of cultural ingredients and foods at lower prices than local grocery stores. Lotte Oriental Supermarket, a Korean-owned oriental foods market with stores in Rockville and Silver Spring, opened a new outlet in Ellicott City. And Jin Mi Oriental Market and Landover Oriental Food are Korean-specialty stores for shoppers in Beltsville and Landover. As immigrants concentrate in suburban areas, they bring the foods and stores that are part of their culture, which are changing the social and cultural dynamic of Maryland and the country.

—Esther Nguonly,
"Immigrant Populations Scatter into Outer Suburbs,"
Capital News Service, April 2007

One-third of Santa Clara County cities will be led by Asian-American mayors in the new year, all immigrants who seized the basics of U.S. civic life and climbed its leadership rungs into political history. Cupertino, Milpitas, Palo Alto, Saratoga and Sunnyvale will usher in 2007 municipal leaders born in Hong Kong, Japan, Taiwan and the Philippines.

—Jessie Mangaliman,
"Asian Americans Leapfrog into Politics:
Success Shows Immigrants Blending into American Life Faster,
Experts Say," *San Jose Mercury News*, December 2006

Asian American Political Pioneers in Suburbia

(clockwise from top left): Current California Assemblyman Van Tran, the first Vietnamese American elected to the Garden Grove, California, city council, in 2000 (photo courtesy of Van Tran); in 2007, Fitchburg, Massachusetts, elects 28-year-old Lisa Wong as the first minority mayor in the city's 243-year history (photo courtesy of Josh Reynolds); Asian Americans in Sugar Land, Texas, mobilize for Daniel Wong, the city's first Asian American council member, during his historic 2008 mayoral campaign (photo courtesy of Jonathan Fong); Kris Wang delivers a veteran memorial speech in Cupertino, California, after becoming the city's first Asian American female and third successive Chinese American council member, in 2003 (photo courtesy of Yeoman First Class Donna Lou Morgan).

Introduction

The United States is a nation of immigrants and suburbs. Every American can trace ancestral roots to an immigrant, and nearly one in two Americans today lives in some type of suburb (Oliver and Ha 2007). Over the past three decades, Asian American immigrants have circumvented the traditional twentieth-century gateways or large metropolises, such as Los Angeles and New York City, for new twenty-first-century gateways embodied in the form of small- to medium-sized suburbs (Li and Skop 2004; Massey 2008; Singer, Hardwick, and Brettell 2008). Such direct migration into small- and medium-sized suburbs is dramatically changing both the demographic and political characteristics of the respective local communities that Asian Americans have chosen to make their new home. Given this trend, I would be remiss to discuss contemporary immigrant politics without focusing on the local context of immigrant-influenced suburbs.

Political scholars have largely ignored the recent immigration trends to the suburbs when discussing immigrant political incorporation by focusing mainly on immigrant communities in large cities. These cities were the primary entryway for a majority of Asian American immigrants arriving in the United States before the Immigration and Nationality Act of 1965. Since this period, however, significant percentages of Asian American immigrants have moved directly to the suburbs due to the quota preferences given to those with high education and wealthy backgrounds as opposed to only those with working-class backgrounds.

The configuration of the Asian American community has been created and re-created through immigration policy since the early twentieth century. Asian Americans, perhaps more than any other racial group, benefited most from the Immigration and Nationality Act of 1965 because it finally allowed them to immigrate to the United States en masse with families and to sustain a future

1

generation after over forty years of racial exclusion dating back to the National Origins Act of 1924 (Chan 1991). Since 1965, Asian Americans have become one of the fastest-growing racial groups throughout the continental United States.

Map 1 illustrates the percentage of the Asian American population in each state and the rapid geographic dispersion of this community throughout the nation. While Hawaii and California respectively contain the largest Asian American populations at 42.8 percent and 12.1 percent, they are by no means alone. Tremendous demographic growth for Asian Americans has occurred in states located in major regions throughout the continental United States, such as Maryland, Virginia, Texas, New Jersey, and Illinois, states that have all seen double-digit growth of their respective Asian American communities from the previous decennial census.

The national geographic distribution of Asian Americans by states is due to the socioeconomic stratifications in their respective ethnic community settlement patterns. For example, while an overwhelming majority of foreign- and native-born Japanese and Filipino Americans choose to settle exclusively on the West Coast, a majority of the Southeast Asian refugee groups, such as the Hmong and Cambodian Americans, are located in the Midwest and the eastern states. Many of these emerging Asian American communities east of California are challenging traditional black and white race relations in their respective regions and cities.

As illustrated in Map 2, a clear majority of the Asian American populations by state are foreign-born or first-generation immigrants. In 2006, approximately 70 percent of the national Asian American population was foreign born, with a majority having been in the United States for less than thirty years. In all of these states, many immigrants have directly entered suburbs where Asian American immigrant social and economic networks exist through the process known as "gravitational migration." Asian American immigrants often do not randomly choose the suburbs they live in, unlike their refugee counterparts, who are typically sponsored by local churches and organizations in various suburbs throughout the nation.

Immigration undoubtedly continues to fuel the growth of the Asian American community today. In 2008, the national Asian American community reached over 14 million, or 5 percent of the nation's population, the largest percentage growth from the previous decennial census for any racial group in the country. During the period 2004 and 2005, more than half (52 percent) of the national Asian American population growth was due to new immigrants (Kelly 2010). Many of these immigrants have a wide range of socioeconomic backgrounds, from the highly educated to political refugees, all of whom have been vetted through a series of seven hierarchical preferences (Chan 1991). As a result of international economic restructuring, which facilitates the movement of transnational capital and skilled laborers, many Asian immigrants are

Map 1 Asian American Populations by States, US Census 2004 (in percentages)

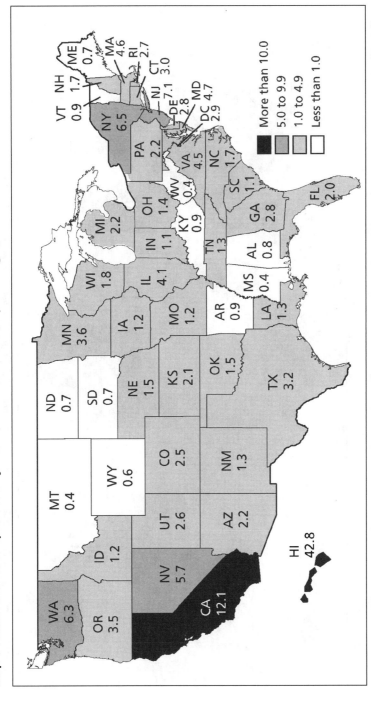

Source: Lai, James S., and Don T. Nakanishi, eds. 2007. *National Asian Pacific American Political Almanac.* Los Angeles, CA: UCLA Asian American Studies Press, p. 57.

Map 2 Asian American Foreign-Born Household Populations by States, US Census 2004

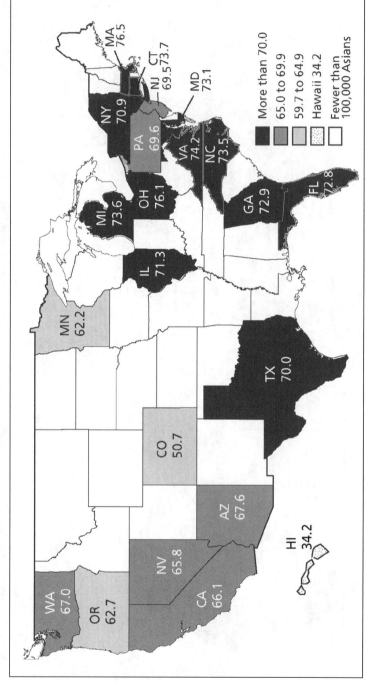

Legend:
- More than 70.0
- 65.0 to 69.9
- 59.7 to 64.9
- Hawaii 34.2
- Fewer than 100,000 Asians

MA 76.5
CT 69.5 73.7
NJ 69.5
MD 73.1
NY 70.9
PA 69.6
VA 74.2
NC 73.5
OH 76.1
MI 73.6
FL 72.8
GA 72.9
IL 71.3
MN 62.2
TX 70.0
CO 50.7
AZ 67.6
HI 34.2
NV 65.8
WA 67.0
OR 62.7
CA 66.1

Source: Lai, James S., and Don T. Nakanishi, eds. 2007. *National Asian Pacific American Political Almanac*. Los Angeles, CA: UCLA Asian American Studies Press, p. 60.

recruited to work in high-tech regions such as Silicon Valley in the Bay Area of Northern California, which currently contains two Asian American majority cities, Milpitas and Cupertino, according to US Census 2010 projections (Li and Skop 2004).

The results of such transnational movements have been major demographic growth in cities throughout California, where Asian Americans account for nearly 5 million of the state's total population (US Census 2004). In particular, Asian Americans are migrating in significant numbers to small- to medium-sized suburbs throughout Northern and Southern California. This effectively is transforming them from mostly white suburbs to Asian American majority and plurality suburbs and, in the process, changing both the demographic and political cultures of these cities.

Twentieth-century gateway cities still remain viable destinations and significant centers for recent Asian immigrant community formation, but this trend is not as large as it was several decades ago. For example, from 2000 to 2004, fewer than half (47 percent) of the Asian American population gains occurred in large cities compared to 53 percent during the 1990s (Li and Skop 2004). The significance of this trend is that suburbs are becoming the primary destination for both foreign- and US-born Asian Americans. According to one study, class issues have less effect on suburban settlement patterns among Asian Americans than in large cities. More affluent Asian immigrants choose to move directly to the suburbs as opposed to large cities because of their desire and ability to pay for newer homes in safer neighborhoods with better public schools, which are all factors that attract residents. Less affluent Asian American immigrants also choose to live in the outer rings of these small- to medium-sized suburbs in rental homes or apartments in order to have access to such public amenities, particularly the public school systems along with the emerging ethnic resources and networks (Li and Skop 2004).

New Asian American Community Formation Patterns, Pre-1965 vs. Post-1965

Small- to medium-sized (30,000 to 110,000 in total population) cities with significant Asian American populations defy the common stereotype of suburbs as mostly containing white populations as attributed to their flight away from metropolises. These Asian-influenced suburbs are also changing the traditional notions of Asian enclaves in large cities with regard to their demographic makeup due to ethnic clustering. Whereas the pre-1965 Asian enclaves composed of Chinatowns, Little Tokyos, and Manila Towns were monoethnic, self-contained urban ghettos, the post-1965 Asian American suburbs tend to be multiethnic and open to attract a diverse representation of Asian immigrants ranging from skill-based preferences to refugee resettlement. Subsequently, this has resulted in unique Asian American community formations and institutional development. With regard to the latter, the emergence of the ethnic media in print and electronic forms has rapidly developed in these small- to medium-sized suburbs that cater to the ethnic markets that are bilingual and transnational in character.

The demographic shifts of Asian American suburbs are only part of a larger picture because they have also served as the primary sites for their political incorporation. In the book, I examine how Asian American immigrants in ten suburb case studies are winning and sustaining elected representation in local governments throughout the nation, which is an important litmus test for measuring a group's political incorporation and power. Asian Americans have not demonstrated this measure of political power at any level in American politics until recently in these Transformed suburbs, which have two classifications, Types I and II. Transformed I suburbs are defined as large Asian American–populated cities where Asian Americans comprise 30 percent or more of the total city population, and Transformed II suburbs are small- to medium-sized Asian American–populated cities where Asian Americans comprise less than 30 percent of the total city population. Both Transformed I and II suburbs have attained medium to strong political incorporation that begins with descriptive, or racial and ethnic, representation that is facilitated by the development of key Asian American political loci (see Chapter 2, Table 2.1).

Unlike in large cities with significant Asian American populations, Asian-influenced suburbs throughout California and other states have witnessed

**New Asian American Community Formation Patterns,
Pre-1965 vs. Post-1965**

On the left, San Francisco's Chinatown, established in the 1840s, is the oldest urban Chinatown in North America. On the right, an Asian megamall in the suburb of Milpitas, California, in the Silicon Valley (photos courtesy of the author).

heightened political mobilization efforts, which have yielded some unprecedented political gains for their respective Asian American communities. Such political gains are sometimes met with resistance from the outgoing demographic majority in these suburbs, and can result in what is termed "tipping point" politics in the form of voter mobilization and retrenchment against Asian American candidates at the voting booth. As newly forming Asian American majorities in these suburbs take shape, it is understandable that such resistance will occur among the outgoing majority, particularly if the latter perceives the former as gaining political power too fast. Tipping point politics is evident in two of the Asian American–influenced suburbs that I examined (Cupertino, California, and Sugar Land, Texas), but remains a cautionary tale for all suburbs that are following similar demographic and political trajectories.

Asian American political incorporation in many of these Asian-influenced suburbs have extended beyond traditional political behaviors such as naturalizing and voting to include latter forms of political behavior, such as running for political office and participating in the making of public policies. The fruits of such local political incorporation efforts in the suburbs have challenged previous political behavior studies in American politics that suggest it takes decades for immigrant groups to become active in politics (Parenti 1967). Instead, it is often first-generation Asian Americans who are the political pioneers in their respective suburbs to run for elected office and mobilize both new and old voters and contributors into the political process along the way.

The political incorporation of Asian Americans in these suburbs does not occur overnight. It is the result of the conflation of the following community factors: substantial demographic shifts over a period of time, the development of Asian American political loci that serve multifaceted roles in the community, and the rise of Asian American candidates. In Chapters 5 through 13, maps are provided to capture these dramatic demographic shifts. Data from the 2000 US Census are used as the source for these maps; only the decennial census contains data for Asian American (racial and ethnic) populations as a percentage of the total population at the census tract level, which are reflected in the maps. Political incorporation begins with gaining Asian American elected representation at the local level, a litmus test for whether Asian Americans are becoming full partners in the democratic and decisionmaking processes in their communities. Central to their local political mobilization efforts are the multiple political loci in the Asian American community that are involved during group political mobilization in suburbs around Asian American candidates' campaigns, which I conceptualize and discuss in Chapter 2. I describe the unique challenges faced in attaining full or strong political incorporation in Asian-influenced suburbs in each of the ten case studies, which reveal both unique and similar internal and external factors.

A large foreign-born population has not completely impeded Asian American political mobilization and incorporation efforts in the suburbs. Newly emerging immigrant groups, along with the US born, have begun to make significant inroads into American politics similar to other minority groups before them. The prior perception of immigrant political behavior was that it was limited to early forms of political incorporation such as US naturalization, campaign contributions, and voting. Subsequent stages of political incorporation such as running for elected positions in local government were reserved for later generations because the immigrant generation either had been interested only in homeland politics or discouraged from participating fully in the political process in its respective homeland, which impeded its participation in American politics. Despite this common narrative, my findings illustrate otherwise.

Location is critical to understanding how Asian American group political mobilization and incorporation are taking shape and most likely to occur. African Americans and Mexican Americans have attained and sustained numerical gains in local and statewide descriptive representatives in both urban and rural contexts. But in contrast, Asian Americans are now demonstrating their ability to maintain and replicate political power in the form of racial and ethnic representatives in local governments to the point where they have attained majority representation within these suburbs. It is this ability to sustain political power that has eluded Asian Americans until recently within the context of small- to medium-sized suburbs, as I will demonstrate in the ten case studies in the book.

The respective histories of Asian American political mobilization and incorporation in these emerging suburbs are distinct. Each contains different Asian American communities, organizations, and political ideologies that have come to symbolize the complexities of this racial group. The development of these political factors that facilitate Asian American political action varies by suburbs, which explains the differences in chapter lengths for those suburbs that are much further along this political trajectory, such as Cupertino (Chapter 5), Garden Grove/Westminster (Chapter 6), and Bellevue (Chapter 10) than in suburbs such as Daly City (Chapter 11) and Fitchburg (Chapter 13). I carefully examine each separate case study to reveal the common and distinct political potentials and challenges of Asian Americans within a theoretical framework of group political mobilization. This framework is nuanced toward understanding Asian American politics in the suburban context due to the different stages of development of Asian American political loci. Only through such a theoretical approach can we understand why the level of Asian American political incorporation in these suburbs varies by city.

While each of the ten suburb cases in this book must be examined separately, comparative analyses can also reveal important insights. Each of the ten suburbs shows many similarities and differences of Asian American political incorporation in local government. Similarities include the incredible dedication of Asian American individual leaders and community groups in achieving this goal. Differences include internal Asian American ethnic group characteristics that may serve as an impediment to local political incorporation.

Despite these similarities and differences, an overwhelming number of Asian American candidates and elected officials whom I interviewed reiterated a common theme as to why they decided to run for local office in their respective suburbs. This theme is the necessity of giving back to the community and country that have given so much to them. This central message is at the heart of the book. Therefore, political incorporation efforts in such suburbs by Asian American groups are not an attempt to empower for group self-interest. Instead, the goal is to transform the local civic institutions so that they will mirror the changing constituency in the form of redistributing substantive policies such as public hiring, better schools, and community redevelopment in order to reflect its evolving needs. It is an effort to rectify the disconnection between the changing demographics of the general community and its elected representatives.

Achieving descriptive representation requires nuanced strategies by Asian American candidates for coalition building across racial lines. In order for Asian American candidates to construct winning local political coalitions in multiracial and ethnic suburbs that reflect these demographic shifts, the following factors must be present within the Asian American community: (1) strong leadership, (2) a unifying political ideology that transcends ethnic interests in favor of racial interests, and (3) a mobilization of developed political loci (e.g., community-based organizations, ethnic media) around the campaigns. These factors of Asian American political incorporation in the suburbs shed light on the understanding of the future trajectory of how successful multiracial coalitions that contain both racial minorities and whites can be constructed and maintained in minority-majority cities and states. As previous studies note, political incorporation is not the end goal, but the beginning, as progressive minority-led regimes must avoid focusing on zero-sum-game politics and instead focus on broader issues that resonate with the broader community to allow minority issues to make their way onto local, state, and national agendas (Hochschild and Rogers 2000). The result for Asian Americans has been a level of group political mobilization and incorporation in local and state politics not experienced before in American politics.

1

The Suburbanization
of Asian American Politics

The two-mile section of Stevens Creek Boulevard that runs through the city of Cupertino, California, reveals the major demographic shifts occurring in many small- to medium-sized suburbs, which have become the initial destinations for a majority of Asian American immigrants arriving in the continental United States over the past three decades. These emerging new gateway suburbs are in stark contrast to the self-contained ethnic enclaves found in large cities such as San Francisco, Los Angeles, and New York City. Cupertino, named by its Spanish settlers after the Arroyo San José de Cupertino, grew from a small rural village among the fruit orchards to a Silicon Valley suburb. Since the 1980s, Cupertino has gradually shifted from a suburb with an overwhelming white majority to one where Asian Americans are the majority as of 2010.

According to the 2000 US Census, Cupertino is currently home to approximately 33,000 Asian Americans, or nearly 45 percent of the city population. The store space that once contained a Le Boulanger sandwich shop is occupied by Lee's Sandwiches, a popular Vietnamese American eatery chain that specializes in French Vietnamese sandwiches and other Asian delicacies. Many of its patrons are white and Asian American. Further down Stevens Creek Boulevard, a variety of Asian restaurants, grocery stores, and small businesses have replaced prior businesses in their respective small strip malls. The economic opportunity to cater to the city's demographic changes has led one Hong Kong investment group to develop Cupertino Village, the city's first pan-Asian shopping and eatery mall, where Korean, Chinese, Taiwanese, Japanese, and Vietnamese restaurants and stores can be found. Many Asian and white faces fill the community pages of the local newspaper, the *Cupertino Courier,* along with home listings that feature many Asian American realtors. One realtor touts that she has a "real Ph.D. with a Ph.D.'s quality of service," and the most ubiquitous and important line in home listings is directly aimed at many Asian American immigrant parents, "located in the Cupertino school district" ("Daphne Chou" 2010). Indeed, Cupertino public schools have earned an international reputation for their consistent placement among the state schools' highest test scores in math and science. And it is not surprising that this reputation has found its way across the Pacific Ocean to major cities in Asia, such as Taipei, Seoul, Mumbai, Ho Chi Minh City, and Hong Kong, due primarily to the ethnic print media, which connects many of its transnational immigrant communities to their respective homelands.

Aside from these demographic and cultural shifts, Cupertino is undergoing political changes as well. This small suburb, which is famous for being the headquarters of Apple Computer, is now also regarded as the archetypeal twenty-first-century California suburb (Brown 2004). Situated at the heart of the city's public affairs is the Cupertino Civic Center, a modest one-story building where the city council and mayor regularly meet, which serves as the epicenter of a dramatic political shift in the city. Cupertino is the microcosm of a larger movement taking shape in Santa Clara County in which the suburb represents one of the most successful sites of Asian American political incorporation of any continental United States city over the past decade. Since 1998, four Asian Americans (three immigrants and one US born) have been elected at different times, paralleling the demographic shifts of this city during the past thirty years. For example, in the November 2007 citywide election, former Cupertino city planning commissioner Gilbert Wong became the first US-born Chinese American to win a city council seat, along with incumbent city council member Kris Wang, who in 2005 became the city's first Chinese American woman to be elected. Three other Asian American candidates were among the field of six candidates, marking for the first time in the city's history that a majority (five) of the city council candidates were of Asian descent (Smartvoter 2007).[1]

The above description of Cupertino could easily be replaced in name by other emerging Asian American–influenced suburbs that have demographically and politically transformed, from Bellevue, Washington, to Sugar Land, Texas, to Potomac, Maryland. The political success of Asian Americans in the suburban context sheds light on the predominant geopolitical site where Asian Americans have achieved the greatest degree of local political incorporation in states like California, where Asian Americans currently account for nearly 13 percent of the statewide population (US Census 2004).

One of the central theses of this book is that the pathways to local political incorporation for Asian Americans are moving faster in the suburban context than in the metropolitan context, which primarily defined this community's development in the previous century. It is precisely within this small- and medium-sized suburban context that Asian American immigrant politics has changed the location and ways that political scientists understand contemporary immigrant political participation in the United States. And as I will argue and demonstrate, this represents the key site for understanding the contemporary and future trajectories of Asian Americans in American politics.

As is true in real estate, the same can be said for Asian American politics: location matters. Where Asian American politics matters most is in the suburbs. This is where Asian Americans have demographically transformed and subsequently have attained the greatest political inroads to achieving local political incorporation beginning with electing Asian American candidates. What differs in this suburban context from that in the urban context is that Asian Americans have been able to sustain elected representation. And in some cities, they have built on this to attain a majority presence on city councils so that decisionmaking on policies takes into account the interests of the entire communities they represent.

The Global and Local Dimensions of Asian American–Influenced Suburbs

What exactly is a suburb? The struggles of scholars and journalists to answer this question are reflected in the competing terminologies used to define a suburb, such as inner suburbs, mature suburbs, true exurbs, edge cities, and outer-ring cities (Lang and Sanchez 2006; Teixeira 2006). In this book, the term *suburb* will align with the US Census Bureau's definition of any city within a metropolitan area with a major city containing a population of a minimum of 50,000 (Gibson 1998). These periphery cities typically are interconnected and dependent on the larger core city in a myriad of economic and political ways, including population size, economic composition, land use, city age, and political institutions (Oliver 2001). Historically, such areas have been racially homogenous, containing mostly whites, but recent immigration trends have found many immigrants from non-European countries, particularly from Asia and Latin America, relocating directly in these types of suburbs due to gravitational migration to preestablished ethnic networks (Massey 2008).

Asian American–influenced suburbs with large transnational Asian immigrant populations represent a new mode of suburb that is not an ethnic enclave associated with the early twentieth century, such as Chinatowns and Japan Towns, but rather a globalized and localized city. Past studies of the pre-1965 Asian American immigrant communities in the United States detail the social structure and development of self-contained "ghettos" (R. H. Lee 1949; Lyman 1970; Daniels 1971). These communities were predominantly composed of Chinese, Japanese, and Filipino contract laborers who comprised the first three major waves to enter the continental United States during the early twentieth century. Since the 1970s, the Asian American community in the continental United States has changed as a result of globalization, transnationalism, and cosmopolitanism (Kwong 1996; Li 1998a, 1998b; T. Fong 2003; V. Miller 2004).

Three important changes that have influenced and impacted Asian American community formation in the United States are the following: (1) the passage of the 1965 Immigration and Nationality Act, which allowed immigration from Asia to be on equal footing with European immigration for the first time in US history; (2) the shift in American attitudes toward Asian people; and (3) the industrialization of Asia.

Recent studies indicate that significant numbers of the contemporary Asian American immigrant communities in the United States, both suburban and urban, are not only localized, but globalized as well (Kwong 1996; Li 1998a, 1998b; T. Fong 2003; V. Miller 2004). Examples of this can be seen in the emergence of international businesses that cater to Asian American immigrant communities. For example, the fast-food franchises of Goldilocks Bakeshop and Jollibee, which cater primarily to the Filipino American communities in Sacramento and Daly City, California, and Vancouver, Canada, are local branches of a global enterprise based in the Philippines. An example in the Taiwanese American community is the Ten Ren Tea Company from Taiwan, which has 110 branches internationally, including 45 branches throughout the continental United States. Asian global banks, such as Far East National Bank and Bank of India, are branching to their respective nationals in the suburbs (Fong 2003). The suburb of Monterey Park, California, located in Los Angeles County, was the first continental US city to take on such global and local dynamics within its majority Chinese and Taiwanese American communities (Li 1998a, 1998b).

The emergence of the ethnic print media, particularly ethnic newspapers, has fostered a global or transnational outlook among many of the Asian American immigrants in these transformed suburbs. Examples of such ethnic newspapers are the *Korea Times,* the *World Journal,* and *Viet Bao,* all of which promote a transnational perspective among their respective Asian American ethnic immigrant and refugee readers through their coverage of global news occurring in their respective native homelands. Such ethnic media also promote existing ethnic networks in Asian-influenced suburbs that facilitate transnational movement toward these cities.

Global and local Asian American immigrant suburbs illustrate the trend that contemporary Asian American community formation in the United States, similar to that of Latinos, is rapidly occurring in the suburban context due to gravitational migration factors rather than the pre-1965 community formation in large gateway cities. This is resulting in a different type of community of Asian immigrants who are more affluent and highly educated, all precursors to political mobilization in local politics. According to one telling 2004 US census finding, 40 percent of immigrants from Asia and Latin America were moving from abroad directly into a suburb in the United States (Roberts 2007). Many of these Asian immigrants, both old and new, purposely chose to live in these suburbs for the same reasons many others chose to live there: the presence of strong public schools and the feeling of safety. However, for Asian

Americans, there are even more reasons to move to these suburbs, such as the establishment of ethnic networks and the presence of strong Asian American communities. Many transnational suburbs develop a local and an international reputation not only for their strong public school systems, which many real estate agents focus on when advertising home sales in international ethnic daily newspapers such as the *World Journal,* but also for being communities that are hospitable to Asian American immigrants and small businesses.

Political Awakenings in Suburbia

Demographic shifts and political mobilization efforts by these emerging communities in the suburbs are part and parcel of each other. For the first time in US history, multiple small- to medium-sized cities throughout California contain significantly large Asian American populations that have allowed Asian American candidates to mobilize Asian Americans and non-Asian constituents through panethnic or multiracial coalition strategies along with the various community political loci that serve as important allies. As a result, Asian Americans are beginning for the first time to elect, reelect, and replace outgoing Asian American candidates in city government in these suburbs. And in some cities, as I will show in Chapter 7 with Japanese Americans in Gardena, a suburb of Los Angeles, they have been the majority racial group on the city council and a strong partner in its governing coalitions for two generations.

Asian Americans have not been able to demonstrate elected sustainability or the ability to replace coethnic elected officials in state- and local-level positions in California, a limitation of group political power and incorporation in American politics. Although California contains the largest percentage of Asian American population of any state in the continental United States, Asian Americans have struggled to replace symbolic Asian American elected officials at the state and local levels with fellow coethnics. This is starkly true for state-level positions such as the California State Assembly. One recent study found that, among the thirteen Asian Americans who were elected to the State Assembly from 1960 to 2004, none were replaced by coethnics. In comparison, 81.3 percent of Latino Democrats and 85.0 percent of black Democrats were replaced by coethnics during this period (Guerra 2004). Reasons why the state level has not been the primary context for Asian American descriptive representation (minority elected representation) are tied to structural barriers such as political redistricting, which has resulted in few Asian American–concentrated state districts due to size of the districts and the geographic dispersion of the Asian American population, along with the need for bilingual voting materials. These factors as well as other cultural factors have contributed to low statewide Asian American voter registration and turnout rates in comparison to other racial groups.

In local-level politics, traditional gateway cities such as Los Angeles, San Francisco, and New York City, which have served as primary entryways for Asian immigrants into the United States, have had little Asian American elected representation during their respective cities' histories. In Los Angeles, only one Asian American (Michael Woo) has served on the fifteen-member city council. In San Francisco, since 2000, only two Asian Americans (Chinese Americans Fiona Ma and Ed Jew) have been elected to the eleven-member board of supervisors. In New York City, only one Asian American (John Liu), who has served in District 20 since 2002, has ever been elected to serve on the fifty-one-member city council. Each of these three cities has had a long history of Asian American immigration and community formation. According to the US Census, both New York City and Los Angeles contain the two largest aggregate Asian American populations in the continental United States (US Census 2004). San Francisco contains one of the largest Asian American populations as a percentage of the total city population at 33 percent for any continental United States city with a population over 700,000 (US Census 2004).

Yet despite these large population bases, why have Asian American candidates struggled in large gateway cities to win elected representation in them? The case study of Michael Woo's 1993 Los Angeles mayoral election in Chapter 4 sheds light on this salient question. Many reasons exist, including the most obvious ones that relate directly to the demographic characteristics of the Asian American community, particularly low US naturalization rates and voter turnout among those naturalized and registered to vote. Other reasons include formal electoral procedures outside of the naturalization and registration argument, such as district elections versus citywide elections. In many large cities, district elections are the norm based on US Supreme Court decisions related to the Voting Rights Act of 1965 and minority voter dilution. For African Americans and Latinos, this approach is logical given their respective community demographic settlement patterns and homogenous socioeconomic characteristics, which tend to create large minority communities.

Since the immigration reforms of 1965, a broader socioeconomic range of Asian immigrants has arrived, consisting of both highly educated and working class immigrants as opposed to the previous working class majority that arrived before the 1960s. As a result, Asian Americans tend to be one of the most residentially dispersed minority racial groups in the United States. Few Asian American majority districts exist in large cities, which makes it harder for Asian American candidates to mobilize their racial and ethnic voters in district elections. The impact of these demographic characteristics and formal election rules in large cities is limited political success of Asian American candidates not only in winning local elected positions, but also in sustaining and building on political representation in city politics throughout the United States. And finally, another important explanation for the lack of Asian American elected representation in large cities is the fact that such cities have entrenched political party machines that have prohibited and intimidated Asian American immigrants from running for office given their lack of the social and political networks that are needed to win in highly contested political districts.

The historic inability to elect and to sustain Asian American elected representation in California statewide positions has not been the case in the state's small- and medium-sized cities. The reason is that these suburbs tend to be recently incorporated cities, often less than fifty years old, that are undergoing constant shifts in their primary economic industries, population size, and racial and ethnic makeup. All of these factors have limited the entrenchment of political machines in the suburbs.

As gravitational migration of Asian American immigrants to specific suburbs has simultaneously occurred during the past three decades due to reasons ranging from emerging ethnic economies to strong public schools, these suburbs have been beneficial to Asian American candidates in the following ways:

1. They have provided Asian American candidates with a sense of political empowerment as they have witnessed their community grow with limited to no political representation in city governments.
2. As a result of the first point, Asian American immigrant candidates have been more inclined to run.
3. Many of these Asian American candidates have been highly educated and economically successful immigrants themselves, which challenges the notion among sociologists and political scientists that immigrants are less likely to participate in the political process as voters and candidates than the second generation. This represents one of the major political behavior characteristics of Asian American immigrants that is uniquely different from other minority immigrant groups because of the high percentages of professionals and highly educated members in their community that have been vetted through rigorous US immigration policies.

The high degree of political participation of Asian American immigrants that extends beyond voting is attributed to what I term the "entrepreneurial spirit." This spirit has defined many of the post-1965 Asian American immigrants or first generation who have left the safe confines of their traditional homelands to seek greater social, economic, and political opportunities in a foreign country where they could not speak the language and had few family members. Such entrepreneurial traits are transferable and advantageous in the electoral arena where candidates must demonstrate the wherewithal to run for public office. For Asian American immigrants who have succeeded in their professions and businesses and have their homes in the suburbs, political participation has provided a perfect way to give back to both the Asian American and general communities.

The success of Asian American candidates in small- and medium-sized suburbs is largely determined by their working in coordination with a complex network of political actors or loci within the Asian American community (see Chapter 2, Figure 2.2). The various Asian American political loci that have formed over the past thirty years include panethnic community-based organizations, the ethnic print media, and Asian American political operatives who understand the nuances of how to reach out to and mobilize the ethnically diverse Asian American communities. Each of these political loci mobilizes community support both within and outside of the city districts around Asian American candidates' campaigns and serves as an important political ally for candidates who choose to utilize them in their campaign strategies.

The size of the Asian American populations in these suburbs is merely a precursor to Asian American political incorporation and not a sole determinant because the racial group must have a large number of registered voters (Browning, Marshall, and Tabb 2003). Asian American candidates must pursue a two-tiered campaign strategy that is necessary for electoral success in cities regardless of the size of the Asian American population. Those tiers are (1) a guiding racialized political ideology that emphasizes Asian American empowerment and mobilization, which attempts to transcend ethnic divisions; and (2) a simultaneous building of cross-racial alliances.

Forming a Critical Mass: The Emergence of Asian American–Majority and –Plurality Suburbs

The suburban dimension of Asian American politics represents an important phenomenon for understanding current and future political and demographic trajectories of Asian Americans in the United States (Oliver 2001; Oliver and Ha 2007). In 2000, 51 percent of Asian Americans nationally lived in suburbs compared to 33 percent of African Americans, 45 percent of Latinos, and 54 percent of whites (Jones-Correa 2004). As a result of the suburbanization phenomenon, Asian Americans have been able to achieve in these suburbs a critical mass of the cities' total populations, which other racial minority groups have historically enjoyed in local politics and parlayed into various levels of local political incorporation (Browning, Marshall, and Tabb 2003). In several cases throughout California, the community formations and settlement patterns have resulted in a new phenomenon: Asian American–majority cities.

Asian American–majority cities are both a suburban and a contemporary phenomenon in the continental United States. In the 1970s, no continental US city contained a majority Asian American population base. In the 1980s, one exception was the Los Angeles suburb of Monterey Park, a city located in the San Gabriel Valley region of Los Angeles County. Monterey Park was labeled the "first suburban Chinatown" and has an Asian American–majority population

(61.8 percent in 2000) that has achieved strong descriptive representation on the city council (Fong 1994). Twenty years later, based on US Census figures, six California cities contained Asian American majority populations.[2] All of the six California Asian American–majority cities are small- and medium-sized in total population, ranging from 30,000 to 110,000 (Lewis and Ramakrishnan 2004). For instance, the small suburb of Milpitas located in Silicon Valley had a total population of approximately 63,000 in 2000, 52 percent of the total population, compared to 12.2 percent in 1980.

As Asian Americans have become the majority or plurality in small- to medium-sized suburbs in California, Asian American candidates have found success in winning and sustaining descriptive representation in citywide offices. According to political incorporation theory, the following three components are necessary for strong minority political mobilization: strong community-based organizations, political maturity in minority communities, and a sizable minority population (Browning, Marshall, and Tabb 2003). Given the right conditions and strategies, Asian American candidates can effectively politically mobilize the majority and plurality Asian American populations. Asian American elected officials on city councils are beginning to challenge and become part of dominant coalitions. This has led to strong local political incorporation, which I define as sustaining descriptive representation, gaining key appointments to citywide commissions, and having a stronger presence on city councils.

Class also plays an important role in the location and context of Asian American community formation. As an Asian immigrant professional and white-collar working class is vetted through hierarchical preferences in federal immigration policy, Asian American political incorporation is occurring more rapidly in globalized and localized sites. For example, according to a 2007 update by the US Census Bureau, Santa Clara County witnessed the nation's fastest-growing Asian immigration for any US county from July 2006 to July 2007, growing nearly 3.3 percent, a total increase of 17,614 Asian immigrants (Swift 2007).

While Asian American–majority cities are prevalent in California, even more suburbs contain Asian American–plurality populations where no majority race exists. In the San Gabriel Valley region of Los Angeles County, for example, Asian Americans have a plurality in the following eight small- to medium-sized suburbs: San Marino (49 percent), San Gabriel (49 percent), Rosemead (49 percent), Alhambra (47 percent), Arcadia (45 percent), Diamond Bar (43 percent), Temple City (39 percent), and Hacienda Heights (36 percent) (US Census 2004). Many of these suburbs are also beginning to witness political transformations as first-time Asian American candidates are being elected to their respective local governments.

The suburbanization of Asian American politics represents a new dimension that is both unprecedented and uniquely different from African Americans and Latinos in local politics. This is due to the fact that the suburbs are the primary level of elected representation for Asian American candidates in American politics today, most visibly coming to fruition in the past decade. For instance, in January 2007, five Asian American mayors (Otto Lee in Sunnyvale, Kris Wang in Cupertino, Jose Estevez in Milpitas, Yoriko Kishimoto in Palo Alto, and Aileen Kao in Saratoga), all immigrants, were sworn into office in Santa Clara County, California, the most for any county at any one time in the continental United States. Such examples challenge the existing notions by social scientists that immigrant incorporation, such as running for elected office, occurs over time—sometimes generations.

Santa Clara County, located in the southern region of the Northern California Bay Area and internationally known as Silicon Valley, is one of the geographic areas most visibly and rapidly undergoing the suburban transformation of suburbs to ethnoburbs in the continental United States. Similar trends are also taking shape in other small- to medium-sized suburbs throughout metropolitan Southern California, particularly in the San Gabriel Valley portion of Los Angeles County and the Little Saigon area of Orange County, as well as in suburbs near large gateway cities in key geographic regions throughout the United States.

Aside from these major demographic shifts occurring in suburbs, little systemic research exists that has examined Asian American or general immigrant political incorporation in the suburban context. Scholars are beginning to study the systemic influences of suburbanization on local electoral politics (Oliver 2001; Oliver and Ha 2007). Others provide unique typologies of understanding residential flight from urbanized core regions into areas such as mature suburbs, inner suburbs, and exurbs (Lang and Sanchez 2006; Teixeira 2006). These studies all offer important insights on race and ethnicity in the suburban context such as the global and local context of suburbs in states like California, where Asian Americans have played an instrumental role in transforming demographically, economically, and politically during the past thirty years. Only recently have political scientists begun to examine the local context of suburbanization in immigrant political incorporation and its barriers (Lai and Geron 2006; Frasure 2007). The tremendous shifts in these small- to medium-sized suburbs throughout the United States, particularly in California, have led to various tensions (both perceived and real) between long-term and recent residents (T. Fong 1994; J. C. Fong 2003; Hwang 2005).

Focus and Organization of the Book

The primary theoretical focus of this book is on the complex processes associated with Asian American political mobilization in the attempts of their candidates to win greater political incorporation in suburbs. I also explain the reasons why Asian Americans have been more successful in gaining the political ends they seek in certain suburbs. The successes and challenges of the local political incorporation attempts by Asian Americans in the suburban context shed new light on immigrant political incorporation of a still relatively understudied racial group, particularly in a state like California where immigrants will become the future majority population. Immigrant politics, both Asian American and Latino, will play an important future role in determining the political trajectory of California. For Asian Americans, local government is where they have a chance to make the greatest influence in California politics and beyond in such suburban contexts.

Half of the suburb case studies in this book are from California because that state remains a central destination within the Asia–United States diaspora and community settlement patterns of Asian Americans, containing 35 percent of the racial group's national population. However, the suburbanization of Asian American politics is not only a California phenomenon. The other suburbs that I examine in the book reflect the major regions of the United States: Sugar Land, Texas (Southwest); Eau Claire, Wisconsin (Midwest); Montgomery County, Maryland (Middle Atlantic); Bellevue, Washington (Northwest); and Fitchburg, Massachusetts (North Atlantic). I look at these five non-California suburbs to show how these sites are similar, dissimilar, or both to the theoretical models developed from the California case studies on Asian American local political incorporation.

While the above suburbs are certainly not the only cities that are undergoing major Asian immigration in the United States, the reasons that I selected these ten suburb cases were based on the criterion that each city has attained some level of political incorporation, beginning with the election of descriptive representatives. Thus, a suburb such as Flushing, New York, would not fit the criterion of Asian American descriptive representation because an Asian American has yet to be elected to a local position, although political mobilization is beginning to occur.

The organization of the book is based on four foundations. In the first foundation (Chapters 1 and 2), I establish the small- to medium-sized suburb as the primary site for Asian American political mobilization, and then offer an analytical framework for examining the suburban dimensions of group political mobilization and define the key Asian American political loci involved during this process. In the second foundation (Chapters 3 and 4), by discussing four historical to contemporary stages, I provide a comprehensive understanding of the evolution of Asian American politics that has led to the suburbs as the primary site. My argument that context (internal and external community factors) is important for understanding why and how successful Asian American political incorporation occurs is framed by the large city versus suburban dichotomy, and is highlighted with the 1993 Los Angeles mayoral election. With these challenges in metropolises, the suburbs allow greater insights into processes of Asian American political mobilization and incorporation, as reflected in the Asian American suburban typologies. In the third foundation (Chapters 5–13),

I examine the ten suburbs through the book's analytical framework (Chapter 2, typologies (Chapter 2, Table 2.1). Each of these typologies helps to explain the external (e.g., the formal rules of a local government) and internal community factors (e.g., political loci) that are necessary for political incorporation to occur. As each of the suburb case studies demonstrates, these external and internal factors play instrumental roles in determining the extent of Asian American political incorporation in their respective cities. In the final foundation (Chapter 14), I discuss the future political trajectories of Asian Americans based on the findings in the ten suburbs and interracial dynamics in multiracial states like California. I also identify the steps that must be taken to ensure continued group political incorporation while participating in multiracial coalitions in local- and state-level politics.

Research Questions

In order to address the main theoretical focus in explaining the processes associated with Asian American political mobilization and incorporation in the suburban context, I address the following research questions:

1. What political loci need to be present in the Asian American community in order for successful group political mobilization and incorporation to occur?
2. What factors exist within and outside of the Asian American community that facilitate and impede political incorporation efforts?
3. How can such Asian American political loci be conceptualized in a suburban model of group political mobilization and incorporation, and how does it differ from previous models for urban cities?
4. What types of campaign strategies do successful Asian American candidates pursue in Asian-influenced suburbs, and how do these differ from other candidates?
5. In what ways do Asian American candidates and the various Asian American political loci, such as the ethnic media, influence group political mobilization and behavior in the Asian American community both within and outside of their respective political districts?

Key Terms and Methodologies

Descriptive Representation and Political Incorporation

One of the key and initial strategies employed by Asian Americans, as seen with other racial minorities, to gain a stronger voice on city councils is running and electing their own racial and ethnic candidates. I refer to this goal as *descriptive representation,* which is defined as electing a representative from one's constituents, including one's racial or ethnic group (Pitkin 1967; Mansbridge 1999). Previous studies have illustrated that minority descriptive representation is the first step to attaining group influence in city governments (Henry 1994; Takash 1999; Pelissero, Holian, and Tomaka 2000).

There are many ways to define the concept of *political incorporation.* One definition of political incorporation is the extent to which a minority group is effectively represented in local policymaking concerning issues of greatest interest to them (Browning, Marshall, and Tabb 1984; Henry 1994). Scholars, such as Lawrence Fuchs, conceptualize the successful political incorporation of immigrants to reflect a three-stage process: (1) the development of various mutual assistance associations that focused on immigrants' initial welfare needs, (2) the creation of economic community institutions such as small banks and ethnic businesses to provide economic opportunities and to address economic needs, and (3) group political mobilization through the American political process (Fuchs 1990, 342–349). In the third stage, group political mobilization, the following outcomes or levels regarding the political incorporation of minority groups in local governments are most likely to occur: (1) exclusion or no political incorporation in which the group is completely shut out by the dominant governing coalition; (2) medium political incorporation, or a minority group's ability to win descriptive representation (coethnic officeholders); and (3) strong political incorporation or substantive authority and influence. The latter refers to the institutionalization of group interests in city politics that extends beyond descriptive representation, as measured by resource allocation, city appointments, and membership in the dominant governing coalition (Browning, Marshall, and Tabb 1984).

Examining Local Political Incorporation Through Case Studies

I utilize case studies in the book to examine and determine the extent of Asian American local political incorporation in each of the ten suburbs. The discussion of the various case studies will help to develop my main thesis that suburban contexts allow for greater mobilization of various Asian American political loci around Asian American candidates' campaigns than do large cities. The Cupertino, and Garden Grove and Westminster case studies (Chapters 5 and 6, respectively) illustrate that Asian American candidates in the small- and medium-sized suburbs can mobilize constituencies and create group consciousness through their campaigns within city limits due to the large Asian American populations. In both case studies, Asian American candidates have been successful, winning key elections and gaining greater political incorporation in city governments. All of the ten suburb cases illustrate the growing influence of both traditional and nontraditional modes on group political mobilization in the Asian American community: the ethnic print media, community-based organizations, and the growing salience of a panethnic Asian American identity among voters, contributors, and candidates.

Despite the relative success that Asian Americans have achieved in certain suburbs, there continue to be many challenges. For example, the Daly City case study (Chapter 11) illustrates the barriers that remain in California suburbs for Asian American candidates. In this case, Filipino Americans lack political representation even though they constitute the city's major ethnic group (31.7 percent) in the largest Asian American–majority city in California. Many of these challenges reflect ethnic-specific barriers that have prevented unified, not necessarily strong, Filipino American community-based organizations from being created, and the subsequent lack of a strong ideology to unify both the Filipino American and Asian American communities in Daly City.

I offer the 1993 Los Angeles mayoral case study (Chapter 4) as an example to illustrate the limitations of Asian American political incorporation in the large city context for Asian American candidates. In this case, Michael Woo realized that, even though it was large, the Asian American population base was not united and was difficult to mobilize due to competing interests and ideologies. This led Woo's campaign consultants to pursue strategies outside of the city limits to tap into Asian American group consciousness in the form of campaign contributions from smaller suburbs in over eleven states.

Panethnicity and the Gradual Formation of an Asian American Group Consciousness in Local Politics

Throughout this book, I use two important terms—*panethnicity* and *group consciousness*—to discuss the impact of Asian American candidates on Asian American populations both within and outside of city districts. Previous studies indicate that such a panethnic identity is taking shape among Asian Americans in general. A groundbreaking 2004 multilingual survey of multiethnic Asian American voters examines the formation of a panethnic identity in large cities like Los Angeles, Chicago, San Francisco, and New York City. The survey investigates panethnic identity in the following three ways: common and shared cultural traits, ethnic self-identification, and shared group fate. The survey results indicate a panethnic identity is gradually forming, particularly in regard to shared group fate. That is, what happens to one Asian ethnic group is likely to adversely affect other Asian ethnic groups (Lien, Conway, and Wong 2004).

Group political consciousness represents self-identification among minorities and helps to promote group mobilization around racialized identities and, ultimately, a group's willingness to participate in the political system (P. D. McClain and Stewart 2006). Minority candidates and their respective campaigns can play an important role in facilitating this process. The formation of racial group consciousness and identity around Asian American elected officials and candidates is a relevant application for understanding Asian American politics in California local elections for several reasons. First, California contains nearly 35 percent of the entire Asian American population in the continental United States. Second, the local level currently serves as the primary and most successful entryway for Asian American candidates into California government. In particular, small- and medium-sized suburbs have been the primary context for successful Asian American campaigns for city council positions in comparison to other larger cities (Lai and Geron 2006).

One theoretical lens often used to examine Asian American group identification has been the panethnic or pan–Asian American identity (Espiritu 1992; Lai 2000a). The impact of Asian Americans on any level of American politics has centered on the important question of whether Asian Americans can vote and form panethnic coalitions as a racial bloc around Asian American candidates and related issues as opposed to pursing divisive ethnic politics (Nakanishi 1991; Lai 2000b). As past elections have demonstrated, the presence of a strong Asian American candidate can bridge cultural and political differences while bringing new Asian American voters into the political process (Rodriguez 1998). The construction of a panethnic identity is slowly emerging among the majority immigrant Asian population in the United States. For example, one recent national study of Asian American voter attitudes found that a majority (60 percent) of its respondents stated that they would vote for another Asian American candidate, regardless of ethnicity, over a non-Asian if the two were equally qualified (Lien, Conway, and Wong 2004).

The term *panethnicity* dates from the late 1960s, and connotes the ability of diverse ethnic groups to view their interests and identities as a collective racial group (Espiritu 1992; Wei 1993; Espiritu and Ong 1994). For Asian Americans, this concept has been operationalized as sociopsychological factors, such as perceived discrimination due to race, knowledge of their leaders, support for race-based policy issues (e.g., affirmative action and the redress movement for Japanese Americans), intermarriage, shared cultural values, and linked fate (Lien 1997; Lien et al. 2001).The underlying goal of those who embrace panethnicity is to unify diverse groups based on their common racial categorization rather than their ethnic heritage. A panethnic strategy represents an important strategy among Asian American political activists due to the lack of Asian-majority districts and an increasingly diverse Asian and Pacific Islander population (Espiritu 1992).

Although panethnicity may represent one means to attain the end of greater political representation, it is by no means a guaranteed strategy of success within the larger Asian American community. The factors that diminish a cohesive racial identity include differences in socioeconomic background, such as education and income, generation issues, and homeland politics (Espiritu 1992; Wei 1993; Espiritu and Ong 1994; Lien 1997; Lien, Conway, and Wong 2004). Cross-ethnic unity in the electoral arena can by no means be taken for granted;

panethnic coalitions do not automatically materialize. They are a constructed phenomenon shaped by the efforts of elected officials and candidates, the ethnic print media, and community-based organization leaders. Despite the gradual construction of a group identity within the Asian American community, group political mobilization around an Asian American candidate will not be possible without the development and support of Asian American elected officials and community leaders. We need only to look at failed panethnic coalitions in California State Assembly districts (e.g., the 1991 District 46 special election and the 2003 District 20 primary election) to see how difficult such coalitions are to construct and maintain.

The development of Asian American suburbs has challenged this perception of the inability to form panethnic coalitions in local politics. This is due primarily to the fact that, in such suburbs, Asian Americans constitute either a majority or plurality and the importance of issue saliency has facilitated group consciousness and mobilization around particular goals or racial projects. The importance of public schools and political representation constitute examples of common issue saliency in California suburbs like Cupertino. In effect, the suburban context has allowed Asian American candidates to consolidate various political loci within the Asian American community around common interests and ideology, which are necessary to building viable coalitions. These factors are more likely to take root in small- to medium-sized cities given the right conditions and candidates.

The existing electoral mobilization literature demonstrates that African American and Mexican American candidates have positive effects on their respective groups' political participation, particularly in voter turnout (Barreto 2007). The theoretical debate on racial and ethnic group mobilization centers on the distinction between group identification and group consciousness (Jackson 1991). Scholars of group identification focus on the unique characteristics that shape and influence racial identity and ultimately impact group behavioral choices of public policies in which race represents an ideological position (Davis and Gandy 1999). For example, it is argued that African American racial group identity is driven by individual self-interest and perceptions of racial group interests in a social construct described as "linked fate" (Dawson 1994, 81). As a result, African American political behavior is shaped by racial self-interest based on the perspective of the success of other African Americans that outweighs other identities based on class, gender, and religion that may influence policy choices (Dawson 1994). Racial ideology has also been linked to large-scale racial projects that seek to organize and redistribute social resources along racial lines (Omi and Winant 1994).

Similar to those who have studied African American and Latino candidates, researchers have examined the impact of Asian American candidates on group political mobilization and group consciousness. The idea of constructing a linked fate or group consciousness among the ethnically diverse and heterogeneous Asian American population has often been referred to as the "panethnic hypothesis or question" (Lai 2000a; Lien et al. 2001; Collet 2005). The monumental Pilot National Asian American Political Survey (PNAAPS) utilizes several windows to examine this hypothesis or question in the nation's first multicity, multilingual, and multiethnic public attitude survey. These windows include the ways individuals self-identify (e.g., Asian American vs. Chinese); a sense of shared culture (e.g., whether Chinese and Japanese Americans have similar cultures); and a sense of common destiny (e.g., whether what happens to other Asian American groups affects what happens in one's life). With regard to the third window, the findings suggest that nearly 49 percent of Asian American respondents in the survey felt a sense of common destiny with other Asian Americans (Lien et al. 2001). This percentage is likely to increase over generations.

Group consciousness represents an underlying force behind the historical elections of African American and Mexican American mayors in various cities. African American and Mexican American elected officials and candidates have been at the center of the development of group consciousness in their respective communities following the civil rights movement.[3] As the leader of one African American organization declared in the late 1960s, "Negro elected officials have, in a significant sense, become the new leadership of the civil rights movement" (Smith 1996, 106). The same is true for Asian American candidates today. With the recent emergence of local political districts in California suburbs that contain large Asian American populations, Asian American candidates are mobilizing this potential voting base around a group consciousness ideology that emphasizes more of a panethnic orientation as opposed to focusing on ethnic-specific interests. This strategic approach of a racialized group consciousness has resulted in Asian American candidates winning elected representation in city government at a greater success rate than ever before. The next chapter conceptualizes how such successful Asian American group political mobilization occurs in the suburban context in the continental United States, shows how Asian American candidates have emerged as the key political players in this theoretical model, identifies the various Asian American political loci involved during this process, and describes the political outcomes.

Notes

1. The three Asian American candidates were Barry Chang, Raj Abhyanker, and Albert Chu, along with incumbent Kris Wang and former planning commissioner Gilbert Wong.
2. According to the 2000 US Census, Asian American–majority cities in the continental United States were the following: Daly City (50.7 percent), Cerritos (58.4 percent), Monterey Park (61.8 percent), Milpitas (51.8 percent), Rowland Heights (50.3 percent), and Walnut (55.8 percent). All of these cities are located in California. Please

note, this list does not include those cities where Asian Americans represent a plurality (relative majority) where no majority (greater than 50 percent) race exists. In the San Gabriel Valley region of Los Angeles County, for example, Asian Americans have a plurality in the following eight cities according to the 2000 US Census: San Marino (49 percent), San Gabriel (49 percent), Rosemead (49 percent), Alhambra (47 percent), Arcadia (45 percent), Diamond Bar (43 percent), Temple City (39 percent), and Hacienda Heights (36 percent).

3. During their respective campaigns, African American and Latino candidates were crucial in mobilizing their community and formed prominent biracial coalitions with white progressives to reform local government to incorporate their interests. In Atlanta, Maynard Jackson was elected the city's first African American mayor in 1973 as a result of the African American community's movement away from a quiet accommodations strategy during the 1940s toward direct-action protests in the 1960s. Los Angeles also elected their first African American mayor, Tom Bradley, in 1973, who would serve as mayor for twenty years, with the support of a biracial coalition consisting primarily of African Americans and white liberals united by common ideology and interests. What made this Los Angeles biracial coalition unique was that it was the first time that it allowed an African American to be its leader and not just a coalition partner. A decade later, in 1983, Chicago and Philadelphia elected their first African American mayors (Harold Washington and Wilson Goode, respectively) through similar multiracial coalitions. In Chicago, Harold Washington's mayoral campaign galvanized a coalition of liberal white city reformers with African Americans who were brought together by the concept of political motivation, which was defined as an analysis, mass education, and thorough assessment of group interest. Underlying the major motivation of African American political actors in Chicago was not merely to increase African American political representation but also to change and to exercise their control over the existing political system. Similar to African Americans, Mexican American elected officials and candidates have had strong mobilizing effects on their communities. Most notably, this was evident with the historic elections of Henry Cisneros in San Antonio, who became the first Latino mayor of a major US city in 1981, and Federico Peña in Denver in 1983, who became Denver's first Latino mayor. The electoral mobilization of Mexican American voters in both cities was instrumental to the electoral successes of Cisneros and Peña. In both of these elections, group consciousness was clearly developed around both candidates within the Mexican American communities in these cities.

2

Political Mobilization and Incorporation: An Analytical Framework

The political mobilization literature suggests that minority elected officials can have a positive impact on group political participation. The debate on racial and ethnic group mobilization has centered on the distinction between "group identification" and "group consciousness" (Jackson 1991). According to group consciousness proponents, a distinction must be made, in which "group identification connotes a perceived self-location within a particular social stratum along with a psychological feeling of belonging to that particular stratum" whereas group consciousness "involves identification with a group's relative position in society along with a commitment to collective action aimed at realizing the group's interest" (A. H. Miller et al. 1981, 495). The theory of group consciousness is suggested as a major influence on the historical election of African American elected officials in large cities. Maynard Jackson was elected Atlanta's first African American mayor in 1973 as a result of the African American community's movement away from a quiet accommodationist strategy of the mid-1940s toward direct-action protests during the mid-1960s (Stone 1989, 25–26, 51–52). Also in 1973, Los Angeles elected its first African American mayor, Tom Bradley, with the support of a biracial coalition consisting primarily of African Americans and white liberals (Sonenshein 1993, 1997). Bradley's successful mayoral campaign was heavily supported by both African American and Jewish American voters. A decade later, in 1983, Chicago elected its first African American mayor through a multiracial coalition of city reformers galvanized by the concept of "political motivation," which is determined only after "analysis, mass education, and a thorough assessment of group interest" (Starks and Preston 1990, 91). According to Starks and Preston, the major motivation among African American political actors in Chicago was not merely to increase their political representation, but to change and to exercise their control over the existing political system.

The Urban Model of Minority
Political Mobilization and Incorporation

Given the above examples of successful minority political mobilization around minority elected officials, scholars have attempted to explain why minority mobilization, particularly among African Americans, has succeeded and failed in various cities during the post–civil rights era. Leading scholars of local minority political incorporation Browning, Marshall, and Tabb argue that two components necessary for successful electoral mobilization at the local level are a sufficiently large minority population base and a large minority electorate as part of that population (1984, 2003).

Figure 2.1 is based on Browning, Marshall, and Tabb's conceptualization of minority political mobilization as traditionally reflected in the African American experience in urban cities (2003). In this model, African American candidates are seen as the essential political agents in gaining political incorporation for the African American community in the post–civil rights era. The two key components, a large minority population and electorate, necessary for this to happen successfully were both present in large cities such as Berkeley and Oakland where African Americans were able to elect their own into city government. In contrast, in other large Northern California cities where minority groups possessed only one or neither of these two components, they were unsuccessful in electoral mobilization. Other factors that contributed to the inability of African Americans to gain political incorporation included weak biracial coalitions between African Americans and white progressives, co-optation of African American elected officials, and the presence of strong governing coalitions that were antagonistic to African American interests (Browning, Marshall, and Tabb 2003).

Toward a Suburban Model of Asian American
Group Political Mobilization and Incorporation

A new theoretical model is necessary to capture the nuances of Asian American political mobilization in the suburban context and to illustrate the various community loci that have emerged to serve as strategic political allies for Asian American candidates. In addition, such a suburban model must illustrate the central role that Asian American candidates play during group political mobilization along with the strategies used by them in seeking political incorporation. Such a suburban model is conceptualized as below.

Figure 2.2 illustrates the triangulation of three emerging Asian American political loci (Asian American candidates, Asian American community-based organizations, and the ethnic media) during group political mobilization in galvanizing Asian American voters and contributors around candidates' campaigns

**Figure 2.1 Urban Model of Minority Political Mobilization and
Incorporation**

| Group mobilization | → | Candidates run for elective office | → | Representation and incorporation into government | → | Government responsiveness on policy |

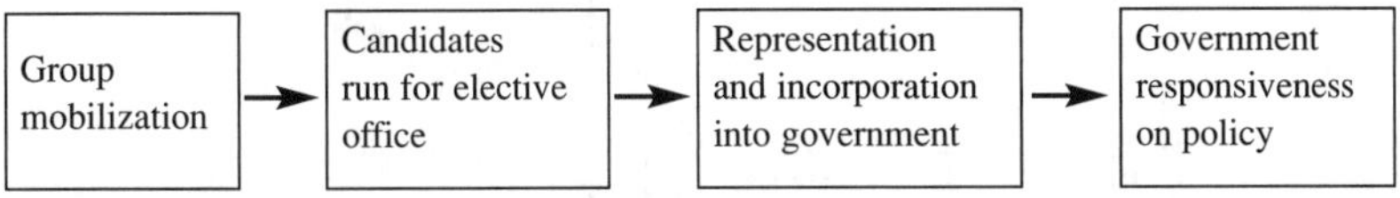

Source: Browning, Rufus P., Dale R. Marshall, and David H. Tabb. 2003. *Racial Politics in American Cities,* 3rd ed. New York: Longman Press, 13.

to achieve the end goal of political incorporation. The presence of a strong ideology (typically, panethnic) and common interests will facilitate this triangulation during group political mobilization. Successful Asian American candidates must be strong leaders—in that they also must hold a strong track record in public service, must have personal charisma, and must demonstrate the ability to form multiracial and multiethnic political coalitions with both non-Asians and the Asian American groups. Without these traits, Asian American candidates will be ineffective in mobilizing the necessary Asian American political loci to be competitive in the elections.

The Asian American community and its candidates do not live in a political vacuum, as they must develop cross-racial coalition-building strategies. Mainstream civic institutions such as state Democratic and Republican Parties and affiliated local groups can play essential roles in helping support Asian American candidates beyond what the Asian American community can provide with regard to votes, volunteers, endorsements, and contributions. The ability of Asian American candidates to appeal to both non-Asian and Asian American groups is known as the two-tiered campaign strategy that many successful Asian American candidates have pursued regardless of district level. A previous study on Vietnamese American candidates in local California politics defines this strategy as "toggling" and discusses such a two-tiered strategy as being necessary for candidates to balance the need for racial and ethnic solidarity with the pragmatic need for capturing non-Asian votes (Collet 2008).

As a result of such toggling strategies, Asian American candidates tend to focus on two primary constituents when tailoring their verbal and symbolic images in their campaign literature: the white and the Asian American communities. With regard to the latter, the role of the ethnic media can help Asian American candidates calibrate their campaign messages linguistically to their ethnic community. This provides an effective strategy for group political mobilization while simultaneously focusing on salient mainstream issues such as law and order, economic or slow growth, education, and accountability of local government officials.

As illustrated in Figure 2.2, the mandatory Tier 1 campaign strategy focuses on the political realities of many diverse suburbs, which are racially and

Figure 2.2 Suburban Model of Asian American Political Mobilization and Incorporation

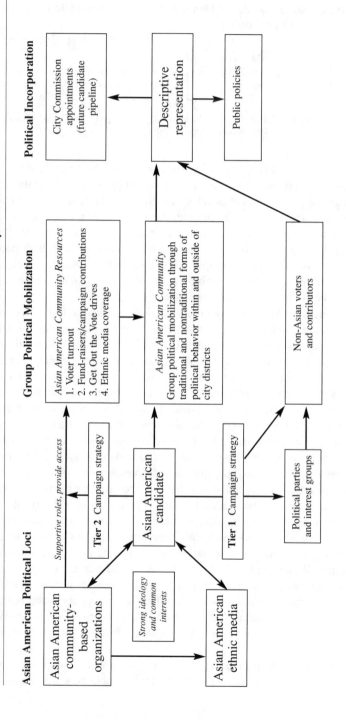

ethnically commingled, unlike the ethnically concentrated urban enclaves of the pre-1965 era. Legitimate Asian American candidates must focus on cross-racial coalition building, particularly with white voters and contributors, if they want to have a chance at winning local- and state-level elections that contain these suburbs. Civic institutions such as state parties and local political clubs are important in providing access for Asian American candidates to their respective partisan mainstream voters and contributors. The challenge, as will be illustrated in Chapter 8's Montgomery County case study, is to gain incorporation into these institutions, particularly when one party dominates a particular region. The mobilization of Asian American candidates on mainstream voters and contributors will be empirically demonstrated in this book's case studies as I examine the campaign strategies and political data of Asian American elected officials and candidates. With regard to campaign contributions, an overwhelming number of successful Asian American candidates receive a majority of their contributions and main political endorsements from non–Asian Americans.

The optional Tier 2 campaign strategy for Asian American candidates focuses on the significant Asian American population in these suburbs. Although typically not the majority voting base, despite its large numbers, this population can play an important role by allowing Asian American candidates to mobilize and gain access to support from the three primary Asian American political loci mentioned above: elected officials, community-based organizations, and the ethnic media. As described above, political mobilization of these three Asian American political loci, as well as others, around Asian American candidates is facilitated by the presence of a strong Asian American ideology that focuses on racial equality and social justice. These Asian American political loci can make the difference in closely contested local and state district elections in which the substantial Asian American population can be the swing vote to tip the election in its favor. Politically savvy Asian American candidates will seek a two-tiered campaign strategy because the Asian American community can be an important swing vote in a closely contested election.

Asian American Political Locus 1: The Impact of Asian American Candidates on Group Political Mobilization

As illustrated in Figure 2.2, Asian American candidates are at the center of group political mobilization (P. D. McClain and Garcia 1993; Lien 1997; Saito 1998). Past studies indicate that Asian American candidates can influence group political mobilization, particularly ethnic campaign contributions, beyond district boundaries (Uhlaner, Cain, and Kiewiet 1989; Lien 1997; Lai 2000b; Wong 2006). The degree of a candidate's influence on Asian American voters within and outside of political districts is bolstered and supported by local and statewide networks of Asian American community elites such as community-based organization leaders, community activists, and the ethnic print media, which provide candidates exposure and access to resources within the Asian American community.

The role of these community elites in politically mobilizing the Asian American community is twofold: (1) to enlist their votes for local and state candidates, and (2) to provide campaign funding and resources to elected officials and candidates who choose to target them. Therefore, these individuals serve as conduits to Asian American candidates who seek to utilize various political networks in their communities. Those who utilize campaign strategies that target Asian American political loci can benefit from them in closely contested local and state elections.

Asian American candidates in small- to medium-sized suburbs may seek to target Asian American political loci (community-based organizations and the ethnic media) that can provide them with access and media exposure to political resources within their respective ethnic communities, as illustrated with the Tier 2 strategy in Figure 2.2. Among the most important of these political resources is campaign contributions, an area where Asian Americans have historically wielded their political muscle in local and state politics (Tachibana 1986; Nakanishi 1991, 1998). Group political mobilization in the form of Asian American campaign contributions often extends beyond district limits to include other cities within and outside of the state. Although this phenomenon does not strictly pertain to Asian American candidates, it has become a key strategy for many of them in these suburbs.

The attempt to construct and to maintain panethnic political coalitions among Asian American voters and contributors is a strategy utilized by many Asian American candidates who pursue the optional Tier 2 campaign strategy. Ultimately, the task of pan–Asian American coalition building in multiethnic suburbs can be difficult for a viable Asian American candidate who must ultimately bridge competing interests, ideologies, and leadership under a panethnic coalition. If any of these three critical components are missing, panethnic coalitions likely will not materialize. This will result in political splintering in the Asian American community, regardless of its population size, as seen in Daly City and the Filipino American community in Chapter 11.

Asian American Political Locus 2:
The Development and Proliferation of
Asian American Community-Based Organizations

The pan–Asian American community-based organization has represented one of the fastest-growing public service sectors in various Asian American communities in the continental United States over the past three decades. For example, in 2008, there were over 250 pan–Asian American organizations in Los Angeles and Orange Counties alone (*Asian and Pacific Islander Community Directory: Los Angeles and Orange Counties* 2008). Given the traditionally weak structure of the Republican and Democratic Parties at the local level in cities like Los Angeles, where elections are nonpartisan, community-based organizations represent an emerging political ally for Asian American candidates running in minority districts.

Politically active community-based organizations play both supportive and proactive roles in the recruitment of future Asian American elected officials (Lai 2000b; Wong 2006). A supportive role entails helping Asian American elected officials and candidates whose campaign strategies focus on their gaining access to important community resources (e.g., votes, campaign volunteers, and campaign contributions). For example, in Los Angeles County, the Asian Pacific Planning and Policy Council, which represents an umbrella organization of over fifty civil rights and social service organizations, plays an integral role in assisting Asian American political candidates through nonpartisan Get Out the Vote (GOTV) drives and candidate forums. A proactive role of community elites (e.g., community-based organizations and elected officials) in recruiting Asian American candidates involves actual training workshops that provide prospective candidates with the skills necessary to run effective political campaigns.

Despite the political roles of Asian American community-based organizations during group political mobilization, it is important to note the gray areas within which they operate. In order to understand the parameters of these gray areas, one must recognize the different classification characteristics of Asian American community-based organizations. Many of these community-based organizations are classified as nonprofit under Internal Revenue Code section 501(c)(3). As a result of their nonprofit status, these groups are prohibited from engaging in partisan political activities. Therefore, the leaders of community-based organizations must differentiate their individual support from their organizational affiliation. According to current California State Assembly member Warren T. Furutani (D-Carson):

> Because of their 501(c)(3) statuses, such groups that conduct political activities cannot be political. However, the types of activities conducted by their leaders can fill this gap. In order to do this, these leaders must differentiate their individual actions from the organizations they represent.[1]

Such political activities by Asian American community-based organization leaders are understandable given that they tend to have contact with American elected officials and candidates. In turn, these leaders have access to political networks (e.g., ability to guarantee a critical mass for campaign fund-raisers) at the local level that Asian American candidates, within and outside of their political district, can utilize during campaigns. As an example, US

Representative David Wu (D-Oregon) from District 1 near Portland holds out-of-state fund-raisers in the suburbs of Los Angeles and Santa Clara Counties with the assistance of Asian American community-based organization leaders and other community activists. For instance, in Silicon Valley, a community-based organization leader, former Santa Clara Board of Education member Barry Chang's principal duty was to ensure that a critical mass of Asian American donors and organizations would attend Wu's local fund-raisers. These fund-raising strategies are optional. But for the Asian American candidates in local-, state-, and federal-level elections who pursue them, Asian American community-based organizations are an important political ally in mobilizing financial support from Asian Americans around their campaigns and result in electoral success.

Asian American Political Locus 3:
The Emergence of the Ethnic Media

The emergence of the ethnic media provides an important political ally for Asian American candidates during group mobilization by connecting their campaigns and messages to the Asian American community, both within and outside of their political districts. The rapid growth of Asian American–influenced suburbs has also fueled the growth of the ethnic media in these cities. A Los Angeles County study found that, from 1965 to 1991, nearly 80 percent of Asian Americans ten years or older were foreign born (Ong and Azores 1991).

This large percentage of foreign-born citizens flowing directly into small-to medium-sized suburbs has spurred a dramatic increase in ethnic newspapers and television programs that cater to them. During 2008, in Los Angeles and Orange Counties, it is estimated that there were nearly 1,000 different Asian and Pacific Islander media outlets, including newspapers, journals, radio programs, and television programs (*Asian and Pacific Islander Community Directory: Los Angeles and Orange Counties* 2008).

In California, the emergence of the Asian ethnic media, particularly the ethnic print media, in suburbs with large Asian American populations provides an important nexus between Asian American candidates and voters during group political mobilization in the suburban context. For example, the *World Journal,* headquartered in Cupertino in Santa Clara County, is the largest circulated Chinese daily newspaper in the United States. And the *Viet Bao Daily,* headquartered in Westminster in Orange County, is the largest-circulated Vietnamese daily newspaper in the United States. The primary role of the ethnic print and electronic media is to cater to a large foreign-born population by providing coverage of economic and political news as well as popular culture stories from their respective homelands. The ethnic print media also focuses on economic and political news affecting the Asian American community in the United States, in particular, stories involving Asian American candidates who are running for local and statewide positions.

Besides giving Asian American candidates access to political resources, the ethnic media can provide them with important media exposure to a large Asian foreign-born, bilingual population. With their strong influence in outreach to the Asian and Pacific Islander foreign-born population, the ethnic media can be an important political ally for Asian American candidates during group political mobilization around their campaigns. Perhaps the first example of the influence of the ethnic media for Asian American candidates in California politics was Matt Fong's 1998 US Senate campaign, in which he targeted the Chinese American print media in order to get his message out to prospective Chinese American voters and contributors. Fong utilized the Chinese American print media to his advantage, and even credited them with helping him win the Republican primary election (S. C. Lin and Galbraith 1998).

The role of Asian American ethnic print media as a political ally for Asian American candidates' campaigns in small- to medium-sized suburbs is manifested in three important ways. First, the ethnic print media provides free or "earned" coverage for Asian American candidates as Asian Americans become politically active in the ethnic suburbs where they are reaching a critical mass. In effect, the ethnic print media becomes an important ally in the mobilization of Asian American voters by providing Asian American candidates with media exposure to a large Asian foreign-born, bilingual population. A 2006 update by the US Census Bureau found that more than 70 percent of the national Asian American population ten years of age or older were foreign born (UCLA Asian American Studies Center 2006). Given this large percentage of foreign-born citizens, as discussed earlier, there has been a dramatic increase in ethnic newspapers and television programs that target them in both large cities and suburbs.

Second, the ethnic print media provides a cost-effective way to reach out to and mobilize the Asian immigrant community through their native language, as opposed to mainstream media outlets. The cost-effectiveness of advertising in Asian ethnic print media versus mainstream print media can be seen in the following example: a full-page advertisement in the *San Francisco Chronicle* costs $55,000 compared to $1,200 for one in the *Sing Tao*, a Bay Area Chinese newspaper with a national circulation of 60,000. This cost-effective strategy of utilizing the ethnic media allows Asian American candidates to mobilize both old and new Asian American voters in the political process as well as contributors within and outside of their political districts.

And third, given the ethnic diversity within the Asian and Pacific Islander community, with twenty-five ethnicities that comprise this racial group (US Census 2008), the ethnic print media helps to foster a pan–Asian American identity among voters, contributors, and volunteers during group electoral mobilization. The ethnic media's coverage of Asian American candidates can provide them with greater visibility to this ethnically diverse and largely immigrant community. Thus, the influence of the ethnic print media in relation to Asian American candidates makes it an important political ally during the political incorporation process.

Suburban Typologies:
Categorizing Asian American–Influenced Suburbs

No two Asian American–influenced suburbs are alike. However, similarities exist among the ten case studies in this book that help explain why certain suburbs are more successful than others with regard to their respective levels of political incorporation, regardless of their geographic locations. As I argue, several factors must be present for Asian Americans to attain medium to high levels of local political incorporation that begin with descriptive representation. Table 2.1 illustrates the emerging suburban typologies of Asian American political incorporation. Each of these typologies is fluid. For example, a suburb that can be classified as Emergent I today may in the near future become a Transformed I suburb, as happened with Cupertino and Garden Grove and Westminster from the 1980s to the present.

The far right column in Table 2.1 represents the level of Asian American political incorporation based on three existing factors within and one outside of the Asian American community. The three factors within the Asian American community are (1) the Asian American population size, which does not guarantee successful political incorporation by itself; (2) the presence of developed Asian American political loci (candidates, community-based organizations, and ethnic media); and (3) the establishment of a strong political ideology to guide the Asian American mobilization efforts. The fourth factor, which is outside of the Asian American community, is political party and interest group support for Asian American candidates in various forms. While many local political elections and offices are nonpartisan, state parties, local political clubs, and interest groups are important political allies for Asian American candidates. They provide access to mainstream registered voters and contributors, all of which are necessary for Asian American candidates to be successful in attaining the Tier 1 support outlined in Figure 2.2.

The confluence of the three factors within and one outside of the Asian American community is reflected in the Class I and II typology groupings. In Class I, there are the following: Transformed I (cities with large Asian American populations—30 percent or greater of the total city population) and II (cities with small- to medium-sized Asian American populations—of less than 30 percent of the total city population) suburbs that have attained medium to strong political incorporation. Only the Asian American population size differentiates these Transformed suburbs because the level of their political incorporation

Table 2.1 Suburban Typologies of Asian American Political Incorporation

Suburban Typologies	Sample Suburbs (chapter in this book)	Asian American Population Size	Asian American Political Loci	Asian American Political Ideology	Asian American Political Incorporation
Transformed I	Cupertino, CA (Ch. 5); Garden Grove/Westminster, CA (Ch. 6); Gardena, CA (Ch. 7)	Large	Strong	Strong	Medium-strong
Emergent I	Montgomery County, MD (Ch. 8); Sugar Land, TX (Ch. 9); Bellevue, WA (Ch. 10)	Large	Weak-medium	Weak-medium	Weak-medium
Delayed I	Daly City, CA (Ch. 11)	Large	Weak	Weak	Weak
Transformed II	Eau Claire, WI (Ch. 12)	Small-medium	Strong	Strong	Medium-strong
Emergent II	Fitchburg, MA (Ch. 13)	Small-medium	Weak-medium	Weak-medium	Weak-medium
Delayed II	Most suburbs	Small	Weak	Weak	Weak

ranges from medium to strong. As mentioned above, population size is not enough to determine the level of Asian American political incorporation, but may help to facilitate political mobilization efforts. Instead, a strong community political locus and a strong political ideology are key within the Asian American community, along with outside party support, in determining the success of Asian American political mobilization efforts beginning with descriptive representation. Having fewer than three of these factors will typically result in weak political incorporation, as demonstrated by Emergent I and Delayed I suburbs with large Asian American populations and Emergent II and Delayed II suburbs with small- to medium-sized Asian American populations. The Delayed II suburbs represent those where Asian Americans are a small percentage, no political loci are present, and there is no political incorporation, which is why a suburb case study of this typology will not be provided in this book.

One major difference between Emergent and Delayed suburban typologies, regardless of Asian American population size, is that the former has the potential to reach Transformed status if a medium to strong ideology and political loci can be established and maintained during group political mobilization. The establishment of a strong ideology to guide its leadership can be facilitated by the actions and rhetoric of influential Asian American political loci, such as community-based organizations and their respective leadership, and coverage by the ethnic media, which can articulate the importance of panethnic support rather than promoting ethnic self-interest that will likely splinter such coalitions. Party linkages with the Asian American community and its candidates must also be developed and fostered by this community leadership, allowing for cross-racial coalitions to develop.

Note

1. Warren T. Furutani, California State Assembly member (D-Carson), personal communication with the author, August 18, 1999.

3

From Exclusion to Inclusion: The Four Stages of Asian American Politics

The contemporary formation of Asian American communities in small- to medium-sized suburbs and their subsequent political developments are inextricably linked to the past. It therefore is important to frame Asian American politics in the United States as an evolutionary process that spans over 160 years, from the arrival of the first wave of Chinese gold miners in California in 1848, who were aliens ineligible for US naturalization, to its current stage of political incorporation in the suburbs (Takaki 1989; Chan 1991). Asian American politics during this period can be characterized by four major stages that embody the political trajectory of this often maligned racial group and foster understanding of why, despite this long history, it is today still a relatively young majority immigrant community. These four stages are the following: Stage 1: Early Forms of Asian American Political Participation in US Political Institutions (Late 1800s to 1950s); Stage 2: Racial Formation and the Asian American Movement (1960s to 1970s); Stage 3: From Protest to Politics (1970s to Present); and Stage 4: New Emerging Sites of Political Incorporation (1980s to Present).

Much of the history of the immigrant Asian American contract laborers of the late nineteenth and early twentieth centuries is filled with discriminatory and exclusionary laws. Underlying these historical racial antagonisms toward Asian Americans were economic fears and xenophobia created and instilled by white labor unions and political opportunists. For example, prior to 1900, Dennis Kearney's California Workingmen's Party in San Francisco touted the platform "The Chinese Must Go!" This campaign served as the political impetus for Congress to pass the Chinese Exclusion Act of 1882, the first law to exclude a group based on its racial background.

Asian Americans comprise the only group in US history to be excluded from immigrating to the country solely on the basis of its racial background by

41

The Chinese Must Go! (1878)
Source: Reprinted with permission from Carl Albert Browne, "Regular Ticket Workingmen's Party California. The Chinese Must Go! 11th Senatorial District." California Historical Society, Fine Arts Collection, FN-30623.

an act of Congress, entitled the National Origins Act of 1924, which stated that any alien who was ineligible for US citizenship was prevented from immigrating to the United States. At the time, only immigrants who were free white persons and those of African descent were allowed to become naturalized US citizens. As a result of the National Origins Act of 1924, Asian Americans were prohibited from immigrating to the United States as a racial group for nearly forty-one years until the passage of the Immigration and Nationality Act of 1965. Underlying the National Origins Act was the "yellow peril"—the image of early Asian immigrants as a threat to the moral ethos and economic health of the United States that justified their exclusion and inability to naturalize. Such national exclusionary laws had a profound effect on the political maturation of early Asian Americans because not only did it deny them basic civil protections and rights, but also prevented them from voting and running for elected positions.

The perception of disloyalty among Asian American immigrants is also a prevalent narrative in US history. This is illustrated by the Japanese American internment during World War II in which two-thirds of the roughly 110,000 interned were US-born citizens as well as the proliferation of hate crimes directed at Muslim Asian Indians in the post-9/11 era. The idea of racial phenotypes having more influence on people's loyalty to their nation has made some scholars label the Asian American as a "permanent alien" (Wu 2002). For example, during the late 1990s, the permanent alien stereotype emerged with highly celebrated political stories, like the 1996 Democratic National Committee campaign finance scandal surrounding Democratic Party insider John Huang, and the espionage trial of former Los Alamos nuclear scientist Wen Ho Lee, who was later acquitted of all espionage charges. The permanent alien and yellow peril metaphors of the early twentieth century remain today in both subtle and explicit forms, and have led to various growing pains in Asian American–influenced suburbs. For instance, the *Wall Street Journal* featured a story entitled "The New White Flight" that chronicled the subtle racial tensions from the outgoing majority (European Americans) to the newly forming majority (Asian Americans) within the suburban context (Hwang 2005). Underlying the article is the theme that white residents feel threatened by a newly emerging Asian immigrant population that is unwilling to acculturate and imposing its cultural values onto cities. As I illustrate in the Cupertino, California, and Sugar Land, Texas, case studies (Chapters 5 and 9, respectively), this perceived group threat by whites in the area of education is spilling over into the local electoral arena in the form of tipping point politics. Despite such perceptions, the case studies provide a cautionary tale to the myriad challenges that suburban transformations pose for race relations in such Asian American–influenced suburbs.

Stage 1: Early Forms of Asian American Political Participation in US Political Institutions (Late 1800s to 1950s)

Early Asian American immigrants in the mid-nineteenth century have been perceived as "apolitical" in the traditional sense of political participation through voting due to their inability to become naturalized US citizens. Although early Asians in the United States were not political in the traditional sense of voting, they did practice other nonvoting forms of political participation in order to protect themselves against discriminatory laws. Due to anti-Asian sentiments in the form of discriminatory laws, early Asian leaders utilized avenues that were available to them, such as the US court system. According to historian Charles McClain in his book *In Search of Equality:*

> The conventional wisdom concerning Chinese and their supposed political backwardness needs to be stood on its head. The nineteenth-century Chinese American community may, because of language, have been more isolated from mainstream society than other immigrant groups in certain respects, but lack of political consciousness was not one of its distinguishing characteristics. There is abundant evidence that the leaders were thoroughly familiar with American governmental institutions, the courts in particular, and knew how to use those institutions to protect themselves. (1994, 3)

Chinese immigrants during this period were outsiders to mainstream political institutions since they could neither vote nor testify in court. Nevertheless, early Chinese community leaders utilized the US court system with the help of white lawyers to contest for constitutional rights, such as the Equal Protection Clause of the Fourteenth Amendment. Many of the late nineteenth-century Chinese leaders arose from labor associations such as the Chinese Consolidated Benevolent Association (CCBA), also known as the Chinese Six Companies in San Francisco. Oftentimes, these interests would have to be pursued in the courts. An important case decided in 1886 by the US Supreme Court was *Yick Wo v. Hopkins* (118 US 356), in which the majority ruled that the San Francisco ordinance requiring wooden laundry facilities to obtain permits unfairly discriminated against Chinese businesses and, therefore, was a violation of their Fourteenth Amendment equal protection status. This stands as an important case and is often cited as legal precedent. The significance of *Yick Wo* is that it is a historical instance when early Chinese Americans challenged discriminatory laws through the US court system to protect themselves from racist laws in coalition with white progressive attorneys. It also shows that early Chinese Americans were indeed politically active in American politics despite the limitations imposed on them by the group denial of basic constitutional rights and protections.

Early Asian American leaders also petitioned the US Supreme Court to argue for extended constitutional rights and protections despite their alien statuses. Perhaps the most vivid examples are the World War II internment cases that were argued before the Court. In the 1944 case, *Korematsu v. US* (323 US 214), the Court used the strict scrutiny standard for the first time in addressing an equal protection violation of the Fourteenth Amendment. Although the Court's majority decided that Executive Order 9066 did not violate equal protection status of US citizens of Japanese ancestry, thereby requiring them to report to relocation centers across the West, the early Japanese American community demonstrated similar use of the US court system to challenge discriminatory laws and to gain greater protections despite their alien status as defined by the National Origins Act of 1924. Forty-four years after the internment, Japanese American community leaders had not given up achieving the impossible dream of redress and reparations for the grave constitutional violations imposed on them through the World War II internment. The culmination of this dream occurred when President George H. W. Bush signed the Civil Liberties Act of 1988, which issued a formal apology to Japanese American survivors and a sum of $20,000 to all internment camp survivors. This act resulted from the efforts of Japanese American national and local leaders who lobbied to rectify this past civil rights injustice by framing the Japanese American internment as a civil liberty issue for all Americans that allowed for multiracial coalition building with groups beyond the Japanese American community (Maki and Kitano 1999).

A successful example of attaining greater civil rights protections through the US court system can be seen in the California Supreme Court cases that challenged the discriminatory California Alien Land Laws of 1913 and 1920. The original 1913 law, passed by California voters, prevented Japanese American farmers, who were of alien status, from owning land and limited the leasing of lands to three years. The 1913 law was later amended in 1920 by the State Assembly to close existing loopholes and prevent Japanese American farmers from purchasing or leasing lands in the names of their minor children who were US born (hence citizens). This legislation represented a direct threat to the state's burgeoning Japanese American population who owned agricultural businesses, precluding them from attaining a livelihood due to their alien status. The laws were eventually overturned in the California Supreme Court case of *Sei Fujii v. California* as a violation of the Equal Protection Clause of the Fourteenth Amendment (Chan 1991).

The experiences of the late nineteenth- and early twentieth-century Asian Americans embodied broader forms of political participation compared to those today. As illustrated by the various legal cases above, this broad Asian American political participation is due to their historical experiences with local, state, and federal discriminatory laws throughout both centuries. Due to their inability to attain US naturalization as a racial group until 1956, Asian American political participation during the late nineteenth and early twentieth centuries focused acutely on nonvoting forms of political participation among its predominantly foreign-born population.

The demographic growth of the national Asian American population remained dormant due to federal exclusion laws and antimiscegenation laws from after World War II to the 1960s. A small second generation of US-born Asian Americans, the offspring of the pioneer immigrants who were able to marry and have children, understood the historic struggles of the preceding generation and the chasm that existed between the Asian American community and civil rights. The animosities of homeland politics that existed and divided their parents' generation in the United States were being replaced among the second generation with an emerging racial group identity along with a common language, English. These two monumental developments would usher in a second stage of Asian American political participation to provide the foundation for its leadership and guiding ideology during the period of the 1960s to the 1970s.

Stage 2: Racial Formation and the Asian American Movement (1960s to 1970s)

The electoral gains made by racial minority groups during the mid- to late 1960s in large cities across the country, along with the passing of federal legislation such as the Voting Rights Act of 1965 and the Immigration and Nationality Act of 1965, embodied a new era for minority political representation. For

Asian Americans, this marked the beginning of a critical period referred to as the Asian American movement, in which Asian American community leaders and activists sought new modes of equality and opportunity in social services, employment, and educational opportunities in large cities throughout the West Coast. In the area of higher education, Asian American young adults were central partners in the progressive multiracial coalitions for racial minorities to attain access to and curricular changes in institutions of higher education. During this period, an emerging racial consciousness took shape among second-generation Asian Americans living in large cities, as expressed through the cultural arts, community-based organizations, and educational curricula (Louie and Omatsu 2001). According to Michael Omi and Howard Winant in their influential book *Racial Formation Theory in the United States* (1994), the dominant paradigm of race relations that emerged with the civil rights struggles of the mid-1960s and, continues today is racial formation theory.

Asian Americans in the United States during the turbulent social movements of the 1960s and 1970s began to mobilize around a common racial identity. They sought to transcend ethnic differences by finding a common struggle with other racial minorities and with progressive whites. As Omi and Winant contend, racial minorities realized that their political influence on public policies and elections depended on their ability to mobilize their interests as a racial bloc around "racial projects" that sought influence on domestic and international policies as well as equitable redistribution of resources along racial lines (1994, 55–56). For many of its participants, the Asian American movement was a microcosm of the civil rights and antiwar movements and would define the next generation of Asian American leadership, whether as community-based organization leaders, labor activists, teachers, professionals, or elected officials, as these young activists came of age. Influencing institutions of higher education around the issues of curriculum in the form of ethnic studies and open admissions to such institutions was central to the student movements of the 1960s.

Another public institution that other racial minorities, particularly African Americans and Mexican Americans, set their collective sights on was elected representation in local and state governments. In 1959, among the 300 most significant elected positions in California, African Americans, Latinos, and Asian Americans held 2, 1, and 0 positions, respectively. In 1969, African Americans, Latinos, and Asian Americans held 14, 2, and 6 positions, respectively. In 1979, African Americans, Latinos, and Asian Americans occupied 26, 10, and 11 positions, respectively (Guerra 1991, 120–121).

Perhaps no other racial group since the civil rights movement has experienced such great electoral success as African Americans. The symbolic gains in African American elected officials during the 1970s and 1980s were also seen outside of California. While African Americans in Los Angeles and Atlanta gained their first black elected mayors (Tom Bradley and Maynard Jackson, respectively) in 1973, Chicago elected its first black mayor (Harold Washington) in 1983 (Sonenshein 1993; Stone 1989; Starks and Preston 1990).

The gains in minority elected representation in key political offices at the local level during this decade were parlayed into further representation in other key cities. In 1983, New York City elected its first African American mayor, David Dinkins (Browning, Marshall, and Tabb 1984). The gains made by African American elected officials in predominantly large African American constituencies heightened political group consciousness. For Asian Americans, the question would be whether they could mobilize as a racial group around the principles of social justice and equality to attain group political incorporation beginning with descriptive representation.

Stage 3: From Protest to Politics (1970s to Present)

The goal for Asian American elected representation is a logical progression of the broader goals of the Asian American movement. The beginning of this period has been characterized for racial minorities as a movement from protests to electoral politics (Browning, Marshall, and Tabb 1984). For Asian Americans, similar to African Americans and Mexican Americans, the period witnessed increased political activity as ethnic candidates began to seek elected office (Wei 1993; Louie and Omatsu 2001). This was evident with the emergence of Asian American elected officials at the federal level in the 1960s. In Hawaii, where Asian Americans represent the majority population, the first Asian American federal elected officials were US Senators Spark Matsunaga (D-Hawaii) and Daniel Inouye (D-Hawaii), both elected in 1962. Patsy T. Mink (D-Hawaii) would be elected to the US House of Representatives in 1964. Many of these Asian American elected officials were the children or grandchildren of the pioneer Asian American contract laborers who worked on sugar plantations and endured institutionalized discrimination.

Despite the gain in the number of Asian American federal elected officials from Hawaii, Asian Americans in the continental United States are generally underrepresented in federal-level positions. Historically, a majority of the few Asian American federal elected officials were from California. S. I. Hayakawa (R-California) served as a US senator from 1976 to 1982. Norman Mineta (D-California) served in the US House of Representatives from 1974 to 1996. The late Robert Matsui (D-California) was first elected to the US House of Representatives in 1978 and eventually served thirteen full terms. Since this period, Asian American federal elected officials have not increased dramatically in the continental United States. In 2009, a total of four Asian Americans serve in the US House of Representatives, with three (Mike Honda, District 15; Doris Matsui, District 5; and Judy Chu, District 32) from California and one (David Wu, District 1) from Oregon. Judy Chu was elected with nearly 62 percent of the vote after a special election in July 2009. She is the first Chinese American woman in the continental United States to be elected to the US Congress. Chu fills the seat vacated by former congresswoman Hilda Solis, who accepted President Barack Obama's appointment to become US labor secretary. Chu began her career at the local school board level, which served as a pipeline to higher elected offices on the Monterey Park City Council and the California State Assembly. Her campaign strategies have always included constructing a multiracial coalition between her large Asian American base combined with Latinos (the majority in the district) and organized labor groups.

In 2008, as shown in Table 3.1, a total of 258 Asian American elected officials in the United States held key positions, ranging from US senator to city council member. This amount is nowhere near the total number of African American or Latino elected officials in the same positions. But it signals gradual political incorporation of Asian Americans in key elected positions beyond the historic base of Hawaii to include nineteen other states. Emerging state districts in the continental United States include those in California, Washington, Oregon, New Jersey, Utah, and Massachusetts. Many of these state political districts contain portions of large cities and suburbs where Asian Americans are a significant population. This has fueled local political incorporation efforts, as witnessed by California's seventy-six city council members and twenty-seven city council members from eleven other states throughout the continental United States. An overwhelming majority of these Asian American local elected officials come from small- to medium-sized suburbs, which have served as cultivating and training grounds for those Asian Americans who seek higher offices like US Representatives Honda and Chu.

Electing Asian Americans at any level of government is a process that involves many key community allies during political mobilization. As mentioned in Chapter 2, one of the key allies for Asian American candidates is the panethnic community-based organization that emerged during the 1960s and 1970s with the sole focus of seeking group empowerment and representation of the marginalized Asian American community. During the transition period between Stage 2 and Stage 3, panethnic community-based organizations and their leadership were instrumental in creating a sociopolitical infrastructure for the largely immigrant Asian American community. These organizations served two primary roles: (1) to fill the direct void left by representing their community's interests to non-Asian elected officials and institutions through organization-sponsored forums and outreach efforts; and (2) to provide resource support for Asian American candidates during group political mobilization efforts through various activities such as fund-raising, registering voters, and staffing phone banks.

Many of these organizations' leaders were Asian American activists during the 1960s and 1970s who sought social justice for their broader racial and respective ethnic communities in gateway cities such as Seattle, San Francisco,

Table 3.1 Asian American Elected Officials in Key Positions by State, 2008

Level	Total	Level	Total
US Senators	2	State Governors	1
Hawaii (2)		Louisiana (1)	
US Representatives	3	City Mayors	24
California (2)		California (18)	
Oregon (1)		Hawaii (3)	
State Senators	21	Illinois (1)	
Hawaii (18)		New Jersey (1)	
Minnesota (2)		Washington (1)	
Washington (1)		City Council Members	123
State Representatives	84	Alabama (1)	
Alaska (1)		Arizona (1)	
California (9)		California (76)	
Georgia (1)		Connecticut (1)	
Hawaii (50)		Georgia (1)	
Iowa (1)		Hawaii (20)	
Maryland (3)		Illinois (2)	
Michigan (2)		Louisiana (1)	
Minnesota (3)		Massachusetts (3)	
Nevada (1)		New Jersey (5)	
New Hampshire (1)		Texas (4)	
New York (1)		Utah (4)	
New Jersey (1)		Washington (4)	
Oregon (1)			
Pennsylvania (1)			
South Carolina (1)			
Texas (1)			
Utah (1)			
Vermont (1)			
Washington (3)			
West Virginia (1)			

Source: Lai, James S., and Don T. Nakanishi, eds. 2007. *National Asian Pacific American Political Almanac.* Los Angeles, CA: UCLA Asian American Studies Press, 82.

and Los Angeles (Browning, Marshall, and Tabb 1984). Underlying these social justice goals was the predominant panethnic ideology among many of their Chinese, Japanese, and Filipino American community leaders. This ideology, centered on the common historical experiences of Asians in the United States communicated through the common language of English, sought to construct panethnic alliances and unity over ethnic division.

The pursuit of panethnic unity at the local level by Asian American community-based organizations in large cities was especially prevalent in the social welfare and electoral arenas (Espiritu 1992). In the electoral arena, politically oriented Asian American community-based organizations emphasized the formation of a racial political bloc as a swing vote. These organizations engage in activities focusing on the political cultivation and education of Asian Americans. An example in Los Angeles is the Asian Pacific American Legal Center of Southern California, which conducts important legal and political activities such as political education forums, Asian American candidate forums, formal exit polling, advocacy on political issues (e.g., bilingual ballots and redistricting), and GOTV drives. Many of these activities attempt to build group consciousness among Asian American citizens and immigrants through their panethnic ideology. However, the challenge in the large cities has been competing ethnic interests, which limit the ability of panethnic coalitions to materialize within the broader Asian American community.

Stage 4: New Emerging Sites of Political Incorporation (1980s to Present)

The fourth stage, which has emerged simultaneously with the third stage, takes place in a different local context—small- to medium-sized suburbs containing significant Asian American populations—in comparison to the primarily large metropolitan context of the previous stage. Since the monumental passage of the Immigration and Nationality Act of 1965, which allowed for family reunification along with mass immigration of families from Asian countries through a preference system that expedited entry for more educated and wealthier immigrants, Asian American–influenced suburbs have become an important site for examining this group's recent political incorporation efforts.

An important distinction must be made between Asian American communities in the past and the contemporary Asian immigrant–influenced suburbs, which have been referred to as global and local cities (J. C. Fong 2003). As discussed in Chapter 1, the term *global and local suburb* refers to cities where localized culture and ethnic entrepreneurship link and intersect with globalized commerce and transnational culture. Most scholars tend to lump Asian urban and suburban communities together. Typically, global and local suburbs are small- to medium-sized, with populations ranging from 25,000 to 100,000 in comparison to the much larger cities that served as primary gateways prior to 1965.

As a result of these demographic trends, these small- to medium-sized suburbs are critical to understanding the current and future political trajectory of Asian Americans in California and other states. In particular, Asian Americans have been able to replicate and build on electoral success in the suburban context in the continental United States, which they have not been able to achieve in the local context outside of Hawaii. This is an important difference historically for Asian American candidates when compared to their African

American and Latino counterparts. In local and statewide politics, African American and Latino candidates have demonstrated their respective abilities to parlay large minority voting bases in city and state districts into political success using successful group mobilization strategies (e.g., voter registration, GOTV, and landmark lawsuits challenging formal election procedures). In contrast, established and large Asian American populations in large cities have struggled to demonstrate sustainability of elected representation of ethnic candidates. This can be seen in Los Angeles and New York City, two cities that contain the largest Asian American aggregate populations, but have elected only one Asian American to their respective city councils. Asian American–influenced suburbs are now demonstrating sustainability of political power in their respective local governments due to the formation of a variety of internal community factors.

Unique community formations with regard to Asian immigrants, capital, and institutions are rapidly taking shape in small- to medium-sized suburbs in major regions in the continental United States, such as California's Santa Clara County. A 2007 update by the US Census Bureau found that Santa Clara County had the nation's fastest-growing Asian immigration of any US county from July 2006 to July 2007, growing nearly 3.3 percent, with a total increase of 17,614 Asian immigrants (Swift 2007). This number outpaced urban gateway areas such as Los Angeles County, which was second in Asian immigration during the same time period. A major force driving this growth is the technology industry in the Silicon Valley (Swift 2007). While Silicon Valley may be unique in this regard, other similar immigrant suburbs are emerging around the technology industry in other major regions in the continental United States, including Bellevue, Washington, and the suburbs in Montgomery County, Maryland.

The emergence of Asian American–influenced suburbs has also resulted in the formation of Asian American political loci, such as community-based organizations and the ethnic media within such suburbs that have facilitated local political incorporation. An example of one Asian American political locus can be seen in Santa Clara County with the Asian Pacific American Silicon Valley Democratic Club (APASVDC). This organization has been successful through a myriad of grassroots activities in helping elect over thirty Asian American candidates, the most of any county in the continental United States since 2002 (Corcoran 2004).

The ethnic media is another Asian American political locus that has formed to accommodate the informational and entertainment needs of predominantly bilingual and transnational communities in these suburbs. Past studies have found that the ethnic media can play an important role in the political mobilization and incorporation of immigrant groups like Mexican Americans (Browning, Marshall, and Tabb 2003). As I will discuss in Chapter 4, these political loci help establish the small- to medium-sized suburb as the primary site for examining contemporary Asian American political mobilization and incorporation in California politics.

4

Locating Contemporary Political Incorporation: The Suburb vs. the Metropolis

Although it is by no means alone, California leads all of the continental states in its total number of Asian American–influenced suburbs. Large gateway cities such as Los Angeles and San Francisco will continue to play an important role in Asian American politics, but they no longer represent the primary focal point where political mobilization and incorporation efforts are taking shape. As discussed in Chapter 1, tremendous demographic shifts are occurring in various small- to medium-sized suburbs in states like California as a result of Asian American gravitational migration during the past thirty years. Such suburbs are now the key to locating and understanding the potential and challenges of Asian American political incorporation efforts in California and other states.

This trend is significant for Asian American political incorporation in California politics because, prior to this period, Asian Americans tended to be residentially dispersed throughout city council districts in large cities such as Los Angeles, and thus did not represent a significant voting bloc in any one city council district (Sonenshein 2005). As a result, their political influence as a potential voting bloc was often limited and unsuccessful. Despite containing one of the largest aggregate Asian American populations of any city in the continental United States, Los Angeles has elected only one Asian American (Michael Woo in 1985) to its city council. Population dilution across districts in large cities that employ district elections is not an issue in small- to medium-sized California suburbs. There, Asian American populations are reaching either majority or plurality status in cities that employ citywide elections as opposed to district elections. Such differences between small- to medium-sized suburbs and large cities have allowed the former to achieve a more rapid and successful level of political incorporation.

Maps 4.1 and 4.2 illustrate the growth of Asian American–influenced sub-urbs in Santa Clara, Alameda, Los Angeles, and Orange Counties. Scholars have termed these suburban cities *ethnoburbs,* or cities transformed by transpa-cific capital and immigration whose economies are interconnected to these linkages (Li 1998a, 1998b; Vo and Danico 2004). Gone are the days of the eth-nic enclaves (e.g., traditional Chinatowns) that were created due to forced seg-regation and exclusion from the mainstream economies.

Asian American candidates in these small- to medium-sized suburbs have begun to demonstrate consistent electoral success by replacing outgoing ethnic city council members with newly elected ones (Lai and Geron 2006). Multiple

Map 4.1 Bay Area Counties and Cities with Majority and Plurality Asian American Populations, 2000

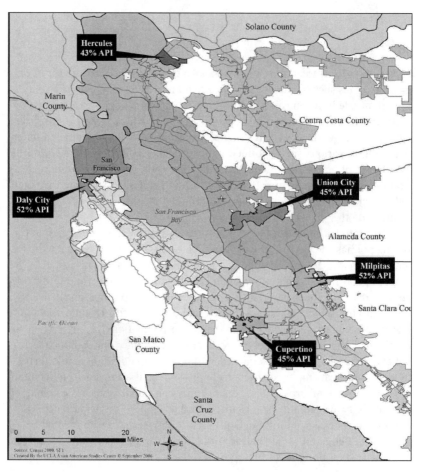

Map 4.2 Los Angeles and Orange County Cities with Majority and Plurality Asian American Populations, 2000

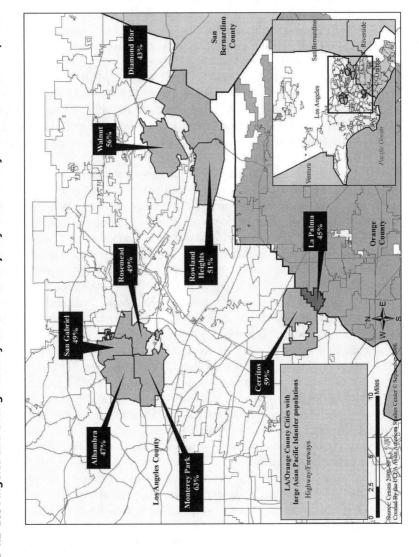

reasons explain why Asian American candidates have done better in the suburban context than in larger urban areas. These include the presence of a majority or near-majority population base in small- to medium-sized cities during the past two decades, the development of key community political loci, common issue saliency, and the existence of few formal electoral procedures to harm rather than help Asian American candidates (Lai and Geron 2006).

One of the most visible examples of strong Asian American descriptive representation and medium political incorporation in Los Angeles County is the suburb of Monterey Park, which was the first Asian American–majority city in the continental United States. In 2000, Monterey Park contained a total population of 60,051, of which 61.8 percent were Asian (US Census 2006a). It is situated next to East Los Angeles and about 10 miles east of downtown Los Angeles. It has been uniquely labeled the "first suburban Chinatown," and has been the site for strong Asian American descriptive representation on its city council (T. Fong 1994).

The Asian American community in Monterey Park has been successful in attaining local political incorporation as measured by its ability to win and sustain descriptive representation on the city council. Between 1970 and 1990, five Asian Americans were elected to the Monterey Park City Council. Among the five is Lily Chen, who was elected to the city council in 1982 and later became the first Chinese American woman to be elected mayor in a continental United States city. During the 1990s, two Asian Americans served on the Monterey Park City Council. Sam Kiang served from 1990 to 1994. Council member Judy Chu was first elected in 1988. In 1998, Chu lost the Democratic nomination for the California State Assembly, District 49, which contained Monterey Park, to Gloria Romero. But she eventually was elected to represent the same district in 2002 and was one of six Asian American members of the California State Assembly. In 2009, Chu was the first Chinese American woman elected to the US Congress in the continental United States. Since then, three Chinese Americans (Vice Mayor Mike Eng, Betty Tom Chu, and David T. Lau) were elected to the Monterey Park City Council. Monterey Park is the first Transformed Asian-influenced suburb in the continental United States in which Asian Americans have a great influence on the city council, local city commissions, and public policy decisions.

Many California suburbs are currently experiencing the same demographic shifts that Monterey Park experienced over thirty years ago. An example is Daly City, which was incorporated in the 1940s as a low-income-housing bedroom community for Italian American immigrants who worked in San Francisco. In 1960, this community was less than 5 percent Asian Americans. In 2000, Asian Americans (with the largest group being Filipino Americans) constituted over 53 percent of the total population of approximately 103,000, making it the largest Asian American–majority city in the continental United States. As a result of the emergence of multiple Asian American–majority and –plurality cities like Daly City, Asian American candidates possess new opportunities and incentives to pursue panethnic strategies to mobilize the substantial Asian American political resources within their respective cities.

Panethnic coalitions within the Asian American community are difficult to construct and maintain during group political mobilization without common issue salience within the diverse Asian American community. Much of the gravitational migration that pulls Asian Americans, both immigrants and US born, to various suburbs throughout the nation is tied to common salient issues, such as the desire for good public schools, affordable housing, low crime rates, and job opportunities (Vo and Danico 2004). With the presence of common issues and the absence of class issues that often divide the broader Asian American community in large cities, panethnic coalitions are more likely to take shape in the suburban context provided that other key factors are present, such as a strong ideology and leadership. In large cities such as Los Angeles, pan-ethnic coalitions have been extremely fragile and difficult to construct due to competing ethnic interests and the lack of consensus around issues pertaining to group interests (Lai 2000a).

Why Asian American Candidates Often Struggle

The most vivid example of the barriers and challenges to Asian American political incorporation in large cities with sizable Asian American populations can be seen in the Los Angeles mayoral election in 1993, one year after the city sustained the 1992 Los Angeles civil riots, the most violent and expensive riots in the history of the United States. Los Angeles is often associated with the potential of Asian American incorporation in California politics for two major reasons. First, it is home to the largest concentrated Asian American population in the United States, at 369,334, approximately 10 percent of the city's total population in 2000 (US Census 2006b). Second, it has served as a major gateway city for many Asian American immigrants on the West Coast during the past thirty years. As Map 4.3 vividly illustrates, much of the Asian American population is geographically dispersed throughout the city's fifteen city council districts, which supports previous findings that Asian Americans tend to be the most residentially dispersed among all minority racial groups.

Yet despite their large aggregate population in Los Angeles, Asian Americans have struggled to gain political representation on the city council. As mentioned previously in this chapter, the lack of a concentrated Asian American city council district in Los Angeles, which utilizes single-district elections for each of its fifteen city council seats, has been a major reason why Asian Americans have not elected more than one Asian American city council member in the past (Sonenshein 2005). Other reasons include fierce competition for city council seats that require strong political networks and coalitions for

Map 4.3 Asian American Population Distribution in Los Angeles County, 2000

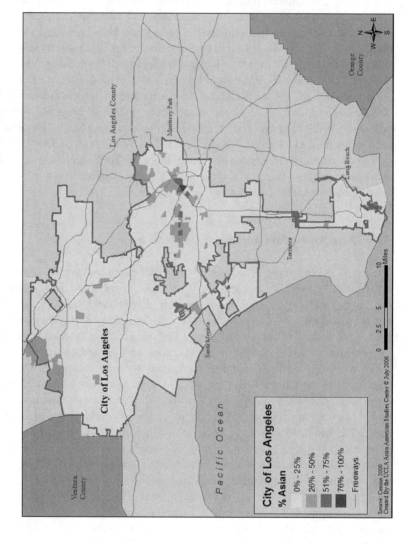

City of Los Angeles

Ventura County

Los Angeles County

City of Los Angeles

Monterey Park

Santa Monica

Pacific Ocean

Torrance

Long Beach

Orange County

City of Los Angeles

% Asian

0% - 25%
26% - 50%
51% - 75%
76% - 100%

Freeways

0 2.5 5   10
Miles

N
W   E
S

Source: Census 2000
Created By the UCLA Asian American Studies Center © July 2006

success, which are not available to political newcomers like Asian American candidates, and the lack of a valid Asian American candidate pipeline in large cities.

At the center of the 1993 Los Angeles mayoral election was Michael Woo, currently dean of Environmental Design at California State Polytechnic University, Pomona. Woo remains the only Asian American ever to serve on the Los Angeles City Council, winning the District 13 seat in 1985. Woo seemed poised to become the successor and to lead the multiracial coalition crafted by popular long-term mayor Tom Bradley. The 1993 Los Angeles mayoral election would serve as a litmus test for the potential of Asian American politics and whether multiracial coalitions could be maintained in Los Angeles. Woo attempted to galvanize, on one hand, both local and nationwide Asian American contributors and voters in his attempt to be the highest elected official in the nation's second largest city. On the other hand, he had to find common interests with the city's African American and Jewish American voters.

As shown in Table 4.1, Woo received nearly 20 percent of his campaign contributions ($2.4 million) from Asian American contributors and nearly 31 percent from Asian American contributors from both outside of Los Angeles County (within California) and outside of California, despite the fact that it was a local election. Seventeen states were represented among those Asian American contributors from outside of California: Illinois, Ohio, New York, Virginia,

Table 4.1 Michael Woo's Asian American Campaign Contributions by Ethnic Group and Geographic Source, 1993 Primary Election

Asian American Contributions	Total Contributions ($)	Percentage of Total Contributions	Percentage of Asian American Total
Ethnic Group			
Chinese American	358,673	14.6	75.0
Korean American	45,125	1.8	9.4
Japanese American	43,475	1.7	9.1
Asian Indian	22,628	0.9	4.7
Vietnamese American	6,700	0.3	1.4
Filipino American	1,630	0.1	0.3
Asian American Total	478,231	19.5	100.0
Geographic Source			
Within LA County	621	68.0	
Outside LA County (within CA)	113	12.4	
Outside California	179	19.6	

Source: Author's coded findings from California Long Form 490, Schedule A, Michael Woo's Los Angeles Mayoral Campaign, 1993.

Texas, Maryland, Washington, Michigan, New Jersey, Arizona, Wisconsin, Missouri, Pennsylvania, Florida, Minnesota, Louisiana, and Arkansas. According to 2000 US Census figures, all of these states contained an Asian American population of less than 7 percent of the total population (Barnes and Bennett 2002). Moreover, none of the contributors were affected by Woo's candidacy except on a symbolic level.

Woo's 1993 campaign contribution findings demonstrate the challenges Asian American candidates face in large cities like Los Angeles. Because the Asian American community is extremely diverse in Los Angeles, where no Asian American ethnic group is a plurality or clear majority, Woo's campaign consultants realized the challenges and limitations in mobilizing this diverse community as the primary strategy. Woo's campaign finance codirector, David Lang, foresaw the need to go outside the political district's boundaries, even as far as the East Coast. According to Lang:

> We specifically targeted Asian Americans outside of California, particularly Chinese Americans. So I drafted up a proposal to Mike in 1990, in which we would begin a cross-country tour. I targeted which cities and we met with various Asian American groups to solicit future campaign contributions. Our strategy was based on cultivating and developing a relationship with Asian Americans, Chinese American in particular. You must earn their support. They [Chinese Americans] have an ethnic connection with Mike because he is Chinese. Also, Mike was one of the few elected Chinese American officials in the country.[1]

Despite the presence of a large Asian American population in Los Angeles, Woo's 1993 mayoral campaign failed to mobilize panethnic support around him at the voting booth. One of the central questions during the election was whether Asian Americans, who represented 12 percent of the city's population at the time, would provide the important swing votes to Woo's campaign. Asian American voters supported Woo over Richard Riordan, 69 percent and 31 percent, respectively, in the runoff election. Although a *Los Angeles Times* exit poll did not operationalize for the ethnicity of Asian American voters, its findings indicated that Woo did not receive their overwhelming support. Given the fact that Woo received 82 percent of the African American vote, one would expect his support among Asian Americans to be even greater. Therefore, why did Woo fail to mobilize an overwhelming majority of the Asian American voters in his favor?

Several complex reasons explain the overall Asian American lack of support for Woo's campaign. The first reason is that the Asian American electorate is ethnically, politically, and economically heterogeneous. As a result of their ethnic and political heterogeneity, a substantial portion of the moderate and conservative Asian American electorate did not vote for Woo. This group most likely accounted for the majority of the 31 percent of Asian Americans who supported Riordan. The second reason is that Woo faced the difficult two-tiered challenge of maintaining a fragile coalition of diverse and competing ideologies and interests in the Asian American community. On one hand, he tried to maintain the multiracial Bradley coalition but, on the other, he was attempting to do this less than a year after the nation's most expensive and deadliest riot. This riot is well documented as a multiracial riot, where the media pitted economically marginalized Latinos and African Americans against Korean American petite entrepreneurs in South Central Los Angeles (Chang 2003). Attitudinal surveys by the *Los Angeles Times* two months after the 1993 Los Angeles mayoral election indicate that these African American and Latino perceived tensions toward Asian Americans, particularly Korean American petite entrepreneurs, were real and increasing (Lien 2002).

And finally, the metropolitan context has been difficult for Asian American candidates, unlike other minority candidates, due to the spatial dispersion among Asian Americans throughout Los Angeles, where there is no concentrated Asian American community outside of Koreatown. In the case of Woo, his main campaign finance strategy toward Asian American contributors was to focus on countywide and national fund-raising. With regard to the Asian American voters in Los Angeles, Woo hoped that they would identify primarily with panethnic identities. But unfortunately issues became important to key Asian American communities, as is demonstrated with the Korean American liquor store below.

As a result of the above three factors, Woo appeared ineffective and contradictory on key issues where contrast instead of agreement existed among Asian Americans, African Americans, and Latinos. And subsequently, he lost their votes. A clear example of this point is the issue concerning the rebuilding of Korean-owned liquor stores that were destroyed during the 1992 civil uprising. Woo's controversial stance on this issue is shown in his statement at a public debate: "I encourage merchants to convert liquor stores to laundromats. . . . We cannot deny that African Americans see Korean Americans as another wave of immigrants who are taking their jobs. It's the same age-old idea of yellow peril" (Cho 1993, 1).

Woo was forced to side publicly with the African American community in District 5, from which any liberal mayoral candidate needed support if he or she was to have a chance of winning, at the expense of alienating the city's Korean American voters (Sonenshein 1993). At 24.8 percent, Korean Americans represent a substantial percentage of the total Asian American population in Los Angeles. Woo's message about the rebuilding of Korean-owned liquor stores in District 5 may have won over 80 percent of the city's African American vote, but it alienated many Korean American voters who were concerned about rebuilding their economic livelihoods and interests in the niche economy that many had entered.

The rebuilding of Korean American liquor stores in South Central Los Angeles demonstrates the challenges that Asian American candidates face in finding salient issues where there is a panethnic Asian American community consensus in large cities due to diverse and competing Asian American ethnic and economic interests. The issue of rebuilding of liquor stores was arguably one of the most salient and contentious issues for the large Korean American community in Los Angeles during the election. However, the liquor store issue was not as salient for other Asian American ethnic groups, particularly the residentially dispersed Chinese, Taiwanese, Japanese, and Filipino American communities throughout the city, whose salient issues were most commonly crime and the economy (Sonenshein 1993). As a result, Woo was unable to mobilize Asian American voters around common interests, which resulted in ethnic splintering at the voting booth, as found in several exit polls. Without such a panethnic base, Woo was unable to capture the multiracial coalition that was crucial for a liberal mayoral candidate to win.

Competing interests among the various Asian American ethnic groups during the 1993 Los Angeles mayoral election were reflected in their respective ethnic newspapers' coverage of Woo's mayoral campaign. For example, coverage by the *Korea Times* (a Korean English daily) revealed the importance of finding common interests in constructing panethnic support. During the entire election period, the *Korea Times* ran eleven articles that featured Woo (five articles during the primary and six during the runoff election). Among these, the fifth article to appear during the campaign period, headlined "Woo Says Liquor Stores Should Convert to Laundromats—Mayoral Candidates Face Off at a Community Forum," appeared on the front page of the March 24, 1993, edition. Woo's statement on this heated issue (see above) came up at a debate in Koreatown that was sponsored by the Korean American Coalition, the Korean American Democratic Committee, and the Korean American Republican Association, three of the most powerful community-based organizations in the Korean American community.

The lack of a dominant panethnic ideology to guide Asian American politics in Los Angeles represents one of the major hurdles that exists for Asian American candidates there as well as in other large cities where panethnic identity and group consciousness are less likely to emerge. Factors contributing to this lack are competing interests among Asian American ethnic groups that are both real and perceived, and a high degree of residential dispersion of Asian Americans throughout these cities' multiple city council districts. Such factors are present in every city with a large Asian American population, but they are more likely to be mitigated with the presence of a strong political ideology that promotes panethnic coalition building instead of competing ethnic interests that result in zero-sum politics. This is key in small- and medium-sized suburbs that employ at-large elections as opposed to district elections, as Asian Americans are able to circumvent their residential dispersion in district elections and to take advantage of entire Asian American city populations.

While the metropolises still matter politically for Asian Americans in today's context, small- to medium-sized suburbs throughout the continental United States have become the primary sites for Asian American community formation and, consequently, they are where group political mobilization and incorporation are most rapidly taking shape. I will develop this thesis in Chapters 5 through 13 by revealing the common and distinct political potential and challenges in each of the ten Asian-influenced suburb case studies. As I will illustrate, the extent of Asian American political incorporation in each suburb is influenced by various internal (e.g., political loci and demographic characteristics) and external factors (e.g., formal government rules and tipping point politics). The demographic and political developments of each suburb vary and, therefore, some of the chapters on the mature Asian-influenced suburbs have more detail and longer political trajectories than those on less mature Asian-influenced suburbs. Nevertheless, all ten suburbs speak to where Asian American political mobilization and incorporation will likely take shape most rapidly and influentially because they embody political incubators for Asian American elected officials who will choose to run for higher elected positions that contain these suburbs in their respective districts.

Note

1. David Lang, Michael Woo's campaign adviser, interviewed by the author, Los Angeles, California, November 7, 1995.

5

Cupertino, California:
A Panethnic Suburb in Silicon Valley

The high-tech Silicon Valley suburb of Cupertino represents the archetypal Asian American Transformed I suburb because it possesses all of the internal community factors (significant Asian American population, strong political loci, and strong ideology) that have culminated in political incorporation that extends beyond descriptive representation. It was estimated that, in 2010, Cupertino would become the seventh Asian American–majority city in the continental United States, with Asian Americans at 56 percent of the city's total population (Swift 2008). During the 2010 election cycle, Asian Americans won a majority (three seats) of the five total Cupertino City Council seats, making it only one of two cities with a majority Asian American city council, the other being Westminster, California.

Cupertino is located in Santa Clara County, California, in an area internationally known as Silicon Valley. Santa Clara County has long been known for its technological ingenuity and its Pacific Rim linkage. In 2000, Santa Clara County had an Asian American population of 435,868, or 25.9 percent of the total population. The largest Asian ethnic groups in Santa Clara County were Chinese Americans (6.9 percent), Vietnamese Americans (5.9 percent), Filipino Americans (4.5 percent), Asian Indians (4 percent), Japanese Americans (1.6 percent), and Korean Americans (1.3 percent). The total Asian American population in Santa Clara County was significantly higher than this group's statewide population of 14 percent (US Census 2006c). Much of the Asian American population growth during the past twenty years in Santa Clara County has been related to the Silicon Valley boom (Park 1996).

The Asian American population in Silicon Valley is both ethnically and economically diverse. It consists primarily of the following groups: highly educated Asians recruited and trained both in the United States and abroad, immigrant entrepreneurs, and blue-collar workers (Park 1996). In 1990, nearly

Map 5.1 Chinese American and Taiwanese American Population Distribution in Cupertino, 2000

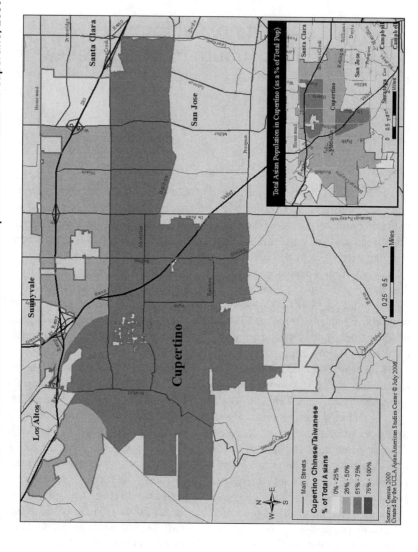

9,000 Asian Americans accounted for 47 percent of the total 19,000 blue-collar workers in Silicon Valley. A majority of these workers were employed in large firms. At the opposite end of the economic spectrum, the Asian American Manufacturing Association found in 1989 that more than 500 Asian American–owned high-tech firms were in the Silicon Valley and San Francisco area, with more than $1 billion in generated sales (Park 1996).

As captured in Map. 5.1, these demographic and economic shifts have transformed Cupertino into a global suburb with a significantly large Chinese and Taiwanese American population. A city best known for being the corporate headquarters of Apple Computer, Cupertino underwent a demographic transformation in the decades that followed the emergence of Silicon Valley with the 1971 invention of the microprocessor. As Silicon Valley progressed, other internationally known companies, such as Hewlett-Packard, Portal Software, and Symantec, began to establish headquarters and satellite campuses in Cupertino.

The rise of Silicon Valley witnessed a simultaneous rise of the Asian American population in Cupertino. In 1980, the Asian American population in Cupertino was 6.7 percent while whites represented 87 percent. Twenty years later, with a total population of approximately 52,000, Asian Americans now account for 44.6 percent (up 69 percent) of the city's total population, compared to whites at 48 percent (down 55 percent). Chinese Americans (23.8 percent) are the largest group, followed by Asian Indians (8.7 percent), Japanese Americans (4.6 percent), Korean Americans (4.2 percent), and Vietnamese Americans (1 percent) (US Census 2006c).

As the Asian American community began to grow in Cupertino after 1980, so did the renowned reputation of the city's two public school districts: the Cupertino Unified School District and the Fremont Union High School District. This attracted immigrant families from Taiwan to Cupertino as the initial high-tech workers began to settle in the city. Cupertino housing listings appeared in daily newspapers in Taiwan and Hong Kong and in brochures at Asian international airports that targeted the wealthy class who could afford multiple residences and sought an initial entryway into US colleges for their children. As a retired Cupertino teacher from this period stated:

> In 1980 when I was teaching at Kennedy Junior High, a Chinese couple came into my science class and told me that they wanted their daughter to enroll in our school. During the 1980s newspaper articles began to appear in newspapers in Singapore, Taiwan, and Hong Kong about the wonderful Cupertino School District. (Sethe 2005)

Since this period, both Cupertino Unified School District and the Fremont Union High School District have developed majority Asian American student populations. Local newspapers, such as the *Cupertino Courier,* highlight the local public school districts with each month's listings of homes for sale, targeting prospective Asian American, domestic, and international buyers.

Racial tensions within the community have increased with the dramatic shift of the Asian American population as it grew from a minority to a potential majority, particularly in the area of public education, where Asian Americans constitute 51 percent of the Cupertino City Unified School District (Hwang 2005). In the civic arena, confrontations have occurred with Cupertino City Council members around the issue of naming a public building after a prominent Asian American community donor (Hosley Stewart 2003). On August 9, 2003, the city of Cupertino sponsored with community organizations a public forum called "A Time to Talk." It included 150 Cupertino residents, mostly white and Asian American, who candidly shared their perspectives and concerns on the changing demographics of the city. Common views shared by old-timers at the public forum were that the city was changing too fast and that they didn't feel it was their home anymore. On this point City Manager David Knapp said that "these problems will never go away and cannot be fixed once [and] for all. These are problems that we need to work on on an ongoing basis. . . . We should be happy that our neighborhoods are reflective of the city's diversity and what we have in common is more than our differences" (Che 2003).

The growing racial tensions, overt and covert, in Cupertino from the 1980s to the present have coincided with the emergence of an Asian American political voice in local government. As Cupertino changed, the Asian American community leadership began to view their interests as muted in city government and have attempted to change this through the establishment of a strong political ideology and group consciousness that could unify and mobilize the community.

Local Government Structure and Asian American Political Incorporation

Cupertino's local government is characterized as a city council and city manager model in which the five city council members create policy that is implemented and enforced by the city manager, who is appointed by the council. The local elected government consists of the five-person city council and the mayor, all of whom are part-time. All city council positions are elected in staggered elections among citywide voters. Each city council member can serve a maximum of two consecutive elected terms, or eight years. Then, they have to wait one election cycle, or four years, to run again. Vacated seats are determined by the largest vote getters. The two main requirements for running for office are that candidates be US citizens (naturalized or US born) and city residents. The city mayor is rotated among the city council members through a nomination and voting process for a four-year term. The vice mayor is appointed by the mayor, typically based on the council member who received the second highest number of votes in the previous election cycle. Public members of city commissions are chosen through an application, interview, and vote by the city council requiring a majority (three votes minimum) approval. Most of the high-profile city commission positions have a four-year term. Commissioners can serve two consecutive terms, or eight years, then wait one year to apply again.

The citywide elections for city council, combined with the large Asian American population, have facilitated heightened Asian American political mobilization and a string of successive Asian American city council candidates running and winning. Table 5.1 captures the sustained political power emerging in Cupertino from 1995 to 2009, which is unprecedented in any continental United States city, suburban or metropolitan. This unprecedented political power is facilitated by the development of Asian American political loci that play the role of key political allies for Asian American candidates. In addition, a strong political ideology has emerged that continues to guide group political mobilization efforts. In Cupertino, a panethnic ideology has been constructed by its strong Asian American leadership to articulate common racial or panethnic interests that attempt to transcend divisive ethnic fault lines.

As Table 5.2 shows, Asian Americans, particularly Taiwanese and Chinese Americans, have built on and exerted their large community presence in key city political institutions during the decade since Michael Chang became the first Asian American elected official in Cupertino in 1995. Prior to 1995, only six Asian Americans served on any of the city commissions. In comparison, since 1995, sixty-six Asian Americans have served in Cupertino. This suggests that descriptive representation is an important first step for group political incorporation into local political institutions that can transform the demographic makeup of city government to the interests of public policies, which I refer to as the final step of political incorporation, substantive authority, and influence. Chang's historic election signified the political awakening of this community

Table 5.1 Asian American Political Power in Cupertino, 1995–2009

Asian American City Council Member	Year Elected	Total Number of Asian Americans on City Council
Michael Chang	1995	1
Patrick Kwok	2001	2
Kris Wang	2003	2 (replaced Michael Chang, whose term limits forced him out)
Gilbert Wong	2007	2 (Patrick Kwok resigned to accept a county appointment in 2007)
Barry Chang	2009	3 (resulted in Asian American majority city council)

**Table 5.2 Asian American Representation on Cupertino City Commissions
and School Board, 2009**

Cupertino City Commissions	Number of Asian Americans	Total Positions
Library Commission	1	5
Housing Commission	2	5
Parks and Recreation Commission	1	5
Planning Commission	2	5
Technology, Information, and Communication Commission	2	5
Cupertino Union School District superintendent	1 (Phil Quon)	1
Cupertino Union School District board members	1 (Ben Liao, president)	5

to non–Asian Americans in the city, as paralleled by the Asian American demographic growth. Such an awakening would not have occurred without a strong political ideology to guide the city's Asian American politics.

Unlike many large gateway cities such as Los Angeles where the Asian American community interests and ideologies are splintered around ethnic factions, in Cupertino Asian American leaders have been able to circumvent ethnic divisions because of the establishment of a guiding panethnic political ideology that attempts to transcend ethnic differences. This ideology and strategy is modeled after the Asian American movement of the 1960s, which advocated self-determination and group empowerment for Asian Americans in civil rights and access to higher education in public universities (Omatsu 2003). In many ways, Cupertino politics today represents a continuation of the movement into the field of electoral politics by its focus on Asian American political incorporation and self-determination in the area of descriptive representation in city government.

One of the most influential Asian Americans who helped to establish the foundation for Asian American politics in Cupertino during the mid-1990s was Michael Chang. The vision that guided Chang to run for city council was based on the need for greater Asian American elected representation in the city. Underlying this need for greater elected representation were the principles of the Asian American movement of the 1960s. According to Chang, "I came out of the Asian American movement [as a student]. I use most of the principles of this student movement as yardsticks for Asian Americans in the political arena."[1]

California State Assembly member Paul Fong from District 22 was another key individual who was instrumental in establishing the Asian American movement as the primary ideology guiding Asian American politics in Cupertino.

Fong, a former professor of political science and Asian American studies at Evergreen Community College, was a participant in the Asian American movement who realized the necessity of establishing an Asian American voice in local politics by creating local political institutions that reflect their group interests and concerns.[2]

Political Incorporation Through the Establishment of Political Loci

The political incorporation of Asian Americans in Cupertino is rare for any continental United States city. It illustrates the local political power that Asian Americans have yet to demonstrate in statewide California districts—the ability to elect and replace Asian American elected officials with coethnics. An Asian American candidate pipeline does not automatically come to fruition because it requires support from the Asian American community in the form of strong leadership and the presence of political loci such as community-based organizations and the ethnic media. The Asian American candidate pipeline in Cupertino and Santa Clara County is facilitated by two Asian American institutions in Cupertino. The first is the Asian Pacific American Leadership Institute (APALI), which was established by former city council member and mayor Michael Chang at DeAnza Community College. And the second is the Asian Pacific American Silicon Valley Democratic Club (APASVDC), a local political organization affiliated with the California Democratic Party. In addition to these two key political institutions, the ubiquitous ethnic media, particularly the daily print media (the *Sing Tao* and the *World Journal*), play a critical role in outreach to the large foreign-born and transnational Asian American population in Cupertino and Santa Clara County.

APALI provides an annual summer program that targets Asian American students of both high school and college age to participate in the public sector. This program, operating out of DeAnza College for the past ten years, has trained a cohort of young Asian Americans who have gone on to serve as political aides and community activists. A recent APALI graduate and fourth-generation Chinese American, Evan Low, ran for Campbell City Council in 2004 at the age of twenty-four. He finished fourth among candidates to fill two open seats. Low ran again in 2006, making history by finishing second to become the first and youngest Asian American city council member in Campbell history.

Chang and Fong were two key Asian American community leaders who helped to found the APASVDC, a chapter of the California Democratic Party located in Cupertino, which has increasingly become a key political player in Santa Clara County politics. With the help of the California Democratic Party apparatus, the APASVDC has been instrumental in helping to elect twenty-seven Asian Americans to local offices throughout Santa Clara County. An overwhelming majority of these Asian American elected officials are Democrats, and this has allowed the California Democratic Party to solidify its political stronghold in the progressive Silicon Valley. Fong believes the success in Cupertino is attributed to groups like the APASVDC's unwavering commitment to the Asian American movement model. Fong states:

> The Asian American movement is something that Michael [Chang] and I believe in and practice since we both participated in the movement. We are just trying to get Asian American elected representation that is proportional to their population. It has been the model that we have established around Asian American politics in the South Bay. Unlike other cities without the presence of a strong political ideology that guides their community's politics, if divisive ethnic politics surfaces around a particular Asian American candidate, we are able to shut that person out of office through our established networks with other racial groups.[3]

The significance of APASVDC is that it has allowed Asian Americans in Silicon Valley to be serious partners in a political region vital to the California Democratic Party. It is clear that Asian Americans are emerging as serious political players in the region's local and state districts, which has expedited their political incorporation in the party, arguably stronger than in any other region in the United States. The result has been civic institutional support behind Asian American candidates with regard to major political endorsements, campaign finance, and important placements on Democratic campaign mailing slates.

The ability to replicate electoral success at the local level is what makes Cupertino an archetypal Transformed I suburb. Such electoral success could not be achieved without emerging political loci that mobilize both the younger and older generations of Asian Americans into the public sector. One example of such a political locus is APALI, which has served an important role in the political socialization and racial identity formation of high school– and college-aged Asian Americans. Each year, Michael Chang and Mae Lee, also a professor of Asian American studies at DeAnza Community College, coordinate a six-week summer program for predominantly Bay Area youth that includes speeches by local-, state-, and federal-level Asian American elected representatives, mentoring by senior fellows in the public sector, and courses in Asian American studies. Some of the recent alumni have run successfully for local office, including Low. Besides the APASVDC's efforts to recruit and develop a future pipeline, on the older generation spectrum current and former Asian American elected leaders, another political locus, have played instrumental roles in helping handpick future candidates. An example is the role that Michael Chang played in appointing Kris Wang to the City Parks and Recreation Commission, which would serve as Wang's introduction into city politics and lead to her historic 2003 election.

Mobilizing Panethnic Support in Campaign Contributions

The role of Asian American contributors in the campaigns of Asian American candidates is a well-documented and vital part of extending candidates' support beyond their political districts. For example, a study found that approximately 38 percent of state-level Asian American elected officials in Washington State received nationwide contributions from Asian Americans (Lai 2000b). Given the small percentage of registered voters and low voter turnout rates among Asian Americans compared to other racial groups, Asian American candidates have relied heavily on racial and ethnic campaign contributions. Past studies indicate that when Asian Americans give, it is usually to Asian American candidates (Tachibana 1986; Tam-Cho 2002). As a result, high-profile campaigns of Asian American candidates can mobilize both old and new Asian American contributors into the political process, particularly if they pursue such a group consciousness strategy.

Kris Wang's inaugural Cupertino City Council campaign in 2003 is an excellent example of the role of Asian American contributions to an Asian American candidate during group mobilization. The Asian American community's mobilization around her campaign extended well beyond the city limits of Cupertino. The campaign contribution findings for Wang's campaign demonstrate that a significant percentage of her funds came from Asian Americans. Wang's largest contributors are identified as individuals who gave at least $100 to her campaign (coded as Schedule A, Line 3 contributions in her public campaign disclosure forms). Surname identification of her contribution disclosure forms indicates that Asian Americans, nearly all of them Chinese or Taiwanese American, provided a clear majority (69.1 percent) of Wang's total Schedule A, Line 3 contributions, $4,700 of the total $6,800 that she received. This should not be a surprise given that the contributions most likely came from her inner circle of supporters.

Two important caveats must be raised with regard to these overall contribution findings. First, the total amount does not include contributions of less than $100, which are not itemized in the campaign disclosure forms. Because they are not itemized, the race of the individuals cannot be determined. These contributions accounted for a total of $13,200. Second, the city of Cupertino imposes a maximum cap for fund-raising ($20,000) in city council campaigns, which Wang was able to meet relatively quickly. Thus, the findings cannot reveal the overall support of Asian and non-Asian contributors to the extent of races that do not have maximum caps, such as Michael Woo's 1993 Los Angeles mayoral campaign. Both Asians and non-Asians who may have wanted to contribute to Wang's campaign were turned away after the $20,000 contribution cap was met. Nevertheless, Wang's contributions from Asian Americans demonstrate their importance in providing the initial seed money during the crucial beginning stages of the campaign. Without the early support from Asian

American contributors, particularly those who contributed $100 or more, Wang's campaign would not likely have been so successful.

The Role of the Chinese and
Taiwanese American Ethnic Print Media

Kris Wang's 2003 campaign demonstrates the political potential of the Chinese and Taiwanese American ethnic print media. It is estimated that nearly 25 percent of the Cupertino total population speak Chinese (Biggar 2006). Because the Chinese and Taiwanese American populations are the largest in Cupertino and Wang is an immigrant from Taiwan, her campaign helped to galvanize the two largest Chinese and Taiwanese print dailies in the United States, *Sing Tao* and the *World Journal*. The *World Journal*, whose corporate headquarters is in Cupertino, was founded in 1976 and currently is the largest Chinese and Taiwanese news daily in the United States. Wang did not spend any money advertising in the ethnic print media, but she received a significant amount of free coverage in both dailies.

Content analyses of both newspapers' coverage of the three-month Wang campaign—from the official announcement of her candidacy (August 2003) to election day (November 4, 2003)—demonstrate that the ethnic print media can be powerful political allies for Asian American candidates. During this three-month period, a total of seventeen Wang-related articles appeared in *Sing Tao* (eight articles) and the *World Journal* (nine articles). For example, on August 7, 2003, an article with this headline appeared in the *World Journal*: "Cupertino City Council Election. Kris Wang Establishes Web Site. Emphasizes That in the Future She Will Represent All Residents. Endorsed by Michael Chang, Patrick Kwok, and Barry Chang" ("Cupertino City Council Election" 2003, 1). The article provided the website of Wang's campaign. Wang encouraged Chinese and Taiwanese American immigrants as well as American readers of the *World Journal* to register to vote: "To vote in the November 4th election, you must register to vote before October 20th . . . and if you won't be in town November 4th, you can also arrange for an absentee ballot in advance, and this way your vote won't be lost" ("Cupertino City Council Election" 2003, 1). Other articles that appeared in both newspapers included coverage of Wang's campaign fund-raisers and political endorsements throughout Santa Clara County, along with photos.

The effect of Wang's exposure in the two largest Chinese and Taiwanese American print dailies was a tremendous windfall for her campaign because it provided free, constant exposure of her campaign to their readers. This was significant in a city like Cupertino where a large foreign-born Chinese-speaking and -reading population became exposed to the significance of Wang's campaign to replace another outgoing Chinese American (Michael Chang) on the city council. Moreover, the ethnic print media helped to promote group consciousness among old and new Chinese and Taiwanese Americans at the local, state, and national levels. It cannot be downplayed how this likely was able to bring successful Asian American community support to Wang's inaugural campaign. According to Wang, the media exposure from the ethnic print media led to statewide support for her campaign: "So many people call me, encourage me. They thank me for running and even [Asian American elected officials] from Sacramento call to encourage me."[4]

The trend of the Chinese newspapers acting as political allies for Asian American candidates continued in the 2007 and 2008 Cupertino City Council elections. In the 2007 election period, all three Asian American candidates (Kris Wang, Gilbert Wong, and Barry Chang) were the focus of earned- or free-coverage articles. For example, during the period from January 2007 to November 2007, the *World Journal* ran a total of thirty-eight articles that focused on the three Asian American candidates. It also ran a total of eight articles from January 2008 to March 2008 during the special election period that focused on two Asian American candidates (T. N. Ho and Chihua Wei). Each of these findings suggests the prominent role of Chinese daily news-papers in mobilizing old and new Asian American voters in the electoral process around Asian American candidates.

Replicating Electoral Success

On November 6, 2007, Gilbert Wong, a second-generation Chinese American, became Cupertino's first US-born Asian American city council member to be elected. In the election to fill two vacant seats on the city council, Wong finished second with 2,534 votes or 18.4 percent of the total. This was thirty-five more votes than third-place candidate Mark Santoro, an electrical engineer and former CEO of a computer company he created, who received 2,499 votes or 18.1 percent of the total. Incumbent Kris Wang easily finished first among the six candidates, with 3,654 votes or 26.5 percent of the total. The three other Asian American candidates finished as follows: Barry Chang, fourth, with 2,266 votes or 16.4 percent of the total; Raj Abhyanker, fifth, with 2,020 votes or 14.6 percent; and Albert Chu, sixth, with 826 votes or 6 percent.

As the first US-born Asian American elected to the Cupertino City Council, Gilbert Wong set an important precedent. His successful campaign symbolizes an emerging cleavage within the Asian American community, as both immigrant and US-born Asian Americans run successful city council campaigns. The election also demonstrates the ability of the Cupertino Asian American community to put forth multiple Asian American candidates (a record five city council candidates among six) and yet fill the two vacant seats with two Asian

Americans. This represents the third time that two Asian Americans have served on the five-member city council at once. Such findings are rare in any US city with the exception of Monterey Park, California, the first Asian American–majority suburb in the 1980s.

Gilbert Wong's campaign galvanized the Asian American community, particularly in the form of campaign contributions. According to public disclosure records for Wong's campaign from January 1, 2007 to June 30, 2007, he received total contributions of approximately $28,000. Asian American contributors accounted for approximately $17,200, or 61.4 percent of Wong's total contributions, which shows that Asian Americans in Cupertino are willing to give money to emerging candidates as well as incumbents.

Wong pursued a two-tiered strategy that focused on winning panethnic support among Asian Americans along with constructing cross-racial alliances with whites. On the panethnic front, Wong's Asian American contributors were not exclusively Chinese Americans. Among the sixty-six Asian American contributors, the ethnic breakdown was the following: fifty-three Chinese Americans (80 percent of total Asian American contributors), five Japanese Americans (7.6 percent), five Asian Indians (7.6 percent), two Vietnamese Americans (3 percent), and one Korean American (1.5 percent). Thirty-two white contributors gave to Wong's campaign, accounting for approximately 38 percent of Wong's total contributors. Non-Asians contributed 17.1 percent of Wong's total contributions by race. This shows that Wong was able to receive cross-racial support from whites in his city council bid. These campaign contribution findings also illustrate that white contributors viewed their issues and agendas as similar to those of Asian Americans. Wong's primary campaign message, particularly in his campaign mailings, focused on the importance of slow growth to maintain Cupertino's small-town feeling and strong public school education, arguably the two most important issues to Cupertino voters.

Gilbert Wong had been perceived by many as the front-runner to win the single open seat in the 2007 election because of his previous political experience serving on the Planning Commission, a springboard position to the city council, but the election results were much closer than expected. Wong won by a mere thirty-five votes over first-time political candidate and outsider Mark Santoro. In fact, Wong and his campaign advisors believed that the closest competitor for the second seat outside of Wang would be Barry Chang, a first-generation Chinese American, because he had previous political experience in local government, having served previously on the Planning Commission. But he finished a distant fourth. According to Wong, the reasons for his close second-place finish with Santoro were these:

It was clear that Barry [Chang] declaring late as a candidate in the 2007 election likely took some votes away from me, particularly among first-generation Chinese voters who could relate to him. Santoro was clearly an anti-Asian candidate, although he didn't run his campaign this way. It just worked out that way because of the five Asian American candidates running.[5]

Aside from Barry Chang taking away votes from Gilbert Wong, the campaign of Raj Abhyanker, an Asian Indian patent attorney, posed a threat of a different kind to Wong's bid—dividing the rising Asian Indian community from the general Asian American community. The Asian Indian community in Silicon Valley is seen as the "center of Asian Indian entrepreneurial power," given that 40 percent of Silicon Valley high-tech start-ups employ an Asian Indian (Kang 2000, 1). This combines with the fact that, during the 2000 presidential race, Bill Clinton raised $1.4 million in two Asian Indian–hosted fundraisers in Silicon Valley (Kang 2000).

In Cupertino city government, Asian Indians are only beginning to awaken politically, as the city has not had an Asian Indian city council member even though this community represents nearly 9 percent of the city population. Raj Abhyanker's 2007 campaign is a reflection of the positive trajectory of the Cupertino Asian Indian community's political mobilization for descriptive representative on the city council. While Abhyanker's campaign and the city's Asian Indian vote did not influence the outcome of the election, Asian Indians are likely to play an important role in the outcome of future city council elections in the form of votes and campaign contributions.

Tipping Point Politics Emerge

As the Asian American population becomes the majority racial group in Cupertino in 2010, will the outgoing majority white voters allow Asian Americans to become the majority on the city council or will a tipping point in Cupertino politics exist? Mark Santoro's surprising third-place finish, nearly thirty-three votes away from capturing the second seat, represents a precursor to this question. The 2008 special election that again pitted Santoro against two Asian American candidates is, by extension, this question's initial answer. Underlying the tipping point politics question is the perspective of white voters who view Asian American political incorporation efforts as a potential group threat in local politics in gaining too much political power too fast. This perspective is an important measuring stick for determining the future of Asian American descriptive representation in immigrant Transformed suburbs.

The 2008 special election was similar to the 2007 election in two important ways. First, Asian American candidates represented the majority in the field of candidates running with two, T. N. Ho and Chihua Wei; the other non-Asian candidate being Mark Santoro. Voters would choose between a majority Asian American candidate and a non-Asian candidate. Second, both Ho and Wei are foreign born. As seen in the past two elections, a shift in paradigms is occurring in Cupertino in which cultural issues (language and closeness of ethnic ties) are becoming as important as the candidates' political platforms for the predominantly foreign-born Asian American community.

Both Asian American candidates possessed previous political experience in local government prior to their 2008 Cupertino City Council campaigns. T. N. Ho, a high-tech professional who emigrated from Taiwan, received his master's degree in computer science and previously had served as a member of the Santa Clara Board of Education for over a dozen years. Two of the biggest criticisms of Ho, despite his previous public service, were (1) that he was perceived as a carpetbagger candidate who moved to Cupertino two years prior to the election, and (2) that he was quoted at a Chinese community event in the October 16, 2007, edition of the *Sing Tao* that he was running "to form a majority of Chinese-Americans in the city council so as to push for programs favoring the Chinese community" (*Cupertino Courier* 2007). This quotation became an issue for white community residents when former Cupertino city mayor Barbara Rogers criticized Ho for his comment. Ho said at a January 23, 2008, candidate forum that the statement was false and that he intended to serve the entire community. According to Ho: "What I actually said was I wanted Barry Chang to be elected with Kris Wang, and I would run in February. I said I hoped the three of us would work together to stop overbuilding. I never wanted to build a Chinese bloc. . . . I've never voted on a racial line" (Lu 2008, 1). After the October 16, 2007, story, *Sing Tao Daily* published two corrections on December 1 and 14, 2007, stating that the comment was never made by Ho (Lu 2008).

The second Asian American candidate, Chihua Wei, is also a former high-tech professional and immigrant from Taiwan who holds a master's degree in electrical computer engineering. Wei, a twenty-four-year resident of Cupertino, previously served on the Housing Commission and focused his campaign platform on smart growth. Wei arguably possessed the most local public service experience among all three city council candidates.

Mark Santoro held a PhD in electrical engineering but, unlike Ho and Wei, had no previous community public service aside from running for city council in 2007. According to his public biography: "The experience of building a home taught him a lot about Cupertino government. He now wants to give something back to the city of Cupertino" (City of Cupertino, City Council Candidate website 2007). Santoro's statement clearly demonstrates his limited political experience in comparison to T. N. Ho and Chihua Wei. Due to his lack of political experience, Santoro focused on a for-the-people campaign mantra in which he said that he wanted to give Cupertino back to the voters rather than to special interests. Santoro publicly refused any endorsements from elected officials and community groups, unlike Ho and Wei, and presented himself as being a candidate outside of the political establishment. Moreover, Santoro downplayed the racial classifications of the candidates in the minds of Cupertino voters. In the January 23 candidate forum, Santoro stated:

"People are talking about whether we are ready for a black or female president. It would be wonderful if we didn't notice they are black or female" (Lu 2008, 1). Santoro also mentioned that he had been labeled as the only Caucasian candidate in both the November election and special election, but that he saw himself and his opponents as just people (Lu 2008).

While the three city council candidates differed in their respective political experiences, the political platforms of Ho, Wei, and Santoro were similar in that they focused on the salient issues of smart growth, maintaining public school excellence, and maintaining affordable family housing, all contentious issues among a majority of Cupertino residents. Ho's public Candidate Statement mentioned the following with regard to smart growth:

> In the past several years, Cupertino officials have increased residential construction even to the degree of rezoning parcels in order to balance declines in sales tax revenues. This shortsightedness has caused undesirable impacts to the quality of our life, including overcrowding of our schools and severe traffic congestion. Cupertino needs a comprehensive, long-range plan with resident and business input. (City of Cupertino, City Council Candidate website 2007)

Santoro's public Candidate Statement also emphasized containing growth:

> Specifically, when looking at building within the city, I have seen large condo developments where neighbors were very much against those projects. I have seen building codes passed, like the 35% upper floor ratio, when most residents of Cupertino were against it. (City of Cupertino, City Council Candidate website 2007)

Wei's public Candidate Statement focused on affordable family housing in Cupertino:

> I have served on the Housing Commission to help create below-market rate housing. . . . I also have many years of senior management training and experience in the computer industry, and extensive training in economic and legal issues in the housing industry. (City of Cupertino, City Council Candidate website 2007)

Given that all three city council candidates focused on the three major issues for Cupertino voters and all had similar highly educated backgrounds, the 2008 election provides an opportunity to examine whether tipping point politics currently exists there. Santoro finished in first place with 5,642 total votes, or 55.4 percent, followed by Ho (3,748, or 36.8 percent) and Wei (802, or 7.9 percent). For the first time in Cupertino history since 1995, an Asian American running for Cupertino City Council failed to be elected.

If the political campaign finances and platforms were relatively equal among all three candidates, what were the deciding factors that allowed Santoro to win on such a convincing margin? The answer lies with the difficult subject of what some have alluded to in Cupertino and other similarly shifting suburbs. In other words, will the outgoing majority of white residents, particularly longtime residents and senior citizens, be ready to accept these changes or will they resist in other forms? In addressing this question, the latter will likely take shape beyond the classrooms and neighborhoods to the halls of city government as future Asian American candidates continue to build coalitions and gain the political trust of white residents and voters in the community.

It is clear that Mark Santoro's for-the-people campaign strategy resonated with voters who were weary of interest group politics in Cupertino. However, it is not conclusive whether this segment of the voter base was enough to sustain his nearly 56 percent vote margin. Other issues, such as perceived group threat among Caucasian voters, likely played a role in Santoro's election. Since no exit poll was conducted, we cannot determine with absolute certainty how racial groups voted for Santoro, T. N. Ho, and Chihua Wei. What can be clearly ascertained by the election results is that Santoro was the favorite among the majority of Cupertino voters and the 2008 election represents an extension of his 2007 campaign. Even though Santoro publicly stated he did not want to be viewed as the Caucasian candidate, race likely played an important role in both of his campaigns, which culminated in the success of his 2008 special election.

Emotional attachments of Cupertino's voters to the three city council candidates' racial backgrounds were central to the electoral outcome in 2008. Santoro's surname in juxtaposition to Ho's and Wei's Asian surnames on the voting ballot most likely played a crucial role in his success, particularly among white voters, who form the largest racial voting bloc among the approximately 27,000 registered voters in Cupertino (CityLab 2010).

A long-term and influential Cupertino resident of Italian descent, with access to many other long-term white residents' opinions through an affiliated community organization, said after the 2008 election: "I believe Santoro was the recipient of white votes because of the concern that Asians are taking over the city council."[6] Such perceptions and concerns of group threat among white voters would be tested in the 2009 Cupertino City Council election when three seats all held by white members opened up due to term limits.

Capturing the Majority

Perhaps the clearest sign that Cupertino embodies a Transformed I suburb is the 2009 city council election, in which Asian Americans became the majority. During this election, seven candidates (four of them Asian American) ran for three open city council seats. Among the Asian American candidates were Cupertino Unified School District trustee Barry Chang (who ran in the previous election cycle), Cupertino Chamber of Commerce board member Mahesh Nihalani,

Cupertino Public Safety Commission vice chair Daniel Nguyen, and the parks and recreation commissioner Darcy Paul. The three non-Asian candidates were incumbents Orrin Mahoney and Mark Santoro along with the planning commissioner Marty Miller.

The 2009 city council election was unique when compared to the previous election cycles with regard to the diverse political platforms among the seven candidates. For example, incumbent Orrin Mahoney's campaign platform focused on improving the city's fiscal position in order to deliver key city services, and enhancing areas for residents to live and work together. But incumbent Mark Santoro focused on a more transparent government, reduced traffic around the schools, and government for the people. Among the Asian American candidates, Barry Chang centered his campaign on health and safety issues, fiscal responsibility, and green and clean environment in the city. Daniel Nguyen concentrated on fiscal responsibility, public safety, and preserving the small city character with smart growth initiatives. Darcy Paul focused on sustainable development and more use of green technology, followed by greater fiscal responsibility. Mahesh Nihalani concentrated on maintaining jobs in the city, introducing a health partnership between the city and small businesses, and managing city resources with sound fiscal leadership.

These divergent political platforms show that race and ethnicity are not enough to sustain support for Asian American candidates among Asian American voters. There has been a gradual political incorporation of Asian American candidates as their respective campaign platforms have become politically indistinguishable from those of non-Asian candidates with regard to the main issues they must pursue to create a two-tiered campaign strategy. Clearly, these issues resonated with the voters because all four Asian American candidates received 13,837 total votes, or 41 percent of all votes.

The results of the 2009 elections were the following: Mahoney (4,882 votes, or 18.1 percent), Barry Chang (4,212, or 15.8 percent), Mark Santoro (4,142 votes, or 15.6 percent), Marty Miller (3,804 votes, or 14.3 percent), Mahesh Nihalani (3,348 votes, or 12.6 percent), Daniel Nguyen (3,309 votes, or 12.4 percent), and Darcy Paul (2,968 votes, or 11.2 percent). Chang's second-place finish allowed him to join Kris Wang and Gilbert Wong on the city council, which provided Asian Americans with the first majority on the council in the city's history. Chang's finish also demonstrates again that multiple Asian American candidates running in Cupertino elections do not necessarily split the Asian vote and prevent an Asian American candidate from winning.

Taking the Next Step

Asian American–influenced suburbs serve as political incubators for training the next generation of Asian American elected leaders who develop the political capital and experience to move up to higher levels. An example is Paul

Fong's 2008 California State Assembly, District 22, campaign. District 22 contains large portions of the suburbs of Santa Clara County, including Cupertino. The seat was vacated in 2008 after term limits forced out Assembly member Sally Lieber. At the federal level, a large portion of Santa Clara County has been able to elect and reelect US Representative Mike Honda (District 15) since 2001. The question of whether the same suburb, Cupertino, could help elect an Asian American to the California State Assembly was now tested.

Local Cupertino politics was well represented in the District 22 Democratic primary election among the four candidates who declared. Cupertino City Council member Kris Wang and former vice president of the Foothill-DeAnza Community College District Paul Fong both declared their candidacies. Interestingly another Asian American, Anna Song, former Santa Clara Board of Education member, also declared to run, giving Asian Americans the majority (three of the four) of the Democratic candidates running, another first for the state district. The fourth Democratic candidate, Dominic Caserta, is a high school civics teacher and Santa Clara City Council member.

As shown in Table 5.3, the three Asian American candidates running in the Democratic primary were Paul Fong (first), Kris Wang (third), and Anna Song (fourth). Fong clearly pursued a two-tiered strategy in which he received mainstream endorsements from former Assembly member Sally Lieber, the Sierra Club, and the California Democratic Party, among many others. The presence of Fong, Wang, and Song likely split the Asian American vote. But this did not prevent Fong from winning the Democratic primary, as has historically been the case for Asian American candidates who relied solely on the Asian American vote in California State Assembly elections. Asian Americans can win in multiple Asian American candidate races as long as they primarily pursue a mandatory mainstream campaign while focusing on building a panethnic coalition among the broader Asian American community. Fong would face another Asian American, Brent T. Oya, who ran unopposed in his Republican primary.

Table 5.3 Results of the California Assembly, District 22, Democratic Primary Election, 2008

Candidate	Total Votes	Percentage
Paul Fong	8,473	35.7
Dominic Caserta	7,115	30.0
Kris Wang	4,123	17.4
Anna Song	4,035	17.0

Source: Santa Clara County Registrar of Voters, November 4, 2008, Primary Elections.

Table 5.4 Results of the California Assembly, District 22, General Election, 2008

Candidate	Total Votes	Percentage
Paul Fong	93,240	76
Brent Oya	29,466	24

Source: Santa Clara County Registrar of Voters, November 4, 2008, Primary Elections.

As illustrated in Table 5.4, Fong easily defeated Oya by winning 76 percent of the total votes in the November 2008 general election. An important aspect of Fong's victory was that it also was a victory for the Asian American political leadership in Cupertino and Santa Clara County. It also demonstrated that local Asian American candidates could reach the next level of State Assembly politics. Previously, Asian American electoral success had been at the city district level, but not at the statewide district level. This has been one of the weaknesses of the Asian American community in California politics that African Americans and Mexican Americans have been able to overcome. Fong's victory affirms that local Asian American elected officials can reach the next level using the same two-tiered strategy that has allowed many Asian American candidates to be successful in suburbs like Cupertino, which serve as political incubators for Asian American elected leadership.

Potential Barriers in Cupertino Politics: Substantive Representation

Asian American candidates in Cupertino have demonstrated political power in their ability to win consistently elected representation for incumbents and new candidates during the past decade in local elections. The next question must focus on whether this has made any difference in descriptive indicators beyond descriptive representation to achieve the highest form of political incorporation in city government—substantive authority and influence. In other words, are Asian Americans represented in city government beyond the makeup of the Cupertino City Council, which includes city employment and is within the governing regimes of key city policy discussions such as community economic development?

As in any suburb like Cupertino, one of the most important issues facing a community has been rapid, smart, or slow economic growth in the downtown areas of the city. Asian American business interests must learn to play the political game and work with city leadership in gaining access to opportunities.

In 2007, for example, even with the presence of two Asian Americans (Kris Wang and Gilbert Wong) on the city council, Asian Americans lacked a persistent voice in key business decisions influencing city redevelopment. That was because Asian American businesses are still learning to play the political game of backdoor politics that have allowed non-Asian businesses to circumvent formal city zoning procedures. Former council member Kris Wang attributes this lack of influence to other factors, such as cultural practices, in which Asian American business interests are not aggressive enough and do not understand how the political system works. A primary example can be seen in the organized special interest groups, such as the Concerned Citizens of Cupertino (CCC), which attempts to limit suburban sprawl in the city, and the Alliance for a Better Cupertino (ABC), a pro-growth group. These groups have circumvented the city council in battling each other to determine what can be built, how it can be built, and other rules governing growth in Cupertino ("CCC Gathers Signatures," 2004). During the January 22, 2004, meeting of the Cupertino City Council, the CCC introduced three initiatives (the Building Height Initiative, Density Initiative, and Setback Initiative) and was able to obtain the required number of signatures to place them on the November 2004 citywide ballot ("CCC Gathers Signatures," 2004). Asian American interests must compete with special interest groups like the CCC that have been successful in circumventing the Cupertino City Council by bringing their initiatives directly to the city voters.

While they have not been full partners with such organized special interest groups in dominating key issues in Cupertino, Chinese Americans (particularly immigrants) have begun to mobilize politically and to create their own organizations. For example, Chinese Americans have taken on city government leaders, including Kris Wang, and other economic development interests in challenging the city's approved zoning for a large-scale Cupertino condominium proposal. An example is Patty Chi, an immigrant from Taiwan who arrived in Cupertino during her senior year in high school, graduated from Santa Clara University, and purchased her first home in Cupertino with her engineer husband in 2000. In 2006, Chi became concerned about the city's rezoning for a 520-unit condominium near her home, which is situated in a neighborhood adjacent to the city's megamall, Cupertino Square. This outdated mall began remodeling in 2005 to attract more retail businesses, an AMC Theatres complex, chain restaurants, and upscale condominiums. Given this rapid development plan that threatened to change the small-town character of the city, Chi helped to establish a community-based organization known as Cupertino Against Rezoning (CARe). Consider the following from a June 20, 2006, article in the *World Journal,* "Patty Chi Can Do Nothing About the Suit Against the City of Cupertino Referenda. The Issue Is Not That She Opposes Vallco Mall Development but There Needs to Be an Overall Plan":

On the morning of April 19, Chi, pushing her two-year-old daughter in a stroller, went with some neighbors to present more than 9900 signatures to Cupertino City Hall. The City Clerk informed them that by law there needed to be two people's names on the initiatives and on the spot Chi and another Chinese-American Helen Luk became the representatives for those filing the petitions and thus they became the defendants in this suit. . . . That year she also swore an oath to become an American citizen, "but I registered to vote last year in order to vote yes on the three ABC initiatives to restrict development. . . . In the past few months I have discovered that there really are a lot of Chinese people in Cupertino, and Asian Americans are registered voters. There aren't as few as I thought, and everyone is enthusiastic." ("Patty Chi Can Do Nothing About the Suit" 2006, 1)

The fruits of Chi's labor in 2006 through CARe have slowed unbridled growth of dense housing in Cupertino through legal wrestling by the competing interests.

Chi's grassroots mobilization demonstrates the potential of Asian American suburban politics and how their group interests can be aligned with white group interests around local development issues. It also shows how Asian American voters became mobilized by grassroots politics rather than descriptive representatives in Cupertino because of Asian American politically active individuals and the ethnic print media. This community is now beginning to exert its political voice beyond electing descriptive representatives to the city council. This will remain a major challenge for Asian Americans in Cupertino, especially the Chinese and Taiwanese American communities, where a large immigrant population exists. At the same time, Cupertino provides a blueprint of an archetypal Asian American Transformed I suburb from which other Asian-influenced suburbs can learn.

Notes

1. Michael Chang, mayor of Cupertino, interviewed by the author, Cupertino, California, September 16, 2003.

2. Paul Fong, board president of Evergreen Community College, interviewed by the author, Cupertino, California, August 8, 2003.

3. Paul Fong, board president of Evergreen Community College, interviewed by the author, Cupertino, California, August 13, 2003.

4. Kris Wang, Cupertino City Council member, interviewed by the author, Cupertino, California, August 8, 2003.

5. Gilbert Wong, Cupertino City Council member, interviewed the author, Cupertino, California, December 6, 2007.

6. Italian American community leader, interviewed by the author, Cupertino, California, February 23, 2008.

6

Garden Grove and Westminster, California: Vietnamese American Political Incorporation in Orange County's "Little Saigon"

Orange County, California, is home to the largest aggregate Vietnamese American population, nearly 136,000, of any county in the continental United States (US Census 2006d). The cities that primarily form the expanding area of Little Saigon are Garden Grove and Westminster, two suburbs where Vietnamese Americans have achieved the greatest level of local political incorporation in the nation. After World War II, the population of Garden Grove was mainly white. However, beginning with the refugee relocation plans in the 1970s after the end of the Vietnam War, Vietnamese refugees have gradually changed the demographic makeup of this city. A gravitational migration facilitated by established community, cultural, and economic support networks has made the Vietnamese Americans a significant population in Garden Grove.

The rise of the Vietnamese American population in Little Saigon has also culminated in its political incorporation in local and statewide districts, which is beginning to rival the level of political incorporation that Asian Americans have attained in Santa Clara County. In November 2008, Vietnamese Americans in Westminster, California, obtained the first majority Vietnamese American city council when Truong Diep was elected. Diep joined two other Vietnamese Americans, Mayor Pro Tem Tri Ta and council member Andy Quach, on the five-person Westminster City Council. The rise of Vietnamese American politics in Westminster has been paralleled by the rise in the number of elected Vietnamese Americans in Orange County. In 2008, ten Vietnamese Americans served on its school boards, city councils, county board of supervisors, and in the California State Assembly (Tran and Berthelsen 2008). By comparison, in 1992, the first Vietnamese American elected official in the United States, Tony Lam, was elected to the Westminster City Council. This positive trajectory in Vietnamese American political incorporation has been due to the emergence

Map 6.1 Vietnamese American Population Distribution in Garden Grove and Westminster, 2000

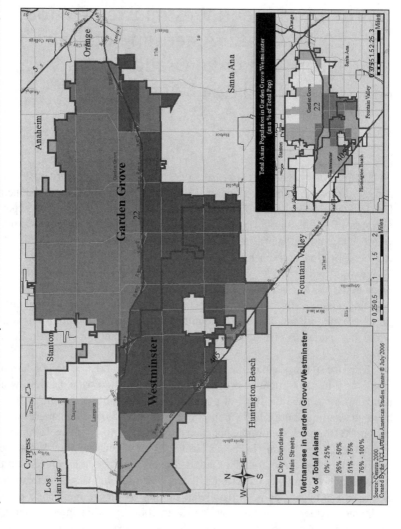

and visibility of the Vietnamese American population and its community institutions in this region, specifically in Westminster and Garden Grove, and the successful integration of Vietnamese Americans in the state Republican Party. As they have gained political success in Orange County, Vietnamese American have been courted by Orange County's white power structure along with Latino elected officials. Vietnamese American voters currently account for 40 percent of Westminster's total registered voters. As California state senator Louis Correa (D-Santa Ana) stated: "I don't believe in central Orange County you can be a successful elected official without the Vietnamese vote" (Tran and Berthelsen 2008, 1).

Map 6.1 illustrates the suburbs of Westminster and Garden Grove as two major destinations of the Vietnamese American refugee community in Orange County. According to the 1990 US Census, the Vietnamese population in Orange County was 71,822, with the two largest concentrations in the suburbs of Westminster and Garden Grove. In 2000, it was 135,548, nearly an 89 percent increase, making Vietnamese Americans the largest Asian ethnic group in the county (Vo and Danico 2004). Westminster, the smaller of the two suburbs, has a total population of 88,207 of which Vietnamese Americans represent 27,109, or approximately 31 percent of the population (US Census 2006e). Garden Grove has a total population of 165,196 Vietnamese Americans (US Census 2006f).

As a result of this demographic boom, the Vietnamese ethnic print media has become equally pronounced. Two Vietnamese newspapers, *Nguoi Viet Daily News* and *Viet Bao Daily* (both located in Westminster, California), are among the largest dailies circulated in Orange County. Their total circulations are 18,000 and 22,000, respectively. *Viet Bao Daily* is the largest Vietnamese American newspaper in the nation, and *Nguoi Viet Daily News* was the first Vietnamese daily outside of Vietnam. Among Vietnamese radio stations, the two most prominent are Little Saigon Radio and Radio Bolsa, which offer twenty-four-hour broadcasts in Vietnamese covering a wide range of issues from politics to popular culture.

Local Government Structure and Formal Electoral Rules

The city government of Westminster consists of five part-time seats on the city council in which each member is elected to four-year terms with no term limits. The citywide elections are staggered (two one cycle, three the following cycle) each election year. The top vote getters determine who fill the open seats. The mayor of Westminster is elected by a citywide vote each election cycle and serves for two years with no term limits. The mayor pro tem is annually appointed by a majority vote of the city council. The two main requirements for all candidates are that they be a US citizen (naturalized or US born) and a city resident. The citizen members of the city commissions are nominated for appointment by a council member, interviewed, and then voted on by a majority of the city council.

In Garden Grove, the local elected government consists of a three-person city council, a mayor pro tem, and a mayor. Members of the city council are elected by citywide vote to four-year terms through staggered elections every two years and have an eight-year term limit. The top two vote getters fill both vacated seats. The mayor pro tem is considered to be a city council member, and is appointed by a majority vote of the council every two years. The mayor of Garden Grove is elected by citywide vote each election cycle and can serve for four consecutive terms, or eight years. Each position requires the candidate to be a US citizen (naturalized or US born) and a city resident. Garden Grove residents are solely appointed by the mayor to the various city commissions.

As in other Asian-influenced suburbs, the citywide election process has facilitated group political mobilization and the development of the key political loci in the Vietnamese American community. Recent political mobilization efforts have allowed Vietnamese Americans to become prominent political players in Orange County and GOP politics. What is fascinating about this is that major obstacles needed to be overcome not only in developing a political consciousness, but also in surviving a violent war, witnessing the persecution of family members, and experiencing the resultant traumatic family disruption as political refugees in the United States.

A Key Political Locus: The Vietnamese American Ethnic Media

The emergence of a significant Vietnamese American population in Little Saigon has generated a proliferation of Vietnamese American ethnic media. Each of these Vietnamese American printed dailies caters to a predominantly transnational Vietnamese American community that is eager to learn about news and entertainment in both the United States and their former homeland. For example, in the area of broadcast television, Little Saigon TV was created in 1986 by John Thai Dinh, who did not like the way in which Vietnamese American refugees were being portrayed on television. In 2004, it was estimated that nearly 250,000 daily viewers watched the one-hour news program that focuses on Vietnam news—one of many daily programs on the network. Aside from challenging stereotypical images of Vietnamese Americans often found in the mainstream, Little Saigon TV plays an instrumental role in the political education and mobilization of Vietnamese Americans by keeping the community connected and informed politically. According to Dinh: "This is what our program has been doing: breaking down the issues for people to help them decide. Little Saigon has been known as Republican country but like everyone else we have matured politically. We don't just vote partisan" (Do 2004, 1).

Little Saigon Radio, also headquartered in Westminster, has emerged to provide radio broadcasts that connect politics, policies, entertainment, news, and culture to its listeners. Founded in 1993, Little Saigon Radio broadcasts to the three most populous regions of Vietnamese Americans: Orange and Los Angeles Counties, San Jose, and Houston. Given the focus and reach of the Vietnamese American political locus, the ethnic media, Little Saigon Radio has become an important political ally for Vietnamese American candidates and their respective campaigns.

The political dimensions of the Vietnamese American ethnic media occur during group political mobilization. Many of the readers, viewers, and listeners of this ethnic media are Vietnamese Americans who reside in regions with large Vietnamese American populations both within and outside of Little Saigon. As a result, group political mobilization around Vietnamese American local candidates in Little Saigon, as facilitated by the Vietnamese American ethnic media, has the ability to reach Vietnamese Americans in a broad geographic context that extends beyond citywide districts. As will be shown below, such was the case with former Garden Grove City Council member and current California State Assembly member Van Tran (R–District 68) during his historic 2004 assembly campaign to become the first Vietnamese American to be elected to the state capitol. Tran's effective use of Little Saigon Radio would bring old and new Vietnamese Americans into the political process, particularly for those outside of District 68, which contains Garden Grove and Westminster, in the form of campaign contributions.

The Sleeping Giant Awakens:
The Quest for Descriptive Representation in Little Saigon

The relocation and settlement patterns of the Vietnamese American community in Orange County have transformed it into a political voice to be reckoned with in local- and state-level politics. Two important events in Westminster signaled the gradual political awakening of the Vietnamese American community in Little Saigon. The first occurred in 1992 when Tony Lam became the nation's first Vietnamese American elected official on the Westminster City Council. Since then, five Vietnamese Americans have run for the city council, with two successes (Tony Lam and Andy Quach). Quach was first elected in 2002 and currently serves on the city council. The second event transpired over a four-month period from December 1998 to March 1999 when anti-Communist Vietnamese Americans protested in front of Hitek Video over the owner Truong Trang's public display of a portrait of Ho Chi Minh and a Communist flag of Vietnam (N.-N. Ong and Myer 2008). This incident was not alone in demonstrating an emerging Vietnamese American political consciousness in Orange County. From 1975 to 2001, there were 209 protest events led by Vietnamese Americans in Orange County (N.-N. Ong and Myer 2008). For

Welcome to Little Saigon
The first Vietnamese American suburb.
Reprinted with permission from City of Westminster.

example, in 1999, Westminster council member Tony Lam became the recall target of anti-Communist Vietnamese Americans who felt he was not vocal enough on the Hitek Video situation.

The political awakening of Garden Grove began when the city elected the first Vietnamese American, Van Tran, to its city council in 2000. When Tran decided to run for the California State Assembly in 2004, the Garden Grove Vietnamese American community helped elect Janet Nguyen, who currently serves the county supervisor. Nguyen is the first woman to serve on the city council in thirty-five years and the youngest to be elected, at the age of twenty-eight years. Previously, Nguyen served on the Garden Grove Planning Commission, an appointment made by Tran, and worked as the district director for former Assembly member Ken Maddox, whom Tran succeeded in 2004.

In November 2006, Dina Nguyen, an attorney in the Orange County Superior Court for eighteen years who previously served on the Garden Grove Neighborhood Improvement and Conservation Commission, became the third Vietnamese American to be elected to the Garden Grove City Council. Similar to the Cupertino case study in Chapter 5, the political incorporation of Vietnamese and Asian Americans in Garden Grove and Westminster extends beyond the city council to representation on influential policymaking city commissions and school boards. For example, in 2006, three Asian Americans (one Vietnamese American) served on the seven-member Garden Grove Planning Commission.

On another high-profile commission, the Neighborhood Improvement and Conservation Commission, two Vietnamese Americans served among the seven members, with one of them (Dina Nguyen) eventually getting elected to the Garden Grove City Council. It is not surprising that Dina Nguyen was nominated by former council member Van Tran. Among the current six school board members who direct the Garden Grove Unified School District, three are Vietnamese American, including school board president Lan Nguyen.

Vietnamese Americans in Garden Grove have clearly attained local political incorporation beyond electing and replacing descriptive representatives to the city council. They have achieved this through a network and alliance among various Vietnamese American community political loci and candidates. Once Van Tran was elected in Garden Grove, he strategically placed other Vietnamese Americans on key city commissions that would provide them (Janet Nguyen and Dina Nguyen) with the necessary political experience and networks to run successful city council campaigns.

A Vietnamese American–Majority City Council in Westminster

The city of Westminster became one of two suburbs with an Asian American–majority city council outside of Cupertino in the continental United States. All three Asian Americans who serve on the five-person city council are Vietnamese Americans (Andy Quach, Tri Ta, and Truong Diep). Quach, a former US Navy officer whose family fled from Vietnam in 1980, was first elected to the Westminster City Council in 2002 after serving as vice chairman of the high-profile Westminster Planning Commission. Tri Ta, a protégé of Quach, was the third Vietnamese American man elected to the Westminster City Council, in November 2006, the same year that Dina Nguyen was elected to the Garden Grove City Council. Ta had previously served as a commissioner of the Westminster Energy Committee and the Advisory Committee for the Disabled. Ta and his family arrived in the United States in 1992 when he was nineteen, and he earned a BA in political science and an MA in international relations from California State University, Los Angeles. Ta gained his initial political experience by working as a legislative assistant for California Assemblyman Jim Morrissey in 1998. Diep was elected to the Westminster City Council in 2008 in a competitive five-person race. His political platform was similar to that of other Vietnamese American elected officials in Westminster, centering on fiscal conservatism with a focus on enhancing public safety and better parks. Diep, a graduate of San Diego State University with a degree in public administration, was also a refugee whose family fled Vietnam in 1991 and relocated in Southern California. Like many Asian American city council members, Diep previously held various high-profile city commission positions, such as vice chairman of the Westminster Traffic Commission, director of the Midway City

Sanitation District, and advisory commissioner in the Orange County district attorney's office. Prior to all of these positions, it is not surprising that Diep's first foray into electoral politics was as a senior field representative for California State Assembly member Van Tran.

As in Garden Grove, Vietnamese Americans in Westminster have been successful in demonstrating electoral sustainability by establishing a pipeline of city commissioners who would later run successful city council campaigns. This pipeline is clearly evident with the current Vietnamese American makeup on the following Westminster city commissions: Water Rate Structure Committee (one among five members), Advisory Committee for the Disabled (two among five members), Community Advisory Group (two among five members), Financial Review Committee (two among five members), and the Mayor's Ad Hoc Zoning Code Update Committee (two among ten members). In short, the presence of Vietnamese Americans has transformed the city government in both Garden Grove and Westminster to one that reflects their group interests. The first step in achieving this transformation is arguably minority elected representation on the city council, which allows minority members to make more appointments to city commissions and at a quicker pace than other coethnics. Many of these Vietnamese American commission members will likely run for future local positions once their appointments end, as seen with Dina Nguyen, Tri Ta, and Truong Diep.

The Vietnamese American communities in the cities of Garden Grove and Westminster have demonstrated the ability to elect and replace outgoing descriptive representatives with other descriptive representatives, an important measuring stick for political power of a group at any level. What is unique about this situation compared to Cupertino is that the Vietnamese American community consists primarily of refugees who began arriving in the United States as recently as the 1980s. Among all the Southeast Asian refugee groups, which also include Cambodian, Hmong, and Laotian Americans, Vietnamese Americans have arguably achieved the greatest level of political incorporation in American politics. Little Saigon represents a political incubator for state-level Vietnamese American elected representatives, as it did for former Garden Grove City Council member Van Tran.

Political Capital in Little Saigon

In 2004, Van Tran, a Republican, became the first Vietnamese American California State Assembly member by winning his first campaign in District 68, which includes Costa Mesa, Garden Grove, Westminster, Fountain Valley, Stanton, Anaheim, and Newport Beach. Tran easily defeated Democrat Al Snook with 61 percent of the total votes. The key to Tran's successful campaign was his ability to form a cross-racial coalition that consisted mainly of whites (non-Asian) and Vietnamese Americans with support primarily from the California Republican Party machine in Orange County. The role of the California Republican Party is unique for Asian American candidates, and explains the limited role that Vietnamese American community-based organizations played during Tran's 2004 campaign. Tran utilized one of the most important roles of community-based organizations for Asian American candidates in the area of fund-raising by focusing on another Vietnamese American political locus, the Vietnamese media, to help raise funds both within and outside of District 68.

These Vietnamese Americans clearly responded to Van Tran's 2004 campaign strategy, allowing him to become the nation's highest elected official of Vietnamese descent. In Orange County, Vietnamese American Republicans overwhelmingly outnumber Democrats by a 2:1 ratio (Tran and Berthelsen 2008). This ratio is even larger when it comes to Vietnamese American elected officials. One of the key factors for Tran was the institutional support provided by the California Republican Party in the form of major political endorsements, campaign finance, and candidate slate placements. Another major factor was the political mobilization of the Vietnamese American community through the ethnic media. The influence of Tran's California State Assembly campaign can be seen in both these areas (campaign contributions and ethnic media coverage) of Vietnamese American group political mobilization.

Table 6.1 demonstrates the monetary influence of the Garden Grove and Westminster Vietnamese American community. Nearly 92 percent of Van Tran's total Vietnamese American contributions ($332,364) came from within the political boundaries of District 68, primarily from Westminster and Garden Grove. Using surname identification to identify Vietnamese contributors, Tran received $74,368 and $59,335 from Vietnamese donors in Garden Grove and

Table 6.1 Van Tran's Campaign Contributions by Racial Group and Location, 2004 Primary Election

Racial and Ethnic Group	Total Funds ($)	Funds Within District ($)	Percentage	Funds Outside District ($)	Percentage
Vietnamese	332,364	306,066	92.0	26,297	7.9
Other Asian	105,499	52,400	49.7	53,099	50.3
Non-Asian	83,140	28,060	33.8	55,080	66.3
Other	300,084	91,409	30.5	208,675	69.6
Total	821,087	477,935	58.2	343,152	41.8

Westminster, respectively, or approximately 40 percent of all Tran's total contribution amounts from Vietnamese Americans.

The amount of monetary support that Van Tran received from the Vietnamese American community is not surprising given his name recognition after a successful 2000 election to the Garden Grove City Council. The ethnic print media, particularly the Vietnamese American print and electronic media, played a key role during group political mobilization around Tran's campaign. Such electronic media networks include Little Saigon TV and Radio Vietnam, both of which have nationwide broadcasts. The exposure and free publicity played a vital role during group political mobilization. For many Vietnamese Americans, Tran's 2004 election extended beyond Little Saigon in Orange County because 64 percent of Tran's total Vietnamese American contributors resided outside of District 68.

Mobilizing the Vietnamese American Print Media

The Vietnamese American ethnic print media played a key role in mobilizing both local and national support for Van Tran's campaign by connecting him to the local, state, and national Vietnamese American communities. According to Tran:

> The Vietnamese American media network is both very insular and national. If I go on Saigon Network, you will hear me in San Jose and on the East Coast. I'm a known quantity in the [local and national] Vietnamese American community. I only go on the air when I need to go on the air. . . . The message becomes very clear to them.[1]

The *Viet Bao Daily* was instrumental in mobilizing Southern California Vietnamese Americans around Van Tran's candidacy. In 2004, there were twenty-three articles related to Tran's campaign. In three of the articles, Tran's picture was also prominently featured. In comparison, the *Orange County Register* printed thirteen articles related to Tran's campaign from January 2003 to December 2004.

Many of the *Viet Bao Daily* articles focused on Tran's historic attempt to become the first Vietnamese American California State Assembly member—for example, March 4, 2004, "Lawyer Van Tran Wins Primary, One Step Closer to Making History." Articles also covered the political mobilization of the Vietnamese American community, for example, January 10, 2004, "1,000 Register to Vote for Lawyer Tran Thai Van"; February 25, 2004, "Last Day to Register for Absentee Voting, Lawyer Van Needs Volunteers"; July 8, 2004, "Lawyer Tran Thai Van to Travel to New York—Visits with Vietnamese Community, Stirs up Support"; and August 30, 2004, "700 People from the North Fundraise for Tran Thai Van."

Content analyses of the *Viet Bao Daily* articles show the overwhelming amount of favorable coverage that Van Tran received on his campaign-related activities during the 2004 primary and general elections. The ethnic print media findings parallel Tran's contribution results in Table 6.1; that is, Tran received national coverage and campaign contributions from both the Vietnamese American media and community. The ethnic print media helps candidates shape and deliver their messages to the Vietnamese American community in the political district and beyond, and represents an important political ally. Vietnamese American dailies like *Viet Bao* provided Tran's campaign with free coverage (also known as "earned" coverage as opposed to "paid" coverage) and name recognition in the Vietnamese American community both within and outside of District 68. Vietnamese ethnic media also served as an impetus for group political mobilization in the form of campaign contributions and voter turnout, the two most important aspects of any campaign. This is particularly important within the suburban context in areas populated by Vietnamese Americans like Garden Grove and Westminster. The effect is that, instead of being a swing vote as in larger districts, Vietnamese Americans can be the majority vote to propel candidates like Tran into elected office more than once. This occurred in 2000 during Tran's Garden Grove City Council campaign, and again in 2004 with his California State Assembly campaign.

Revisiting the Multiple Racial and Ethnic Candidates Scenario

The inevitable trend that is taking shape in the Vietnamese American communities of Westminster and Garden Grove is being witnessed in similar Asian American Transformed I suburbs, as seen in Chapter 5 with Cupertino, which has multiple ethnic candidates running against each other for higher elected offices beyond the local level. This trend can be seen as the by-product of successful local political incorporation in the region, and again tests the prevailing assumption that multiple ethnic candidates are likely to cancel each other out because they will split the votes. In Orange County's Forty-Seventh Congressional District, which includes Little Saigon, State Assembly member Van Tran and another Republican challenger, Quang X. Pham, are attempting to unseat current Democratic congresswoman Loretta Sanchez in the 2010 election. Pham, a decorated US Marine veteran, is a health care entrepreneur. He is the author of a widely acclaimed book, *A Sense of Duty: My Father, My American Journey*, which tells the story of his flight with his family to the United States as a refugee (Pham 2005). According to June 30, 2009, campaign disclosure records, Tran, who is endorsed by the Republican Party and a member of the National Republican Congressional Committee's Young Guns program, had already raised $254,000. To counter this, Pham contributed his own personal wealth to his campaign war chest to meet his $250,000 goal.

However, in March 2010, Pham bowed out of the Republican primary, citing the need to focus exclusively on running his company (Moxley 2010).

Similar to Paul Fong's 2008 California State Assembly District 22 race that pitted him against three other Asian Americans, the fact that two Vietnamese Americans were running against each other in the Republican primary election should not be seen as the result of a divided community. Rather it should be thought of as the natural progression from a medium to strong level of political incorporation of one of the region's most influential groups in the Republican Party. As a result, it is likely that such multiple-candidate scenarios will be overcome because, similar to Asian Americans in Cupertino and Santa Clara County as seen in Chapter 5, Vietnamese Americans in Orange County have become politically entrenched in one of the major parties in the region. What will be interesting to observe in the 2010 election will not be whether a Vietnamese American will successfully emerge in the Republican primary election, but whether that candidate will be successful in defeating the incumbent Democrat Sanchez, who won 60 percent of the district's vote in the previous general election.

Barriers to Vietnamese American Political Incorporation in Little Saigon

Overall, Vietnamese Americans in Little Saigon have achieved great inroads to full political incorporation given both the length of time they have lived in the United States and their refugee status. It is a true testament to this community's resolve. In both Garden Grove and Westminster, Vietnamese Americans have attained a degree of political power that is more than symbolic, as witnessed by their ability to replace outgoing ethnic representatives with coethnics. This was the case with Janet Nguyen winning a seat after Van Tran left the Garden Grove City Council to seek a State Assembly seat. After Janet Nguyen left her position, Dina Nguyen was elected in November 2006. In Westminster, since the historic election of Tony Lam to the city council, several Vietnamese Americans have served, including current city council members Andy Quach and Tri Ta. These findings strongly suggest that the Vietnamese American communities in both cities have achieved more than symbolic representation. In fact, they have demonstrated over a period of time the ability to replicate electoral success in their respective local governments. Moreover, these cities have also been able to support a state-level candidate (Van Tran) and play an important role in winning statewide positions in their districts.

While Vietnamese Americans in both Westminster and Garden Grove have enjoyed unparalleled political success in these suburbs, they have not yet achieved full political incorporation. A large percentage of Vietnamese Americans remain unnaturalized US citizens and the community still suffers from relatively low voter turnout. Moreover, Vietnamese Americans are highly underrepresented on citywide commissions in both cities, as noted earlier, which may have an impact on establishing a formal pipeline of Vietnamese American city council candidates in the future. And finally, perhaps the biggest barrier to full political incorporation of Vietnamese Americans in Westminster and Garden Grove rests with the political cleavages that exist within this community. Such divisions include the Old Guard elite with strong ties to Vietnam's past Communist regime, the anti-Communist faction, and an emerging Vietnamese American community composed of young, mostly US-educated professionals who no longer cling to homeland politics, but see their interests more aligned with other Asian American or other racial groups. The latter group is likely to emerge as the most prominent faction within Vietnamese American communities in the future.

Without a doubt, the Westminster and Garden Grove cases illustrate the political awakening of the Vietnamese American community with institutional support from the local and state Republican political machinery, which has lessened Vietnamese American candidates' heavy reliance on ethnic community-based organizations as seen in other Asian American–influenced suburbs. The current political status of Vietnamese Americans is testimony to the resiliency of a community that arrived in the United States as political refugees, not immigrants. This makes their political successes even more remarkable given the short period since their arrival in the 1970s. Despite this high level of political incorporation, political barriers are emerging within the Vietnamese American community in both Orange County and Santa Clara County, which contain the largest Vietnamese American populations in the United States, at 130,000 and 110,000 respectively.

One of the most visible barriers is the ideological division between the Old Guard (anti-Communist Vietnamese refugees who fled Saigon) and the New Guard (Vietnamese Americans who are too young to remember their homeland or were born in the United States) around political and cultural issues salient within the Vietnamese American community. All former refugees, the Old Guard Vietnamese American leaders are entrenched in the symbolic politics and meanings of their past, as in the term *Little Saigon*. Elected officials such as Tony Lam, the first Vietnamese American city council member elected in the continental United States, and current California Assembly member Van Tran, who began his political career on the Garden Grove City Council, are members are of this generation. Much of their political mobilization centers on the older Vietnamese American community members who vividly remember their lives in Vietnam, the fall of Saigon, political persecution, and being displaced throughout the world. As a result, they are deeply anti-Communist. This emotional attachment to the metaphor of Saigon through labels like "Little Saigon" underlies their strong anti-Communist beliefs. This has made the Republican Party a political recruiting machine for mobilizing the Vietnamese

American community to vote for and contribute to both non-Asian and Vietnamese American candidates throughout Orange County.

The emerging New Guard Vietnamese American leadership is embodied in the contemporary Vietnamese American candidate who either fled as a young refugee or was US born and educated, such as Garden Grove City Council member Dina Nguyen and Westminster City Council members Andy Quach and Tri Ta. They rely less on the older Vietnamese American community by focusing on mainstream voter issues. Many of the New Guard candidates are a product of their acculturation experiences of growing up in the United States and, thus, tend to have less emotional attachment to the symbolism of Saigon. In contrast to the Old Guard, the emerging leaders of the New Guard realize foremost the political necessity to build cross-racial alliances with whites as opposed to focusing solely on ethnic issues.

Such ideological divisions recently manifested in the large city of San Jose, California, which is located in Santa Clara County and is home to the largest aggregate population of Vietnamese Americans (84,635 in 2005) of any US city. At issue was the renaming of a large Vietnamese American business district in South San Jose as "Little Saigon." Interestingly, Madison Nguyen, San Jose's first Vietnamese American city council member, opposed this name because the district also contains Latino and white businesses, preferring the name "Vietnam Town Business District." The San Jose City Council initially did reject wishes of many Vietnamese Americans to have the business area officially named Little Saigon. This was perceived as a slap in the face by many community members and activists. Subsequently, on March 2, 2008, approximately 3,000 Vietnamese Americans ascended the steps of San Jose City Hall where the San Jose City Council meets, to demonstrate for the official name of Little Saigon (Molina 2008a). Two days later, after a six-and-one-half-hour meeting with hundreds of Vietnamese American community members sitting in the city council chamber, a 7-to-4 majority of the San Jose City Council voted against officially naming the district Little Saigon, but also voted to establish formal guidelines for allowing the district's businesses and the community members to have some influence in the official naming of public areas (Molina 2008b). While the door was temporarily closed on renaming the business district area Little Saigon, this controversy nevertheless shows the growing ideological divisions in the emerging generational cleavage between the Old Guard and New Guard that can be found in all Vietnamese American communities.

At the center of the Little Saigon controversy, which has become one of the major local issues in San Jose and has garnered national and international attention in Vietnam, is Vietnamese American city council member Madison Nguyen. According to Nguyen: "I want to be able to represent all of the constituency and not its particular segment since you have people from different communities, different walks of life, you have to be able to please as many people as possible" (Ustinova 2008, D1). Nguyen clearly represents the New

Guard perspective of prioritizing her multiracial constituents over ethnic allegiance, and this has clashed directly with Old Guard nationalism and pride. In response to her stance against renaming the district Little Saigon, members of the Old Guard have mobilized against Nguyen for failing to understand their wishes. Even though the Old Guard clearly supported Nguyen in the historic 2005 city council election, they now formed a political group (San Jose Voters for Democracy) calling for Nguyen's resignation from the San Jose City Council. According to Barry Do, the organization's leader: "Little Saigon is a symbol—it's like our identity. We are the political refugees, and if anything, we will never forget why we are here" (Ustinova 2008, D1).

The Little Saigon controversy illustrates the developing political cleavage between two generations of Vietnamese Americans, the older refugees and the second generation, around cultural and political issues stemming from the former's anti-Communist feelings and the latter's acculturation in American politics. Newly emerging Vietnamese American elected officials in city government face cross-pressures similar to those of other Asian American candidates in that they must pursue a two-tiered strategy that courts both white voters and Asian American voters, often the two largest racial groups in California suburbs. When an issue becomes public, such as the official naming of a business district in San Jose, New Guard leaders like Madison Nguyen must walk a tenuous line between these two tiers, sometimes sacrificing one for the other. In other cases, New Guard Vietnamese American candidates choose not to address ethnic issues for fear of being typecast as only a Vietnamese candidate instead of a mainstream candidate. This belief is reflected by Lan Nguyen, a trustee of the East Side Union High School District in San Jose, who ran for the open San Jose City Council seat in District 8:

> This whole thing about Little Saigon is like a cloud over everybody's head. I am running not as a Vietnamese American candidate, but as the most qualified candidate. It doesn't make sense to me to go out there and support and campaign for Little Saigon when, for me, personally, the most important issue is how to resolve the budget issues we have right now. (Molina 2008c, 1B)

On March 3, 2009, San Jose voters in District 7, which Madison Nguyen represents, decided on whether to recall her from the San Jose City Council, only the sixth time in the city's history that such an election had occurred. Behind this recall election was Nguyen's once-proud power base—the older-generation Vietnamese American leadership that had enthusiastically supported her with both votes and contributions so that she could make political history. In the end, Nguyen survived the recall attempt by a vote of 55 percent to 45 percent (Santa Clara County Registrar of Voters 2009).

The recall election of Madison Nguyen did not prevent or slow down the political incorporation of Vietnamese Americans in San Jose, just as it was not curtailed by the February 1999 Hitek Video store incident described above.

During this incident, Truong Trang's actions provoked dramatic and unprecedented demonstrations among thousands of anti-Communist Vietnamese Americans of all generations that reverberated throughout this group in Orange County and the rest of the continental United States. In retrospect, Vietnamese American political mobilization and incorporation in Orange County increased to unprecedented levels, culminating in a majority Vietnamese American Westminster City Council and strong incorporation in the region's Republican Party. The Nguyen recall election in San Jose will serve as a teachable moment for future Vietnamese American candidates. These candidates will likely be from Nguyen's generation, with weaker symbolic ties to homeland politics and ideological issues when balancing heated topics that exacerbate generational cleavages.

Many of the issues faced in San Jose's Vietnamese American community are a reflection of the growing pains of political incorporation after successfully electing its first Vietnamese American elected official, Madison Nguyen. The weak political incorporation of Vietnamese Americans in San Jose is a reflection of many of the challenges associated with large cities, such as the presence of entrenched political interests that intimidate Asian immigrants and refugees from mobilizing effectively and the presence of single-district elections. In addition to these metropolitan barriers, the large San Jose Vietnamese American community is not entrenched in either the state Democratic or Republican Party, which exacerbates the ideological differences along generational lines that have divided the community on salient issues.

In contrast to the city of San Jose, Vietnamese American electoral success in Little Saigon, combined with the group's incorporation into the established regional political party, has allowed it to temper, not prevent, such ideological divisions in this community. However, even in Orange County's Little Saigon, ideological divisions will likely continue within the Vietnamese American community around generational issues and public policies in the near future because, for the first time, the larger US-born population exceeds those who fled as refugees from Saigon. The challenge for its elected leadership will be how to rectify the two competing perspectives between the Old Guard and the New Guard in order to continue its upward political trajectory in the region.

Note

1. Van Tran, California State Assembly representative (R–District 68), personal communication with the author, August 8, 2005.

7

Gardena, California: Two Generations of a Japanese American Majority City Council

The suburb of Gardena, California, is arguably the oldest Asian American Transformed I suburb in the nation, spanning over three generations. The city currently has nearly 60,000 residents, covers 6.2 square miles, and is located approximately 20 minutes south of downtown Los Angeles. Gardena was incorporated into Los Angeles County in 1930, and has become home to a racially diverse population. In 2000, the population of Gardena consisted of the following: Latinos (31.8 percent), Asians (26.8 percent), blacks (26 percent), and whites (23.8 percent) (US Census 2006g). At approximately 20 percent, Japanese Americans represented the majority ethnic group among the city's total Asian American population. Map 7.1 shows the concentration of the Japanese American population in census tracts within Gardena, ranging from 0.4 percent to 32.3 percent. One census tract (see inset in Map 7.1) contained a total Asian American population of 52 percent.

While most Asian American–influenced suburbs are a post-1965 phenomenon, the historical formation of the Japanese American community in Gardena occurred well before that period. With many Japanese Americans immigrating from Japan and Hawaii to the continental United States as agricultural workers in the early 1900s, Gardena, once known as "Berry Valley" for its abundance of berries (particularly strawberries), became the logical destination for small Japanese American farming families and businesses seeking an economic livelihood in Southern California. This continued even after the devastating effects of World War II internment of the Japanese American community, as many Gardena residents chose to return to the suburb that had been so good to them.

Japanese American Community Formation in a Post–World War II Suburb

World War II disrupted early Japanese American community formation in Gardena, as well as on the entire West Coast, when Japanese Americans were forced

Map 7.1 Japanese American Population Distribution in Gardena, 2000

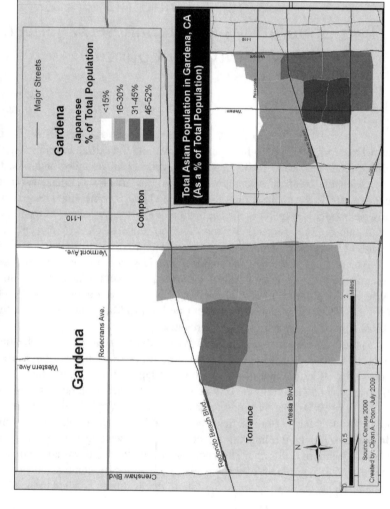

to enter internment camps. Beginning in the late 1950s, a large Japanese American community consisting of immigrants, or first-generation (Issei), and a US-born second generation (Nisei) began to settle in Gardena (Okamoto 1991). Real estate developers advertised in the *Rafu Shimpo,* a Japanese American newspaper, with the intent to target many of the second-generation Japanese Americans who were coming of age and looking for a community to live in during the 1950s and 1960s. According to Bruce Kaji, former city treasurer and the first Japanese American elected official in Gardena: "Gardena was the only community in the Los Angeles area where developers sought to sell homes specifically to the Nisei. There was a strong element of new homes targeted to them, whereas the Nisei did not feel welcome anywhere else."[1] Since this period, Gardena has been the only city outside the state of Hawaii in which Japanese Americans have represented the majority on the city council for two successive generations. Currently, the influence of Japanese Americans in city hall can be felt from the city clerk's office to the mayor to the institutionalization of many Japanese American community organizations and elected officials throughout the city's public sector.

The early history of Japanese Americans in Gardena began in 1911 with the founding of the Moneta Japanese Institute through donations from the Japanese American community for lots, a schoolhouse, and living quarters for the teacher (County of Los Angeles Public Library 2010). In 1916, the parents' association founded the Gardena Japanese School. The normal lives that many Japanese Americans enjoyed in this community abruptly ended with the World War II internment, and many who returned to Los Angeles tried to rebuild their lives in Gardena, one of the few communities in Los Angeles to openly reach out to them.

The ability of the Nisei to form a community set the foundation for their political incorporation in Gardena. Their influence is apparent in a report by the Los Angeles County Commission on Human Relations, which investigated the burning of the Gardena Buddhist Church in the early 1980s: "The contributions of the Japanese American to the growth, stability and vitality of the area are substantial. . . . The presence of Japanese Americans in the professional and business communities is pervasive in the Gardena Valley area" (Olive 1982, 14). The incorporation of Japanese Americans in this post–World War II suburb was unprecedented during the two generations that spanned from 1960s to the present as both the Nisei and Sansei (third generation) came of political age.

Local Government Structure and the
Pioneer Generation of Japanese American Elected Leadership

The city of Gardena's local government consists of four part-time seats on the city council, a mayor pro tem, and a mayor. Council members and the mayor have term limits of twelve years. Elections are citywide and staggered, with the top vote getters filling the number of vacated seats each election cycle. The council members can nominate residents for city commission positions, with a majority vote (three) needed for confirmation.

The Gardena Japanese American community has been able to translate its significant population size during citywide elections into two generations of majority representation on the city council. As the Japanese American community developed, so did its descriptive representation at the city level. Currently, Japanese Americans comprise 43.3 percent of the total Asian American population in Gardena, the largest of any Asian American ethnic group, and 11.3 percent of the city population.

Table 7.1 indicates why Gardena is characterized as an Asian American Transformed I suburb by vividly showing the extent to which Japanese Americans have won key elected positions beyond the city council in Gardena from 1960 to 2007. Ken Nakaoka was the first Japanese American to be elected to the Gardena City Council, in 1962. He won the mayoral election in 1972, making him the first Japanese American elected city mayor in the United States. He later served as a role model for Paul Bannai, a second-generation Japanese American who was the second Japanese American elected to the Gardena City Council, in 1972. Bannai ran in the following year for the California State Assembly seat that included Gardena and served three terms. Although a resident of Gardena, Bannai credits social organizations, such as the Lions Club, Kiwanis, and Nisei Veterans Association, as forming the foundation for his political life. According to Bannai:

> All of the service organizations in our community, such as the Lions Club, were not primarily what you would call Japanese-American clubs. From an economic and business standpoint, it was good to belong. [I]f you are active, then you can contribute to the benefit and growth of the community. Once you get in, and find that you want to contribute, you are pushed up the ladder, so to say. (Douglass 1989, 92)

Membership and activity in these organizations allowed Bannai to be recognized and eventually appointed to the City of Gardena Planning Commission in 1969, which later served as his springboard to the city council.

The legacy of Bannai and Nakaoka marked the beginnings of strong descriptive representation for Japanese Americans in Gardena politics. Masani (Mas) Fukai joined the council in 1974, Vince Okamoto served on the city council beginning in 1978, and George Kobayashi served as city treasurer. Paul Tsukahara became the third Asian American to serve on the Gardena City Council, in 1980.

The influence of Mas Fukai is well-known among veteran Asian American political circles in the Los Angeles area. Fukai was picked by Los Angeles County supervisor Kenneth Hahn to join his staff in 1974, and became his

Table 7.1 Two Generations of Japanese American Elected Officials in Gardena, 1960–2009

	Year Elected
City Treasurer	
Bruce Kaji	1960 (resigned in 1962)
George Kobayashi	1974 (appointed), 1976–1988
J. Ingrid Tsukiyama	2001
City Clerk	
May Doi	1980 (retired in 1999)
City Council	
Ken Nakaoka	1966
Paul T. Bannai	1972
Masani Fukai	1974
Vince Okomoto	1976
Paul Y. Tsukahara	1980
Terrence Terauchi	1999
Paul Tanaka	1999
Grant Nakaoka (son of Ken)	2001
Ronald K. Ikejiri	2001 to present
Paul Tanaka	1998–2004
Mayor	
Ken Nakaoka	1972
Terrence Terauchi	2001
Paul Tanaka	2005 and 2009

chief deputy in 1987. Fukai gained a reputation as a consummate fund-raiser a supporter of many local Asian political candidates by the late 1980s (Goodman 1989). Fukai left the city council in 1998. During 2004, the five-person Gardena City Council was a majority-led Japanese American council (Mayor Terrence Terauchi, Mayor Pro Tem Ron Ikejiri, and Paul Tanaka) with one African American (Steven Bradford) and one Latino (Oscar Medrano Jr.). In 2007, Ikejiri and Tanaka remained on the city council when term limits forced Terauchi out of office. Tanaka currently serves as city mayor, the second Japanese American to do so, after being elected in 2005 and reelected in March 2009.

Sustaining Descriptive Representation and Becoming the Majority on the Gardena City Council

As of 2009, Japanese Americans constituted half of the four-member Gardena City Council, with Mayor Paul Tanaka and City Council member Ron Ikejiri. The other two representatives are African American (council member Steven

Bradford and Mayor Pro Tem Rachel Johnson). Outside of the city council, another Japanese American, J. Ingrid Tsukiyama, is city treasurer. The ability of Japanese Americans to maintain and sustain descriptive representation in the most powerful city positions of the Gardena City Council and the city treasurer's office for two generations is an impressive feat for Asian Americans in California local politics. Several reasons help to explain how the Gardena Japanese American community has been able to achieve this distinction. Council member Ikejiri offers this primary explanation: "The political history of Japanese Americans is due to the Sansei [third generation] staying in Gardena."[2] Because the Sansei chose to remain in Gardena as Japanese Americans attained greater socioeconomic status, instead of moving to another more affluent suburb, third-generation Japanese Americans like Ikejiri allowed the elected leadership to continue what the Nisei began after World War II. This represents one of the latent advantages of the small- to medium-sized suburbs for Asian American political incorporation in that such cities are often the final destination for many Asian American families, immigrant and US born, to settle down over generations because of the advantages that surround strong public schools, established ethnic networks, and low crime. Gardena is the oldest Asian American suburb that I examined among the ten case studies in that it has served as a central suburb for Japanese American community formation over three generations. As a result, previous group incorporation efforts can be sustained, as seen in Gardena with the Nisei efforts in political incorporation, so that succeeding generations can have increased representation. The established track records of Nisei elected officials clearly benefited future Sansei elected officials in a city where Japanese Americans had gained respect. According to Bruce Kaji: "Japanese were clearly accepted in Gardena, which made it easier for them [Sansei] to get elected."[3]

Another reason that has contributed to the recent Japanese American majority on the city council is the group's primary reliance on cross-racial coalitions. Despite Japanese Americans being only approximately 11 percent of the city's population, Japanese American candidates in Gardena have been able to sustain and build on descriptive representation over time through cross-racial coalitions, particularly with the majority Mexican American population and whites. One factor that has contributed to Japanese American candidates' cross-racial support is their professional status. As former Gardena mayor Terrence Terauchi explained: "Japanese Americans have to be able to cross over and obtain broad support. . . . Also, we are all well-educated professionals. . . . We are people who[m] the entire community can be proud of."[4] Terauchi's campaign strategy has been to create a base support of Japanese Americans with broader community support. As he stated: "You cannot focus on Japanese Americans. But they were my biggest supporters. They put the word out and volunteered to help my campaign."[5]

Uncontested Power

For several months prior to the November 2008 deadline for declaring his 2009 mayoral candidacy, Paul Tanaka declared that he would not seek reelection to the city council when his first four-year term expired. Tanaka eventually decided to run when no likely challenger emerged. Interestingly, during the short period of time from November 2008 to March 2009, Tanaka raised nearly $130,000 in campaign contributions even though he needed only his own vote to win the 2009 mayoral election. According to Tanaka: "When I made a decision on the very last day [to file nomination papers], I picked up the phone and called about ten of my friends. Once I found out that I did not have an opponent [the same day], I said, 'I don't need any more money'" (Mazza 2009, 1). Despite no longer needing any campaign contributions, Tanaka received campaign contributions totaling $130,000 from the Gardena sheriff's department (over $1,000) and business owners in South Bay cities such as Rolling Hills, La Crescenta, Tarzana, and Sherman Oaks (over $500 each).[6] Tanaka eventually donated all of his campaign contributions to charities. In comparison, current Gardena City Council member Steve Bradford, who also ran unopposed in 2009, raised less than $1,000 in total contributions.

The significance of Tanaka's 2009 campaign contributions shows both his political strength and the political incorporation of Japanese American elected officials. Even if a challenger emerged in 2009, it would have been difficult to unseat the popular mayor given his longtime affiliation with Gardena's residents, local government, law enforcement, and civic organizations. Without a doubt, Tanaka's twenty-six-year career in law enforcement with the Los Angeles County sheriff's department helped him to raise campaign contributions and gain a key city endorsement. However, Gardena had been Tanaka's home for forty-one years as well as his parents' home. The longtime connection as a resident allowed Tanaka and other Japanese American elected officials before him to participate in mainstream civic organizations and, thus, develop the necessary social and political networks to later propel them during their professional civic careers.

Japanese American Community-Based Organization and Mainstream Civic Institutions in Gardena

Japanese American community-based organizations such as the Gardena Valley Japanese Cultural Institute (GVJCI) have taken shape as this community developed. For many Japanese Americans in Los Angeles County, the GVJCI remains the key locus for community forums. On January 17, 2010, over 1,000 Japanese Americans convened in a town hall meeting to discuss the future fate of the region's oldest bilingual daily, *Rafu Shimpo*. According to its mission statement, the GVJCI seeks to (1) provide programs and activities, sensitive and relevant, to the needs of senior citizens and youth; (2) offer use of facilities and support to community organizations that foster the best interests and welfare of the community; and (3) promote an environment for better intergenerational understanding, cultural pride, and respect for all humanity. Through a multitude of cultural and recreational activities, the GVJCI has become a prominent fixture in local politics by historically providing Japanese American candidates with direct political access to the community through their affiliation with the institute. For example, former Gardena City Council member Terrence Terauchi was a member of GVJCI and served on its board for several years.

As both the Nisei and Sansei acculturated into professional and civic leadership in Gardena, so did their participation in the city's mainstream civic institutions. Through their membership in professional organizations and participation in community groups, Japanese American elected officials in Gardena have become successful at developing cross-racial networks to their political advantage. As in the above discussion about Gardena pioneer Paul Bannai, past and current Gardena City Council members have also been active in mainstream community-based organizations. For example, former city council member Terrence Terauchi was a member of the Optimistic Club, Elk's Club, Chamber of Commerce, YMCA (executive board member), and Japanese American Citizens' League. Candidates' affiliations with such mainstream organizations are another aspect of the two-tiered campaign strategy.

The image of a nonthreatening racial candidate has played a role in the success of past and present Japanese American candidates by allowing them to build and foster cross-racial coalitions. Such coalitions would not have been as likely without the first generation of Japanese American elected officials in Gardena. As Gary Kohatsu, editor of the *Gardena Valley News,* points out:

> There is a sense of a comfort zone among the older [non-Japanese American] Gardena voters regarding having a strong Japanese American presence on the city council. The first generation of Japanese American leaders from Ken Nakaoka to Paul Bannai was responsible for allowing this to be accepted without question.[7]

The unprecedented success of Japanese Americans in Gardena to elect and sustain descriptive representatives over two generations has led to mixed results with regard to their local political incorporation. On the one hand, the current success of Japanese Americans on the city council has led to increased political incorporation in Gardena politics, as seen in the appointment of numerous Asian Americans to influential city commissions. All city commission appointments in Gardena are made by the mayor and city council members. The presence of Asian Americans, and especially Japanese Americans, on the several influential city commissions is noticeable. For instance, the five-member

Planning and Environmental Quality Commission, one of the most powerful commissions, has two Japanese American members. A total of eight Asian Americans, the second largest number among all racial groups, serve on all five city-wide commissions. On the other hand, Japanese Americans are still not part of the dominant coalitions that influence key city policies.

Barriers to Future Political Incorporation

Despite the appointments of Japanese Americans to key city commissions by the Japanese American city council members, questions remain as to whether Japanese Americans can become a part of any of the ruling coalitions in Gardena politics around the key policy issues. One common explanation for this offered by the recent group of Japanese American elected officials is the presence of cultural barriers within the Japanese American community. Former Gardena City Council member Grant Nakaoka believes that the traditional Japanese culture practiced by the older generation inhibits many community members from seeking special interest favors from the Japanese American city council because such behavior is discouraged.[8] Mayor Paul Tanaka, a fourth-generation Japanese American, echoed similar sentiments: "I was not raised by my conservative Japanese American parents to stand out and to challenge the system, but to change it through peaceful ways. . . . I believe in being a champion of all people, not just the Japanese American community."[9]

Due to such cultural beliefs, many Japanese Americans in Gardena are less likely to organize and lobby city council in favor of such interests. Instead, their impact on the city council agenda has been subtle. Japanese Americans account for nearly one-third of the Gardena electorate, and the influence of this significant Japanese American voting bloc on city policies can be seen with issues pertaining to the elderly. Gardena currently boasts one of the most comprehensive senior programs among all cities in the South Bay region of Los Angeles County. Much of this can be attributed to the political influence of the growing number of elderly within the Japanese American community. According to Mayor Tanaka:

> In most cities, crime is the top concern among residents with issues regarding the elderly far below. In Gardena, according to one confidential public opinion poll by the city, issues concerning the elderly rank at the top. The influence of the Japanese American community is one of the key reasons why this is the most important issue.[10]

The locations and participants of the various citywide senior citizen programs demonstrate the influence of Japanese Americans. For instance, the Gardena Community Action Meal Program offers free daily meals to senior citizens over the age of sixty at the Japanese American Cultural Institute and the Paul

Nakaoka Community Center. The Senior Citizens Program, also located in the community center, provides daily, monthly, and yearly activities ranging from flu immunizations to a senior health fair. Many of the volunteers and participants are Japanese American.

Education, particularly the public high school system, has not been a major issue for the Japanese American community in Gardena. That is primarily because the city's main high school, Gardena High, is not owned or operated by the city, but remains under the control of the Los Angeles Unified School District. As a result, the Gardena City Council has been powerless in its ability to address the recent decline of Gardena High and its rising dropout rates. Many Japanese Americans in Gardena have chosen to move away to allow their children to attend better high schools instead of addressing the current ills of Gardena High. The flight of younger Japanese American families away from Gardena likely will negatively impact the future growth of the Japanese American community in Gardena and reduce the probability of a third generation of majority Japanese American city council members.

Another reason that may explain the invisibility of the Japanese American influence in key policy areas is that few local issues are specifically defined as Japanese American. This has not been the case at the federal level, as seen with the national redress and reparations movement, which began after World War II with the incarceration of Japanese American citizens and eventually resulted in the American Civil Liberties Act in 1988.

The Japanese American community is one of the most socially and economically assimilated groups among all Asian American ethnic groups, given its long history in the United States. Many of its key issues are often conflated with the mainstream in areas such as education, crime, and employment. As Gary Kohatsu pointed out: "Unless it's about tearing down a Japanese American retirement home or a cultural institution, you are not likely to see Japanese Americans organize and try to influence the city council."[11] Having to contend with such cultural factors, the Japanese American community has been a less visible partner in the dominant coalitions in Gardena politics, but this does not indicate its lack of influence beyond descriptive representation.

Perhaps the greatest barrier to full political incorporation of the Gardena Japanese American community is its dwindling numbers coupled with the rise of other racial minority communities, particularly Latinos, who will begin challenging descriptive representation on the city council. As the third- and fourth-generation members of the Gardena Japanese American community progressively move away from Gardena to more affluent Los Angeles suburbs, the challenge for the Gardena Japanese American community will be to maintain some level of Asian American representation on the city council. This situation makes the Gardena case study unique when compared to the other cases that I examined in this book because it has attained the longest period of Asian American political incorporation, one unrivaled by other suburbs. And in this important way, it serves as a litmus test of whether Japanese Americans have attained power beyond descriptive representation (substantive authority and influence). The verdict at this point is mixed because, while Japanese Americans have become part of the mainstream in city government and culture, the political voice of this community has been muted due to internal community cultural and political barriers. Moreover, these barriers are not likely to be mitigated by future political mobilization as the community shrinks in both number and influence.

The degree of political incorporation that the Japanese American community has achieved over two generations is unprecedented and has undoubtedly transformed Gardena's local government. Since the post–World War II era, Gardena has remained the suburban center of the Los Angeles Japanese American community. During the past decade, other Los Angeles County suburbs like Torrance have emerged to contend with Gardena. Recently, a number of Japanese corporations, such as Toyota Motor Corporation, Mitsubishi, and Sapporo, have chosen Torrance as the location for their US corporate headquarters. This has spurred new Japanese immigrant–influenced suburbs to rival Gardena. Nevertheless, Gardena and its longtime Japanese American community have witnessed both demographic and political transformations that are unrivaled in any suburb or major metropolitan area in Southern California. This is clearly seen in the myriad Japanese American community institutions that remain in Gardena as well as in the many forms of public recognition for the contributions that Japanese Americans have made to the city. Japanese Americans who have chosen to remain in Gardena no longer need to rely solely on descriptive representatives to be part of the decisionmaking process. The sustained political legacies of the first- and second-generation Japanese American leadership have become part of mainstream Gardena politics, and they are not likely to leave the city's conscience for a long time even if the faces change in the local government.

Notes

1. Bruce Kaji, former Gardena city treasurer, personal communication with the author, July 22, 2004.

2. Ron Ikejiri, Gardena City Council member, personal communication with the author, July 22, 2004.

3. Ron Ikejiri, Gardena City Council member, personal communication with the author, July 22, 2004.

4. Terrence Terauchi, former Gardena City Council member, personal communication with the author, August 4, 2004.

5. Terrence Terauchi, former Gardena City Council member, personal communication with the author, August 8, 2004.

6. Terrence Terauchi, former Gardena City Council member, personal communication with the author, August 8, 2004.

7. Gary Kohatsu, editor of the *Gardena Valley News,* personal communication with the author, July 21, 2005.

8. Grant Nakaoka, former Gardena City Council member, personal communication with the author, July 25, 2005.

9. Paul Tanaka, Gardena mayor, personal communication with the author, July 27, 2005.

10. Paul Tanaka, Gardena mayor, personal communication with the author, July 27, 2005.

11. Gay Kohatsu, editor of the *Gardena Valley News,* personal communication with the author, July 25, 2005.

8

Montgomery County, Maryland: Emerging Asian American Suburbs Inside the Washington Beltway

As illustrated in Map 8.1, one of the fastest-growing and most racially diverse counties in the continental United States is Montgomery County, Maryland. Whether it is in the famous business district along Rockville's Pike Road, where Asian ethnic restaurants and specialty stores can be found, or in the growing Chinese American student body at Potomac's famous Winston Churchill High School, Asian Americans represent one of the emerging communities in the suburbs and townships throughout Montgomery County, where they currently account for 13.2 percent of its total population (US Census 2006h). Factors similar to those in the other suburb case studies have pulled Asian Americans, particularly Chinese Americans, Asian Indians, and Korean Americans, to this region. These include Montgomery County's strong public school systems, ethnic networks, and economic opportunities as it transforms itself into a location for biotechnology, nanotechnology, and information technology industries that draw highly educated Asian Americans to the area. This major population boom of Asian American immigrants in Montgomery County over the past twenty years is beginning to bear the fruits of Asian American elected representation at the state and county levels whose districts contain these suburbs.

Montgomery County illustrates why a case study approach is important to understanding the local context of a particular region. The county contains nineteen municipalities: Barnesville, Brookeville, Town of Chevy Chase, Chevy Chase View, Chevy Chase Village, Section 3 Village of Chevy Chase, Section 5 Village of Chevy Chase, Gaithersburg, Garrett Park, Glen Echo, Kensington, Laytonsville, Martin's Additions, North Chevy Chase, Poolesville, Rockville, Somerset, Takoma Park, and Washington Grove. One of the unique characteristics among these municipalities is that their boundaries segue into each other, which blurs the traditional divisions between municipalities. Among

115

Map 8.1 Chinese American Population Distribution in Greater Washington and Baltimore Area, 2000

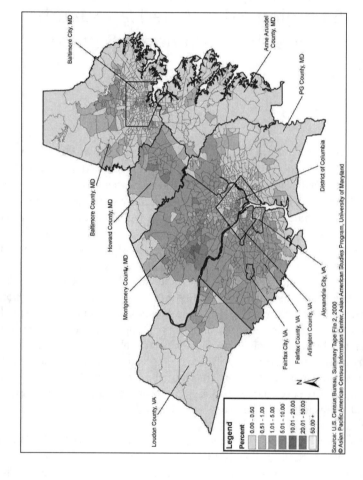

Source: U.S. Census Bureau, Summary Tape File 2, 2000
© Asian Pacific American Census Information Center, Asian American Studies Program, University of Maryland

Source: Reprinted with permission from Shinagawa, Larry H. 2008. *A Portrait of Chinese Americans.* College Park: Asian American Studies Program, University of Maryland. Available at http://www.aast.umd.edu/ocaportrait.html (accessed June 16, 2009).

the Montgomery County municipalities are the incorporated cities of Gaithersburg, Rockville, and Takoma Park, along with thirty-two unincorporated areas, including Potomac and North Potomac, twelve towns, and four villages (Montgomery County, Maryland 2009).

These blurred geographic boundaries, combined with the dispersed residential settlement patterns of Asian Americans in the area, have presented a demographic community profile of overlapping multiple Asian American Transformed suburbs throughout Montgomery County. Unlike the other regions that I examine in this book where there is one particular suburb that is the focus, Montgomery County presents multiple Transformed suburbs, which is why I look at Montgomery County as a whole. In particular, the center of these Transformed suburbs is a 2.8-mile area that overlaps the suburban areas, both incorporated and unincorporated, that include Rockville, Potomac, and North Potomac.

Government structuring predominantly at the county level has given these multiple townships and cities a collective identity as "Montgomery County." Many of the townships and cities have no city governments, with cities like Rockville being the exception. In Montgomery County, the key local elected positions are on the Montgomery County School Board and the Montgomery County Council, while at the state level, the Maryland House of Delegates is the key elected position.

The 2.8-mile area of Rockville, North Potomac, and Potomac, where nearly half of the current Montgomery County Asian American population lives, is an area known as Census Tract 7006.07. It consists primarily of upper-middle-class, highly educated professionals and represents one of the fastest-growing Asian American communities in the Middle Atlantic region. Many of its residents are attracted to the strong public schools in these suburbs. Other emerging suburbs with growing Asian American communities, such as Silver Spring and Gaithersburg, are also taking shape due to similar factors that draw this group to these areas.

Montgomery County is unique from the other non-California cases that I examine in this book because it is an ethnically diverse suburb with no one particular Asian ethnic group being a majority. Figure 8.1 shows that, in 2006, the ethnic breakdown of the Asian American community in Montgomery County was (from largest to smallest): Chinese (except Taiwanese), 30.2 percent; Asian Indian, 22.3 percent; Korean, 15 percent; other Asian, 12.9 percent; Vietnamese, 8.4 percent; Filipino, 7 percent; and Japanese, 4.1 percent. Because of this ethnic makeup, it is paramount that Asian American candidates simultaneously focus their campaign strategies on two major areas: (1) building panethnic alliances in the Asian American community, and (2) pursuing cross-racial alliances with other racial groups during group political mobilization. From 1980 to 2000, the Asian American community in Montgomery County more than quadrupled, with nearly half of Maryland's Asian population residing

Figure 8.1 Asian American Ethnic Populations in Montgomery County, 2006

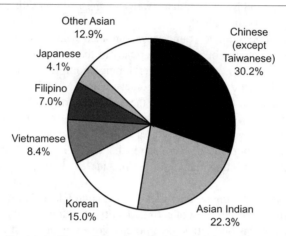

Other Asian 12.9%
Japanese 4.1%
Filipino 7.0%
Vietnamese 8.4%
Korean 15.0%
Chinese (except Taiwanese) 30.2%
Asian Indian 22.3%

Source: Reprinted with permission from the Asian American Health Initiative. 2008. *Asian American Health Priorities: A Study of Montgomery County, MD*. Rockville, MD: Asian American Health Initiative, p. 20.

in Montgomery County (Montgomery County Department of Park and Planning 2000).

The Making of a Global County: The Suburban History of Montgomery County

Prior to becoming a central area for the Asian American suburban community inside the Washington Beltway, Montgomery County had undergone demographic changes since its founding in 1776. After World War I, Montgomery County experienced a boom in population and land development. In the twenty years preceding the Great Depression, land values more than doubled, but government debt increased more than seventeenfold. When the Depression forced property values down, Montgomery County witnessed a growing opposition to tax increases and bond issues, agricultural prices dropped, and farmers were among the hardest hit. With its close proximity to Washington, DC, a large number of federal employees cushioned some of the economic effects and, by 1935, housing starts began to increase and the population grew. African Americans, many of whom were farm workers, left the county. By 1940, the African American population had declined from 17 percent to 3 percent. Montgomery County increasingly became a suburban community with a growing dependence on federal employment. During World War II, many of Montgomery

County's eligible draftees left to fight in the global conflict, and housing construction and suburban growth came to a halt (Montgomery County Historical Society 1999).

After World War II, Montgomery County shared the national suburban growth trend of the late 1940s and early 1950s, but with a difference. Returning veterans and city residents moving to the suburbs constituted only a small portion of the new arrivals. Most of the new homeowners were also new to the region, coming from all parts of the United States to work for the federal government. This suburban growth produced a decline in farming. As land values increased, farmers sold off their land to developers. The US Census in 1950 showed 164,401 people in Montgomery County, only 10,000 of whom were African Americans. Schools were racially segregated and the National Association for the Advancement of Colored People (NAACP) began the first efforts there to protest the quality of African American schools. By 1958, all of the public schools were desegregated as a result of *Brown v. Board of Education* (Montgomery County Historical Society 1999).

During the 1970s, the population growth rate slowed from the previous pace of doubling every decade, but continued strong. Suburbanization gave way to increased density of population. The US Census in 1980 showed a population of 579,000, which reached 665,000 by 1990. Asian Americans, Latinos, and Jewish Americans became part of the demographic landscape as these immigrants began to settle and establish communities. It is estimated that over 63,000 foreign immigrants moved to Montgomery County during the 1990s, representing 186 countries, with 62 countries providing more than 100 immigrants each. No single country contributed more than 8 percent of all immigrants and no region of the world contributed over half. El Salvador sent the greatest absolute number of immigrants, but accounted for only 8.4 percent of total immigration, followed by China with 7.1 percent, India with 7.0 percent, and Vietnam with 6.4 percent. Forty-three percent of the county's immigrants came from Asia; 31 percent from North, Central, and South America; and 13 percent each from both Africa and Europe (Montgomery County Department of Park and Planning 2000).

Figure 8.2 captures the population growth for African Americans, Asian Americans, and Latinos, while the non-Hispanic white population gradually decreased in Montgomery County during the period from 1990 to 2006. The gradual influx of these racial groups has also transformed the demographics of its public school system and workforce. For instance, Montgomery County's public school system had grown to be among the twenty largest in the nation, with more than 96,000 students and 13,000 staff members in 155 schools (Montgomery County Historical Society, 1999). During the 1970s, the district's enrollment was 95 percent white. Whites currently make up less than half of that proportion (43 percent) while African Americans (22 percent), Asian Americans (14 percent), and Hispanics (20 percent) continue to grow in representation. As

Figure 8.2 Demographic Shifts in Montgomery County, 1990–2006

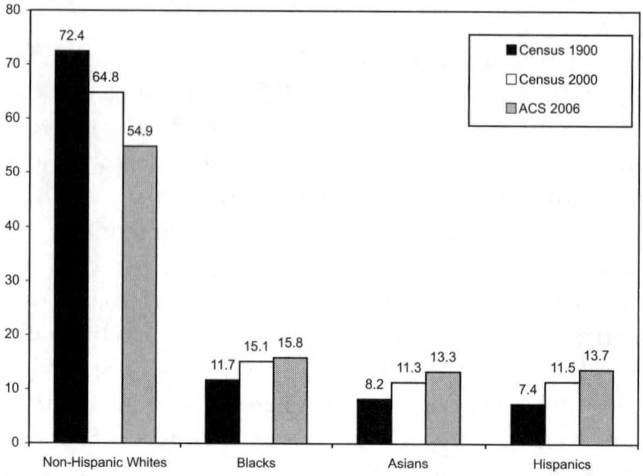

Source: Reprinted with permission from the Asian American Health Initiative. 2008. *Asian American Health Priorities: A Study of Montgomery County, MD.* Rockville, MD: Asian American Health Initiative, p. 19.

a result, it is one of the nation's most diverse school districts, with nearly 140,000 students attending during the 2005–2006 school year, representing 160 nationalities and 120 languages (Montgomery County Historical Society 1999). This demographic shift in Montgomery County was facilitated by immigration laws, such as the Immigration and Nationality Act of 1965 for Asian Americans and Latinos, but also was due to a strong and growing economy. Between 1980 and 1990, the number of residents in the workforce grew by 43 percent (Montgomery County Historical Society 1999).

Asian Americans have become a prominent racial group in Montgomery County during the past forty years, as a new cohort of educated professionals and service industry workers began to arrive during this period. Currently, the largest workforce sector for Asian Americans in Potomac consists of professionals, scientists, and technical services, with 26 percent men and 19 percent women ("North Potomac Maryland" 2009). With this growth of the educated professional class, Asian Americans have begun to make political inroads into statewide politics.

Asian American Descriptive Representation and Government Structure in Montgomery County

The growth of the Asian American community in suburbs like Potomac has facilitated their political action for descriptive representation in Montgomery County. The result has been mixed, as Asian Americans have been successful in certain positions and struggled in others. In Montgomery County state politics, the two major political entities are the Maryland House of Delegates and the Montgomery County Council. The Maryland House of Delegates, which meets three months of the year from mid-January to mid-April, consists of multiple district seats that are spread out through Montgomery County. Three Asian Americans, Susan C. Lee (D–District 16), Kumar P. Barve (D–District 17), and Saqib Ali (D–District 39) currently serve in the Maryland House of Delegates from Montgomery County. Lee, a second-generation Chinese American who previously served as an attorney for the US Commission on Civil Rights, was elected in 2002; Barve, a second-generation Asian Indian, was elected in 1991; and Ali, a second-generation Asian Indian, was elected in 2007.

Kumar Barve is one of three representatives from District 17 in Montgomery County. The two key cities in his district are Gaithersburg and Rockville. District 17 has a total population of 110,712 with the following racial groups: 69,111 (62.4 percent) are white; 13,718 (12.4 percent) are African American; 15,715 (14.2 percent) are Asian American; and 17,519 (15.8 percent) are Latino.

Susan C. Lee, a third-generation Chinese American who was born in San Antonio, Texas, and raised in Potomac, Maryland, is one of three representatives from District 16. Also located in Montgomery County, District 16 contains Oakmont, Bethesda, Drummond, Somerset, Glen Echo, Potomac, and Friendship Heights. The district has a total population of 107,658 with the following racial groups: 91,754 (85.2 percent) are white; 3,217 (3 percent) are African American; 8,996 (8.3 percent) are Asian American; and 5,865 (5.4 percent) are Latino. Lee, a longtime member of the Maryland Democratic Party, had all of the right credentials as well as the right timing to become the second Asian American, and first Asian American woman, to be elected to the Maryland House of Delegates from the region.

Saqib Ali, a software engineer, represents the new generation of Asian American elected leadership that is emerging in Montgomery County. Winning elected office at the young age of thirty-one, Ali had a campaign that demonstrated how grassroots politics, through a two-tiered campaign strategy in the non-Asian and Asian American communities, can be effectively pursued despite the lack of political experience and networks of his opponents in January 2007. According to longtime Asian American community leader and activist, Michael Lin, the executive director of the panethnic Organization for Chinese Americans (OCA):

> Saqib Ali ran his campaign the right way, unlike previous Asian American candidates who assumed that the Asian American community would automatically rally behind him. Ali went directly to the Asian American and mainstream communities and mobilized them with his charisma and political vision.[1]

The elections of Kumar Barve, Susan C. Lee, and Ali from primarily suburban districts in Montgomery County speak to the political potential of this region. However, their electoral successes mask some of the potential barriers for Asian Americans. As mentioned above, the Maryland House of Delegates is one of two major state political institutions in Montgomery County, the other being the Montgomery County Council.

The Montgomery County Council is the legislative branch of county government. It has nine members, all elected at the same time by the voters of Montgomery County for four-year terms. Five members of the council are elected by the voters of their respective council districts. Four members are elected at large by all the voters of the county. The council officers are elected by the council from among its members in December for a one-year term. Unlike the Maryland House of Delegates, which meets only three months of the year, being on the Montgomery County Council is a full-time job. As a result, many local and state political experts agree that the latter is both more competitive and prestigious given that it represents a full-time political position as opposed to a part-time position. Often this results in a greater number of highly qualified candidates running for the county council in comparison to the Maryland House of Delegates.

No Asian American currently serves on the Montgomery County Council, despite the demographic shifts occurring in the region. While several Asian Americans have run in the past, all have been unsuccessful because they did not have any grassroots networks in the Asian American community, which limited their appeal, and they were not politically entrenched within the Maryland Democratic Party to receive its endorsement.

Another elected political institution that serves as a benchmark for Asian American local political incorporation in Montgomery County is the Montgomery County School Board. As is the case for all groups, school boards represent a springboard for many aspiring politicians because they are less competitive, require less money to run an effective campaign, and often offer multiple elected positions compared to other local political institutions like the city council. Montgomery County contains one of the most diverse student bodies in the nation among its 140,000 students, of which Asian Americans account for 14 percent. Yet in the history of the seven-member Montgomery County School Board, only one Asian American, Alan Cheung, a first-generation Chinese American, has been elected, nearly twenty years ago. Cheung broke the glass ceiling in 1991, serving for eight years or two terms.

Unfortunately for Asian American political incorporation efforts, Cheung's tenure did not coincide with the recent demographic boom that the suburbs of Montgomery County have been witnessing, which limited his ability to tap into the emerging Asian American community at the time. The Asian American community was in its infancy. As a result, Cheung was a cross-racial mainstream candidate who won the support of whites and African Americans in Montgomery County. Whether Cheung could have taken his political name recognition to the Montgomery County Council was never tested. Cheung stepped out of the political spotlight after his final reelection to the Montgomery

County School Board, despite a later interest in running for the Maryland House of Delegates in 2002.

Henry Lee, a second-generation Chinese American who is a dentist by profession, became the second Asian American to serve on the Montgomery County School Board. Lee was not elected, but appointed by the Montgomery County School Board to fill a vacated position in 2001. The Asian American community, most notably the Asian Pacific American Political Alliance, mobilized with Chinese American community leaders to lobby school board members to appoint an Asian American to fill the vacancy to reflect an emerging community that is the largest racial group in the school district. Much to the disappointment of the Asian American community, Lee served for only a few months because he was forced to resign to address a family crisis. In 2006 and 2008 an Asian American candidate, Vietnamese American Tommy Le, ran for the one available at-large seat on the Montgomery County School Board, finishing second both times with 37 percent and 32 percent of the vote, respectively.

While Asian Americans have struggled to win elected seats on the general Montgomery County School Board, this has not been the case for Tim Hwang, a second-generation Korean American seventeen-year-old senior at Thomas Wootten High School, who was elected to the student member position in the April 29, 2009, election. Hwang thereby became the thirty-second member of the Montgomery County School Board, with nearly 56 percent of the secondary school vote. He defeated Jiayi Yang, a junior at Richard Montgomery High School, who received 43.5 percent of the vote, and became the fourth Asian American to be elected as a student member.

The sporadic number of Asian American candidates who have run for various county- and state-level positions shows the lack of a formal candidate pipeline in Montgomery County. This can be attributed to several factors in Montgomery County, such as the gradual political maturation of a relatively recent and residentially dispersed Asian American immigrant community and its various community-based organizations. Perhaps the most important contributing factor has been the political entrenchment of the Democratic Party in Montgomery County, which has limited Asian American political incorporation. This is beginning to change, as Asian Americans are working within the Democratic Party establishment and attempting to give Asian Americans greater credibility. One Asian American who has done this is Susan C. Lee, a member of the Maryland House of Delegates.

Mobilizing the Montgomery County Asian American Immigrant Community from Inside the Maryland Democratic Party

Delegate Susan C. Lee (D–District 16), the first Asian American woman to be elected to the Maryland House of Delegates, in 2002, has been an instrumental force in the mobilization of the Montgomery County Asian American community. Lee has served as the deputy majority whip since 2003 and is regarded by many as one of the key Asian American leaders in the Maryland Democratic Party, which has dominated Montgomery County politics during the past decade. This is an important point particularly at the state and county levels because it makes it extremely difficult for any group to gain political incorporation without first becoming a party insider. In Montgomery County, this point is even more acute, as shown by the fact that no Republican currently sits on the county council or is a delegate from this area. Kumar Barve, the first Asian American elected to the Maryland House of Delegates, and Saqib Ali are also Democrats, but arguably neither is as entrenched as Lee.

As with all of the successful Asian American candidates whom I describe in this book, Lee is a two-tiered candidate who focuses first on the mainstream community and then on the Asian American community. In regard to Tier 2, the Asian American community, Lee's candidacy has been instrumental in mobilizing old and new Asian Americans to the political process.

As illustrated in Table 8.1, contributions to Susan C. Lee's 2006 campaign show that the two-tiered candidate can mobilize both non-Asian and Asian American contributors. Her Asian American contributors, who accounted for 66.4 percent of Lee's total contributions, reflect the diverse Asian ethnic makeup of Montgomery County, with over six ethnic groups represented. An overwhelming majority of the Chinese American contributions came from within Montgomery County and the state of Maryland. While it is not surprising that Chinese Americans represented the largest percentage of Lee's Asian American contributors, Korean Americans were the second largest Asian ethnic contributors, at 9.1 percent. One of the primary reasons for this is that Chung Pak, a Korean American, was one of Lee's primary campaign advisors, which served her well with the growing Korean American community in both the county and state. Unlike the other candidates throughout the case studies in this book, Lee's non-Asian contributors did not represent the largest percentage of her total contributions, but only 33.6 percent.

The primary election results in Table 8.2 demonstrate Lee's crossover appeal, which allowed her to finish in 2006 with the second largest number of votes in District 16. All three Democrats who ran in the District 16 election were elected. Entrenchment within the Democratic Party has its clear advantages, as Lee was part of the Democratic candidate mailing slates to registered Democratic voters in Montgomery County.

The ability of Lee to present herself as a mainstream candidate is reflected in her legislative track record as a delegate from District 16, which is transforming itself into a major technological hub in the Middle Atlantic region. Lee has recently authored several state bills that position her as an expert on Internet fraud and identity theft in the Maryland House of Delegates. For example, during the 2004 session, Lee was one of the authors of H.B. 194, an Internet fraud bill that would provide law enforcement officers with the tools to

Table 8.1 Susan C. Lee's Maryland House of Delegates, District 16, Campaign Contributions, 2006 Primary Election

Racial and Ethnic Group	Contributions Received Within Maryland (percentage of total)		Contributions Received Outside Maryland (percentage of total)		Total Contributions (percentage of total)	
Asian Americans	$115,405	(58.4)	$15,705	(8.0)	$131,110	(66.4)
Chinese Americans	$95,320	(48.3)	$11,940	(6.0)	$107,260	(54.3)
Korean Americans	$15,100	(7.6)	$2,800	(1.4)	$17,900	(9.1)
Asian Indians	$3,250	(1.6)	$50	(0.03)	$3,300	(1.7)
Vietnamese Americans	$350	(0.2)	$150	(0.08)	$500	(0.3)
Pakistani Americans	$600	(0.3)	$300	(0.2)	$900	(0.5)
Japanese Americans	$785	(0.4)	$465	(0.2)	$1,250	(0.6)
Non-Asians	$51,145	(25.9)	$15,250	(7.7)	$66,395	(33.6)
Total (Asians and non-Asians)	$166,550	(84.3)	$30,955	(15.7)	$197,505	(100)

Sources: University of Maryland, Baltimore County, National Center for the Study of Elections Campaign Finance Database, "Friends of Susan C. Lee Contributions Dataset."

**Table 8.2 Results of the Maryland House of Delegates, District 16,
           Primary Election, 2006**

Candidate	Total Number of Votes	Percentage of Votes
Marilyn Goldwater (D)[a]	28,607	25
Susan C. Lee (D)[a]	28,474	25
William Bronrott (D)[a]	28,439	25
Robert Dyer (R)	9,519	8
Other	17,682	16

Source: "Election 2006." washingtonpost.com. Available at http://www.washingtonpost.com/
wpsrv/metro/elections/2006/results/general_montgomery.html.
Note: a. Elected to Maryland House of Delegates, District 16.

fight and prosecute online fraud. The bill successfully passed in 2004. The
mainstream appeal of Lee is also reflected in the major political endorsements
she received during her 2006 reelection bid, which included the following interest groups: Maryland State Teacher's Association; Sierra Club, Maryland
Chapter; Progressive Maryland; Service Employees International Union Local
500; Hispanic Democratic Club of Montgomery County; and the Coalition of
Asian Pacific American Democrats of Montgomery County.

The Emergence of Key Asian American
Political Loci in Montgomery County

As I argue in the book's theoretical model and typologies of Asian American
suburbs (Chapter 2, Figure 2.1 and Table 2.1), three key political loci must
emerge within the Asian American community in Montgomery County in order
for successful group political incorporation efforts around Asian American
candidates to occur. The three political loci are (1) an emerging critical mass
of Asian Americans, (2) strong community political loci that mobilize this critical mass in different ways, and (3) the presence of a strong panethnic ideology. The last two loci are beginning to take shape in Montgomery County and
will likely be ready to prime and mobilize the Asian American community
over the next decade. An example of a panethnic community-based organization that works toward the goal of Asian American political incorporation
at the county level is the Asian Pacific American Political Alliance. It is a
community-based organization established in 1998 that consists of panethnic
representation of community leaders who recruit potential Asian American
candidates by providing them with the necessary linkages with mainstream
elected officials and the Asian American community. Michael Lin, who is the

national director of the Organization for Chinese Americans, also serves as the executive director of the Asian Pacific American Political Alliance. According to Lin:

> We are a panethnic organization that attempts to facilitate Asian American leadership by providing them with the necessary networks to both the mainstream and Asian American communities. The Executive Board purposely consists of a panethnic representation of Asian American community leaders. We don't secretly pick a candidate but meet with him or her and ask them if they are ready to run. The challenge is finding the right person who is ready to run, which is not easy. Once we find that person, the mechanisms go into place to support that candidate in the Asian American community. I have a selective e-mail list of around 100 to 150 Asian American community leaders in Montgomery County that also contains a pool of prospective Asian American candidates who are invited to formal gatherings with mainstream elected officials.[2]

The Asian Pacific American Political Alliance seeks to achieve greater political representation for the Asian American community in Montgomery County through two primary efforts. The first effort is organizing formal gatherings that include mainstream elected officials (whites and nonwhites) and Asian American community leaders to provide a forum for substantive discussions to take place. It is the hope that such discussions will facilitate the necessary cross-racial political networks that are successful for Asian American political mobilization. This results in a win-win situation for both realms. Those mainstream elected officials who participate in these gatherings realize the importance of the emerging Asian American constituency while those Asian American community leaders gain access and familiarity with the local elected officials. The second effort is to recruit potential Asian American candidates from the selective pool that Michael Lin has put together. Thus far, no Asian American candidate has emerged from this pool, but the chances are likely in the near future.

The Coalition of Asian Pacific American Democrats (CAPAD), a panethnic umbrella organization that operates within the Maryland Democratic Party, represents arguably the most effective Asian American political community-based organization at the state level. CAPAD is an officially recognized Democratic club within the powerful Montgomery County Democratic Central Committee. According to its mission statement:

> The purpose of this organization is to help promote, support, and advance the interests of the Democratic Party in Maryland by promoting, supporting, or conducting activities and programs to encourage and promote the education and participation of primarily Americans of Asian and/or Pacific descent in the affairs, activities, programs, and endeavors for the Democratic Party. (Montgomery County Democratic Central Committee 2009)

CAPAD was founded by a dozen core community-based organizations and leaders in the Asian Indian, Chinese American, Korean American, and Vietnamese American communities. Its panethnic membership is by design, as is the top-down pyramid approach spearheaded by Judge Chung Pak, one of its founders along with Delegate Susan C. Lee. According to Pak:

> If you bring the right people together as cofounders of the organization, they each can bring their ethnic constituents to support our main goals and you will be able to give them ownership while creating a panethnic identity. Asian Americans have to work together if we are going to get within the State Democratic Party apparatus that dominates Montgomery County politics.[3]

The panethnic structure of CAPAD has been effective in mobilizing its diverse Asian American coalition partners for and against specific legislation. A recent example is when the Maryland House of Delegates considered legislation that would require employees of cosmetology businesses (e.g., hair and nail salons) to take extended education courses in order to renew state licenses. Many Vietnamese Americans own cosmetology businesses that would have been adversely affected by such legislation. When Delegate Lee was informed of this legislation, she relayed it to Judge Pak, who was able to communicate to and mobilize CAPAD's coalition partners against it. Hoan Dang, a former Vietnamese American refugee who directs a Vietnamese American community-based organization, recalled the following:

> One day, I get a phone call from Chung Pak informing me about the cosmetology legislation, and asking me to bring Vietnamese Americans to testify against the legislation. In five days, I was able to mobilize over 100 Vietnamese Americans who testified against this legislation. I conducted special training classes with them to teach them what to expect during the hearings so they would be prepared. We beat the bill while it was in committee, which is rare, and it was the first time that I felt that Vietnamese Americans in Montgomery County were active and understood the importance of civic engagement, because they saw firsthand what they could achieve if they became involved.[4]

CAPAD has also been effective in fighting against anti-immigrant state legislation through cross-racial alliances with labor unions and African American and Latino organizations. Examples include collaborative efforts (1) with labor organizations on state legislation concerning affordable housing and the minimum wage; (2) with Latino organizations around anti-immigrant policies (in 2007, approximately twenty-five anti-immigrant bills were initiated in the state legislature, all of which were defeated by this cross-racial coalition); and (3) with the NAACP around racial profiling and minimum wage. The role of CAPAD in these multiracial coalitions is to support the other group around its specific concerns. As Pak stated: "We [CAPAD] need to show the African American and Latino communities first that we can help them before we ask for their help."[5] Indeed, this has been the case around state legislative efforts by CAPAD. An example of this is the Maryland state official proclamation of an annual Lunar New Year celebration throughout the state. In achieving this goal, CAPAD worked closely with the NAACP and obtained insight from its leaders, who were successful in establishing the Martin Luther King Jr. holiday in the state. Many of the NAACP leaders understood the symbolism and political importance of an annual Lunar New Year celebration by state proclamation in order to educate the general mainstream population in Maryland about the importance and contributions of Asian Americans.

The ability of the CAPAD leadership led by Delegate Lee and Judge Pak to create both cross-racial and panethnic alliances demonstrates the necessity of such strategies in suburbs like those in Montgomery County that tend to be ethnically and racially commingled communities. As shown in Figure 8.1, the demographics of the Asian American community in Montgomery County determine the importance of panethnic coalition building because the county's two largest Asian American communities are Asian Indian (22.3 percent) and Chinese American (30.2 percent). No Asian American ethnic community can go it alone. And no panethnic coalition can be successful without cross-racial alliances to obtain the numbers necessary to get the attention of the Maryland state Democratic Party and the Maryland House of Delegates, whose leadership is still dominated by whites.

Since its existence, CAPAD has been instrumental in promoting nearly a dozen Asian Americans in key positions throughout the Maryland Democratic Party. A primary example is former Vietnamese American refugee Ngoc Quang Chu, a dentist and a clinical assistant professor at the University of Maryland's School of Dentistry, who served as cochair of CAPAD. He was elected in 2007 as second vice chairman of the Maryland state Democratic Party, becoming the first Asian American to be elected to a position in the party. According to Maryland Democratic Party chairman Michael Cryor:

> We strive to ensure that our leadership truly represents all the people of Maryland with the finest individuals willing to serve. Dr. Chu not only brings unequalled professional, community and life experiences to this position, he brings tremendous intelligence and integrity, for which we are very grateful. ("Ngoc Quang Chu" 2007)

The establishment and political emergence of Asian American community-based organizations like CAPAD and its leadership over the past decade will facilitate and mobilize local political incorporation efforts by the Asian American community around future Asian American candidates. Involving the Asian American youth and young adults, in particular, is part of this mobilization.

Since 2002, CAPAD has worked with local organizations such as Asian American Leadership Empowerment and Development (LEAD), which was founded in 1998 to promote the well-being of Asian American youth and families through education, leadership development, and community building. The organization incorporates Asian American youth in its civic education strategies through a high school internship program. In 2002, for example, nearly twenty-five Asian American high school students were placed in internships in mainstream organizations and with non-Asian delegates. In 2006, the number of participants increased to 120 high school students and it has become one of the state's most popular community internships. In return, these students received community service hours and credits, along with the important experience of civic education and engagement. The result has already paid dividends because past interns have been appointed to key state Democratic Party positions. Moreover, in a practical sense, many of these students have developed their own political identities through these experiences outside of the home. Delegate Susan C. Lee laughingly recalled:

> A student and former intern of mine grew up in a household with parents who are conservative Republicans, but became a Democrat and a progressive radical as a result of working in coalitions with labor unions around fair wages and working conditions. Her parents now jokingly tell me that they wished she were moderate and not so radical.[6]

In order for organizations like CAPAD to have influence in state- and county-level politics, they must gain access to and recognition within the Maryland Democratic Party, which currently dominates Montgomery County politics. This has presented a formidable challenge for Asian American political incorporation efforts in the form of elected representation, appointments, and influence on public policies.

Delegate Lee's presence in the Maryland House of Delegates is important as I argue through this book's theoretical model of Asian American political mobilization in the suburbs, which is candidate centered. Lee's presence in the House of Delegates gives her access to political power within a civic institution that makes key decisions, and she has the opportunity to influence it from within as an individual legislator and in coalition with others. While these factors alone do not guarantee political transformations of civic institutions, it nevertheless is an important step in the political incorporation of any group.

Potential Barriers to Future Political Incorporation: Democratic Party Entrenchment in Montgomery County Politics

The past decade has witnessed a shift away from a competitive two-party system to an entrenched Democratic Party in Montgomery County. Currently, no Republican sits on the Montgomery County Council. In many ways, this shift is part of a larger trend that reflects the changing demographics of this region. As Asian Americans, African Americans, Latinos, and other nationalities immigrate in heavy numbers to Montgomery County, the region has transformed from red to blue in its political partisanship.

An entrenched party in Montgomery County politics has potential detrimental effects on Asian American political mobilization efforts in the suburbs. If Asian Americans are to win descriptive representation to achieve greater political incorporation in local politics, the first challenge is to attain incorporation within the Democratic Party so they can have a chance to win. Delegate Susan C. Lee is a vivid example. She was a Maryland Democratic Party insider who was in the right place at the right time. Her appointment to fill one of the three seats from her district that had been vacated was a logical choice given the facts that she was an Asian American woman in a district with many Asian Americans who had no representation and she was a Democrat. Whether Lee would have received the appointment if she had not been a Democrat is an important question. Of the many foreign-born Asian Americans who form a large portion of the Asian American community in Montgomery County, few are key members of the Maryland Democratic Party. This poses a major challenge for future political action efforts for descriptive representation regardless of whether key Asian American political loci such as a guiding political ideology are present or not.

Fortunately for Asian Americans, descriptive representation is slowly occurring in the Maryland House of Delegates for Montgomery County and nearby Prince George's County, where the Asian American population is also growing. Kris Valderrama (D–District 26) was elected from Prince George's County in January 2007 and is the eldest daughter of former Maryland delegate David Valderrama. Four Asian Americans, all Democrats, currently serve in the Maryland House of Delegates (Kumar Barve, Susan Lee, and Saqib Ali from Montgomery County; Kris Valderrama from Prince George's County). This is by no means a critical mass, but it certainly is a beginning for the relatively immigrant Asian American communities throughout the suburbs of Maryland. The key will be whether successful Asian American candidates can emerge in elections for the Montgomery County Council, which is arguably more competitive than the Maryland House of Delegates, and for the Montgomery School Board, where the presence of Asian American students is undeniable. Not only has the Asian American community in Montgomery County been hampered by the entrenchment of the Maryland Democratic Party, but it is also limited in its development of the mandatory three factors that I discussed in Chapter 2. These factors are a large Asian American population, the presence of strong community political loci, and a strong ideology to guide political incorporation efforts. With regard to the third factor, which is seen in more successful suburbs, no pan-Asian ideology permeates Montgomery County politics. This is mainly because of the ethnic diversity in the region's Asian American community, where no one Asian ethnic group dominates. According to Kumar Barve:

Pan-Asianism really has not come to fruition in my opinion. The Asian community is broken up into four, and maybe more, very distinctive groups in
my area. They are in no particular order: one, South Asian Hindus primarily
Indian-American; two, South Asian Muslims primarily from Pakistan; three,
East Asians (Chinese, Korean, and Japanese); and four, South-East Asian primarily Vietnamese. These groups no longer dislike each other, they get along
very well, but they are not an integrated whole. Nor are they ever likely to
be because, frankly, they are very different people. Their needs, languages,
objectives and self perceptions are very different. Also, there is very little
intermarriage. Each of these groups is more likely to marry into the white
community than with each other. This is a distinct difference with a heterogeneous ethnic grouping, like say, the Hispanic community.[7]

This has historically been the panethnic challenge for the Asian American
community. It makes community-based organizations and community leadership important in setting a panethnic tone in their actions by reaching out to a
broader Asian American constituency through fund-raisers, candidate forums,
and coalition-building efforts. In particular, Asian American candidates and
elected officials have the greatest influence in mobilizing a broader pan–Asian
American constituency through their campaign and voter turnout strategies.
Given this argument, it is clear that within Montgomery County, Susan C. Lee
and community-based organizations such as CAPAD are at the forefront of es-
pousing a pan-Asian ideology through their campaign and mobilization strategies. However, they cannot act alone. Other organizations that exist under the
CAPAD umbrella must continue to espouse such an ideology and explain why
it makes sense to their respective ethnic communities.

A formal Asian American candidate pipeline is also necessary to establish
a foundation for sustained successful political incorporation efforts. In Montgomery County, this issue raises an interesting debate about local and national
politics in the region. The next section addresses some competing arguments
that are unique to this region and why such a candidate pipeline has not come
to fruition as quickly as in similarly Transformed suburbs with large populations of Asian American immigrants.

The Long Shadow That Washington, DC,
Casts over Montgomery County Politics

Washington, DC, is located twelve miles from Montgomery County and casts a
long shadow over its surrounding suburbs. The ability to create a viable and
competitive Asian American candidate pipeline in Montgomery County is inhib-
ited in part by the aura, power, and limelight of Washington politics. Being located within the Washington Beltway where federal politics reigns supreme in
both prestige and economic opportunity, many qualified Asian Americans have
opted to pursue the federal political pathways to fulfill their career political and

public service aspirations. Many local observers believe that a hierarchy exists within the Washington Beltway in which local politics is looked down on. According to Paul Tiao, an assistant US attorney and longtime community leader:

> Many Asian Americans would rather work in the federal government in Washington, DC, because the political prestige and pay [are] greater than any local position. If you choose to run for a local position such as the Maryland House of Delegates, you are not taken as seriously. It is sort of political snobbery that exists in Montgomery County.[8]

As a result of this competing pipeline, many qualified and talented Asian Americans choose to work in federal government and pursue a Washington career as opposed to focusing on a local political career in the suburbs of Montgomery County. This is highlighted by the fact that the federal government is the largest public employer in the Montgomery County region. The rise of the Washington career among Asian American government executives can be seen in Washington professional organizations like the Asian American Government Executives Network (AAGEN). According to its website (Asian American Government Executives Network 2009):

> AAGEN was founded in September 1994, is a 501(c)3 non-profit, non-partisan organization of the highest ranking Asian Pacific American career and appointed executives, foreign service officers, legislative and judiciary members, and military officers in the Federal, state, and local governments. . . . In early 1994, several Federal Asian American senior executives met informally to become better acquainted, to explore the possibilities of setting a more structured network, and to find ways to identify other executives. It was agreed that through a network, we would be able to establish a high level voice and representation for ourselves and other Asian Americans in Federal service, to help each other, and to maintain visibility that other similar organizations have achieved for their respective interests. In the ensuing months, the group grew quickly with executives representing more than 20 Federal agencies, and the network was formed.

While many talented Asian Americans inside the Washington Beltway have chosen to pursue a career in both federal government and nongovernment agencies, they are still severely underrepresented at key levels of the federal executive positions. In a sobering 2003 report by the General Accounting Office (GAO) on diversity in the Senior Executive Service (SES), which is the highest-ranking corps of executives who have the strongest influence in the daily decisions and operations of the federal government, only 100 Asian Americans were serving in such a capacity, or about 1.7 percent, which is less than half of the Asian American representation in the US population (US General Accounting Office 2003). The same GAO report also found that approximately 82,000 Asian Americans work in the civilian segment of the federal government, and another 54,000 serve in active military forces.

Despite the imposing competition of Washington, DC, politics, it is likely within the next five years that more Asian American immigrant and nonimmigrant candidates will begin to emerge and run for elected offices in the suburbs of Montgomery County. This process is already occurring, as two Asian Americans, Susan C. Lee and Kumar P. Barve, are among the seven members of the Maryland House of Delegates from Montgomery County, and as the demographic growth continues in small- to medium-sized suburbs like Rockville, Potomac, North Potomac, Springville, and Gaithersburg.

Others, like Michael Lin, believe that while Washington, DC, does siphon away talented Asian Americans who choose to be career federal government executives, there are enough talented and motivated Asian Americans who work in the suburbs to provide a potential candidate pool. Regardless, one thing is certain: Asian American candidates must be groomed by current Asian American elected officials in Montgomery County, particularly at the state level, beginning with the Asian Americans who currently serve in the Maryland House of Delegates. As seen in the suburb case studies of Cupertino and Garden Grove and Westminster, current Asian American elected leaders play an important role in appointing qualified Asian American candidates to high-profile city commissions because they will likely seek higher elected positions.

The Future Trajectory of Asian American Political Incorporation

It is easy to characterize Montgomery County as containing Emergent I suburbs. Given the large percentages of Asian Americans in Montgomery County, on the surface level it should be shocking that only one Asian American has been elected to either the Montgomery County School Board or Montgomery County Council. This has been due to several factors: the gradual, but slow, political maturation of the Asian American immigrant community; the formal political rules of Montgomery County that make county-level positions the initial entryway as opposed to local positions like the city council; the overshadowing of nearby Washington, DC, politics, which competes with Montgomery County politics for talented Asian American candidates; and the political stranglehold of the Maryland Democratic Party on county and statewide positions in the region. Within the Asian American community, these challenges are further amplified and muddled by the slow and gradual development of the three key community factors necessary for Asian American local political mobilization efforts: a large Asian American community, the establishment of Asian American political loci, and a strong political ideology to guide it.

While Asian American political loci in the form of community-based organizations are slowly developing in Montgomery County, no strong pan–Asian

American ideology guides the local politics beyond community-based organizations like CAPAD, which is situated within the Maryland Democratic Party and not within the Asian American community, because of its political influence in county and state politics. Thus, such organizations are limited in their scope and outreach to the broader Asian American community. CAPAD attempts to influence the community through its linkages with community-based organizations through voter education and registration activities revolving around Asian American candidates and substantive issues that affect Asian Americans. Such an ideology is not likely to permeate the large immigrant-born population if Asian American candidates, community leaders, and community institutions do not lead the charge.

The suburbs in Montgomery County represent an Asian American community in transition from an Emergent I to a Transformed I suburb. It is likely that, within the next decade, the Asian American community as well as the Latino community will begin to tap into their vast political potential given that the factors necessary for political incorporation are in place. But it will take time to develop them into insurgent political agents within the community. It is only a matter of time before Asian Americans emerge as important constituents and key political players that even the Maryland state Democratic Party will not be able to deny or take for granted.

Notes

1. Michael Lin, executive director of the Organization for Chinese Americans, interviewed by the author, April 13, 2008.

2. Michael Lin, executive director of the Organization for Chinese Americans, interviewed by the author, Washington, DC, June 16, 2008.

3. Chung Pak, judge, interviewed by the author, Rockville, Maryland, June 18, 2008.

4. Hoan Dang, board member, Maryland Vietnamese Mutual Association, interviewed by the author, Silver Spring, Maryland, June 17, 2008.

5. Chung Pak, judge, interviewed by the author, Rockville, Maryland, June 18, 2008.

6. Susan C. Lee, member of the Maryland House of Delegates, interviewed by the author, Rockville, Maryland, June 18, 2008.

7. Kumar Barve, member of the Maryland House of Delegates, personal communication with the author, July 6, 2008.

8. Paul Tiao, assistant United States attorney, interviewed by the author, Washington, DC, May 14, 2008.

9

Sugar Land, Texas:
The Political Awakenings of
Asian Americans in a Houston Suburb

The Houston–Sugar Land area represents a unique case study of political symbiosis between the large city of Houston and the small suburb of Sugar Land, Texas, in which the former has been able to provide the impetus and set the tone for political incorporation efforts in the latter. Houston ranks as the seventh largest city in the United States, with a total population of 2.14 million. In contrast, as illustrated in Map 9.1, the nearby suburb of Sugar Land holds approximately 73,000 residents, with an Asian American population of nearly 24 percent (US Census 2006i). Since the late 1990s, the political symbiosis has been mutually beneficial between both the large core city and its peripheral suburb with regard to Asian American community mobilization around Asian American candidates concerning campaign contributions and other coordinated mobilization efforts. For example, Asian American candidates who run in Sugar Land will likely receive campaign contributions from Asian Americans in Houston and vice versa. The relationship between Houston and Sugar Land makes this case study important for understanding how Asian American political incorporation, with regard to sustained Asian American descriptive representation, can be achieved in a suburb outside of California.

The gradual influences of Asian American immigrants on Houston can be seen when driving along Interstate 59 from the Little Saigon Radio signage that prominently boasts its presence in the Harris County area to the emergence of Asian Indian, Pakistani American, and Taiwanese American restaurants throughout the city's downtown area. The metropolis of Houston and its Asian American community show the diversity of post-1965 Asian American immigration to the United States. Prior to 1965, the Asian American community in Houston was relatively sparse, with the first public sighting in the 1870s being 250 Chinese railroad laborers who were passing through the city. Census records reveal that the first Asian American born in Houston was a

137

Map 9.1 South Asian and Asian Population Distribution in Sugar Land, 2000

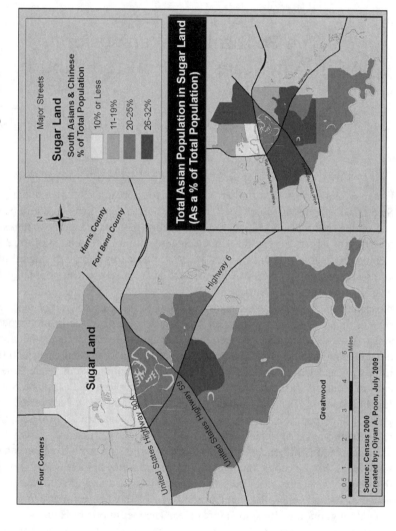

Four Corners

Sugar Land

Harris County
Fort Bend County

United States Highway 90A

United States Highway 59

Highway 6

Greatwood

N

Major Streets

Sugar Land
South Asians & Chinese
% of Total Population
10% or Less
11-19%
20-25%
26-32%

**Total Asian Population in Sugar Land
(As a % of Total Population)**

0 0.5 1   2   3   4   5
Miles

Source: Census 2000
Created by: Oiyan A. Poon, July 2009

Chinese American named Lincoln Yuan, who was born in 1880, the son of a Chinese merchant and Caucasian mother (Chen and Von Der Mehden 2009).

During World War II, the Chinese American community was estimated to be 121 individuals. Many of these immigrants came to Houston from neighboring states like Arkansas, Louisiana, and Mississippi as well as other parts of Texas. For their livelihoods, most worked at or operated ethnic-owned businesses such as restaurants and laundromats predominantly in African American neighborhoods. By 1955, the Asian American community peaked at 1,000 (Chen and Von Der Mehden 2009).

Immigration reform and a robust local economy of the aeronautics and technology sectors eventually diversified and internationalized the Houston citywide demographics. Oil was the initial industry that allowed Houston to grow into a major urban city. Its location along the Gulf of Mexico allowed it to become a central trading hub for the Southwest, but it has been the growing influx of aeronautics, including the National Aeronautics and Space Administration (NASA), that has attracted the recent influx of highly educated and professional Asian American immigrants to Houston, particularly from Taiwan and India. Currently, Houston boasts the most Fortune 500 corporations of any US city besides New York City.

While economic opportunities have attracted Asian American immigrants to Houston, economic issues such as the lower cost of living have also played an important role in the recent influx and growth of this community. In particular, large waves of Vietnamese Americans have begun to move from Southern California and San Jose to Houston due to cost-of-living issues (Tran 2008). As a result, Houston had the third largest Vietnamese American population in the nation with approximately 85,000 in 2006, a nearly 33 percent increase from 2000. Many of these individuals are professional and educated (Tran 2008). Changes are clearly evident throughout pockets of Houston's suburbs with emerging Vietnamese supermarkets, large Vietnamese Catholic churches, Pho Saigon Noodle Houses, and Vietnamese real estate agents who are targeting this community and its upper-middle-class clientele. A new thirty-two-acre, $300 million New Saigon Shopping Plaza is currently in development, which seeks to make Houston's Little Saigon the premier one in the United States (Tran 2008). This new Vietnamese American community profile is in stark contrast to the original Vietnamese American refugees who settled near Houston and engaged in the fishing and shrimp industries to survive in their new country.

Federal immigration reforms in 1965 also contributed to the Asian American community's growth in Houston as immigration exclusion laws were lifted. The post-1965 period brought with it diversity of the Asian American community as East Asian immigrants (China, Japan, and Korea), Southeast Asian refugees (Vietnam and Thailand), and South Asians (India and Pakistan) arrived and made suburban Houston their home. In 1965, the Houston Asian

American community was 2,500, compared to 106,620 in 2000, or 5 percent of the city's total population. Houston currently boasts the second largest Southeast Asian American refugee population behind the city of Los Angeles. Given the relatively small percentage of Asian Americans in the community since 2000, it might be thought that their political incorporation in city government was nonexistent. But the thesis of this book is understanding why focusing on large cities such as Houston is not the ideal indicator of understanding the site of Asian American political mobilization. Instead, we need to focus on suburban areas where Asian Americans have had their greatest growth, and in the Southwest, where no other suburb has achieved such rapid Asian American population growth in the past decade as Sugar Land. And with this growth has come some degree of Asian American local political incorporation.

Setting the Tone: The Beginnings of
Asian American Descriptive Representation in Houston

Among all of the major large cities, Houston has elected more Asian American city council members than cities more famous for Asian American immigration such as Los Angeles, New York City, and Chicago. The historic 1993 Houston City Council campaign of Martha Wong, a second-generation Chinese American woman raised in Houston with a self-admittedly strong Southern accent, showed that an Asian American could win in the predominantly white and conservative city. Wong represented the perfect Asian American candidate to break the city's glass ceiling and defy political pundits. She had strong local ties to Houston mainstream organizations with great political clout, such as the city's homeowners' associations, but she also was able to mobilize the city's growing multiracial population because of her minority background. After Wong's city council tenure ended in 1999, she ran a successful campaign for the Texas House of Representatives from the Houston district in 2002 by mobilizing the district's majority conservative population while holding on to her longtime supporters.

Martha Wong's historic city council seat marked the beginning of Asian American representation on the Houston City Council. Immigration law attorney Gordon Quan, who grew up in the Latino east end of Houston after immigrating from China at an early age, won an at-large seat in 2000. He was unanimously approved by the city council in 2002 to be the city's first Asian American mayor pro tem. Quan was able to mobilize a multiracial, progressive coalition in the city's at-large district due to the political networks that he developed as a well-respected immigration law attorney. Asian Americans played an important role in Quan's election, in particular those Asian Americans in the nearby suburb of Sugar Land. According to Quan: "A majority of my Asian American contributions came from Sugar Land because while many

Asian American Political Power in Harris County, Texas
The Houston–Sugar Land political symbiosis: former Houston City Council member and Mayor Pro Tem Gordon Quan (third from far left), first and former Houston City Council member and former Texas State Representative Martha Wong (middle), current Houston City Council member M. J. Khan (sixth from far left), current Texas State Representative Hubert Vo (immediate right of Martha Wong), former Sugar Land City Council member Daniel Wong (fifth from far left), and current Sugar Land City Council member Tom Abraham (third from far right). Reprinted with permission from the Asian Houston Network.

Asian Americans live there, many owned businesses and worked in Houston, so they identified with my campaign."[1] Quan was followed by M. J. Khan, a Pakistani American who holds a professional engineering degree and is president of a civil engineering company in Houston. Khan was elected in District F in 2003 and currently serves on the city council. Building on a multiracial campaign, Khan was able to become Houston's third Asian American city council member in the past decade.

Perhaps a strong indicator of the emerging potential of Vietnamese American politics in the broader Houston area known as Harris County is the 2004 election and 2006 reelection of Hubert Vo, the first Vietnamese American and second Asian American to be elected to the District 149 seat in the Texas House of Representatives. Vo set a major precedent for Texas state politics in 2004 by becoming the state's first Vietnamese American member after winning a major contested battle with the House's most entrenched member, Republican incumbent Talmadge Heflin, a twenty-two-year political veteran who was then chairman of the House Appropriations Committee, by a razor-thin margin of three votes (20,695 to 20,692). Despite potential political lawsuits that contested the margin of victory and grassroots countermobilization by

Asian American community organizations and activists, the final result stood. Vo demonstrated that he was not a "one-hit wonder" by winning his electoral rematch with Heflin in 2006 by 54 percent of the total votes.

The success of Vo in his 2004 and 2006 campaigns shows how Asian American voters likely were the swing vote that made the difference in both elections. Incumbent Heflin's District 149 was changing as new immigrants began to settle, and many of them connected with Vo's campaign message about incorporating immigrants into the political system. This district contains a large portion of the multiracial Harris County, which is a minority-majority district, along with the predominantly conservative white suburbs of Alief and Katy. Vo was also able to win moderate to liberal Democrats, mostly whites, who sought to end Heflin's political entrenchment in the district.

In both the successful inaugural and reelection campaigns of Martha Wong and Hubert Vo, Asian Americans demonstrated the ability to get elected and reelected, an important measure of political power, in multiracial districts where Asian Americans are nowhere near a substantial portion of the city population. Wong and Vo focused on cross-racial coalition building by presenting themselves as mainstream candidates while attempting to mobilize a panethnic coalition among Asian American voters. According to Vo: "These are consequences of the racial and ethnic transformation in some districts. It's fascinating because things are changing so rapidly. There's a demographic transition in that district, and it's changing the face of the city" (Stinebaker and Rodriguez 2004, 1). In the Harris County area of Houston, Vo's greatest political allies are the Asian immigrants who are changing the face of the district, most evidently in the areas surrounding suburbs.

Emerging Asian American
Political Loci in the Houston Suburbs

The success of Asian American political incorporation in the nearby suburbs of Houston is tied strongly to the rise of the various Asian American political loci, particularly the ethnic print media, community-based organizations that focus on political mobilization (e.g., the Houston 80-20 Asian American Political Action Committee), and the prominent role of established community leaders. The Houston 80-20 Asian American Political Action Committee is a perfect example of the political linkages between Houston and Sugar Land Asian American politics. The board members of this political action committee (PAC) are primarily panethnic, with key members being leaders of the Chinese American, Taiwanese American, Asian Indian, Pakistani American, Vietnamese American, and Filipino American communities. The orientation of this PAC is strongly pan–Asian American, and they seek to promote greater Asian American political representation in the Houston area. The suburb of Sugar Land is one area that the Houston 80-20 Asian American Political Action Committee sought to be involved in, as they officially endorsed Daniel Wong for Sugar Land mayor in the May 2008 election and helped finance a campaign consultant, Mustafa Tameez, to work with Wong's campaign.

Another key Asian American political locus in the Houston-area community is the ethnic print media. As shown in Cupertino (Chapter 5) and Garden Grove and Westminster (Chapter 6), all suburbs with large Asian immigrant populations, the ethnic print media is an important political ally for Asian American candidates and elected officials in mobilizing both old and new Asian Americans into the political system through their campaigns. With their large foreign-born population, the rise of ethnic print media in these communities is inevitable. For example, in the majority foreign-born Asian Indian community in Houston, three Asian Indian newspapers currently exist. The largest is the *Indo American News,* which prints nearly 50,000 copies a week and is distributed at fifty location points throughout southwest Houston, primarily at ethnic markets, restaurants, and community centers. The same is happening in every one of the major Asian American ethnic communities, as the ethnic print media market is beginning to catch up to the demands of the community for ethnic-related news and entertainment.

Although the city of Houston has been able to defy the challenges of Asian American political incorporation faced by similar large cities, the most important question has yet to be addressed: whether it can sustain elected representation and even build on it, a true test for measuring group political power in local politics. Concerns are justifiably raised by Asian American community leaders in the Houston area as to whether a formal Asian American pipeline has been created. Without such a pipeline, future Asian American political incorporation is limited, as articulated by past and current Asian American elected officials. Martha Wong, the city's first Asian American council member, states:

> Although I have mentored Asian American candidates like Gordon Quan, I think it is important that we begin a political network of past and present Asian American elected officials in the area so that they can serve to mentor others about what it takes to get elected. I have my own opinions about what it takes to get elected that I share with prospective candidates about everything from their clothes to their facial hair.[2]

According to Rogene Gee Calvert, a board member of the Houston 80-20 Asian American Political Action Committee who works in the Houston mayor's office, such formal pipelines are beginning to happen:

> It is important to have such formal pipelines and we are beginning to create them with 80-20. We recently had in February 2008 a "Lunch and Learn" that I led about Municipal Utility District Boards and how to run for them. Such

boards are important stepping stones for Asian American candidates seeking higher office.[3]

Despite appointing Asian Americans and other racial groups to key city commissions, Houston City Council member M. J. Khan is concerned about whether any will run in the future. Khan stated: "I have personally appointed Asian Americans and other minorities to key city commissions but whether they run is another issue. It takes a lot of risk and courage to run and so far no one has done so."[4] If no foreseeable qualified Asian American candidate decides to run once term limits force Khan out of office, the potential for another Asian American candidate will be diminished over time. According to Mini Timmaraju, former director of field operations for Congressman Nick Lampson, the challenge becomes greater because the Houston community is constantly changing:

> Approximately six thousand new residents move to Houston each year, which makes it increasingly challenging to maintain the same coalitions that elected M. J. Khan and Gordon Quan. It becomes increasingly difficult for another Asian American to run as other racial and ethnic groups begin to emerge and want to support their own candidates.[5]

With these future challenges of sustained descriptive representation facing the Houston Asian American communities, the political momentum that began with Martha Wong and continued through M. J. Khan will likely shift to the nearby suburbs, which will become the center of Asian American political incorporation efforts in the general area of Houston known as Harris County. The Asian American political incorporation efforts in Houston are having significant repercussions for Asian American communities in nearby suburbs such as Sugar Land, Fort Bend, and Stafford. For many of the Asian American leadership in these suburbs, the prevailing question is, if Asian American candidates like Wong, Quan, and Khan can get elected in a heavily conservative white city like Houston, why can't Asian Americans in these small suburbs do the same, especially when they have such large population bases? The above-mentioned electoral successes of Asian American candidates in Houston had significant repercussions for various Asian American communities in the suburbs outside of Houston, in particular Sugar Land, Fort Bend, and Stafford. Among these suburbs, Sugar Land has demonstrated what few suburbs, even in California, have been able to achieve; that is, sustained elected representation of Asian American candidates in local government.

An Emerging Asian American Southwest Suburb of Houston

Twenty-two miles south of Houston is the suburb of Sugar Land, which got its name from the city's early industrial economy of the Imperial Sugar Company.

The city's history began in 1835 when Stephen F. Austin was awarded a land grant from the Mexican government that allowed for 300 families to settle in the area ("Sugar Land Annual Report" 2007). Prior to the early 1900s, the city remained predominantly underdeveloped with little economic industry until the Imperial Sugar Company opened its doors in 1908. The area then transformed into a company town in which the Imperial Sugar Company provided housing, schools, a hospital, and various businesses for its workers. In 1950, the Imperial Sugar Company sought to expand its housing, resulting in the subdivision of homes known as the Venetian Estates, which got its name from its man-made lakes that served as backdrops to the new houses. Another housing subdivision, known as Covington Woods, emerged in the 1960s and focused on affordable housing in the area. Sugar Land gravitated toward becoming an upper-middle-class planned master community like the nearby community of Sugar Creek. In 1977, Sugarland Properties Incorporated began the first stage of the master planned community process, which would last for thirty years.

Sugar Land is witnessing the same suburban transformations that similar suburbs in California, such as Cupertino, Garden Grove, Westminster, and Daly City, are undergoing. In many ways, Sugar Land's demographic makeup makes it look more like a typical Asian American–influenced California suburb that happens to be located in the southwest part of Texas. Over the past thirty years, Sugar Land has become a suburban destination for all racial groups, particularly Asian American immigrants who are highly educated professionals and entrepreneurs attracted to the city's country living, strong public schools, affordable housing, and close proximity to Houston. During this period, the city's total population grew to 79,943 in 2006 when the Asian American community represented 23.8 percent of the city's total population, the second largest racial group behind whites. The influx of Asian Americans into Sugar Land due to gravitational migration has also been felt politically because Asian Americans have become the suburb's second largest racial group. The racial breakdowns in the four city council districts of Sugar Land, excluding the two at-large districts, are District 1 (non-Hispanic whites, 63.3 percent; Asians, 15.8 percent); District 2 (non-Hispanic whites, 59.9 percent; Asians, 26.1 percent); District 3 (non-Hispanic whites, 55.7 percent; Asians, 29.7 percent); and District 4 (non-Hispanic whites, 62.9 percent; Asians, 25 percent). These districts will serve as political battlegrounds between white and Asian American candidates as the latter continue to become more politically active.

These demographic shifts altering the general Sugar Land community have garnered national attention. Sugar Land became the first US city to achieve the distinction of a "Community of Respect," which is part of the Anti-Defamation League's initiative to help governments, nonprofit organizations, and institutes of higher learning "to create an atmosphere that rejects prejudice and fosters respect and an appreciation of diversity" ("Sugar Land Annual Report" 2007, 30). While Sugar Land has a large Asian American foreign-born population (69 percent foreign-born Asian and 34 percent Pacific Islander), many of them have become naturalized US citizens. In fact, more than half of the foreign-born Asian Americans in Fort Bend County have become naturalized citizens ("Sugar Land Annual Report" 2007).

Local Government Structure and Formal Electoral Rules

The city of Sugar Land is a city council–and–manager system. Six part-time members make up the city council, which appoints a city manager to execute the city policies created by it. Two members of the council are elected from at-large districts, with the remaining four from citywide districts. All council members serve two-year terms with term limits of eight years. The mayor is elected for a two-year term, and must win by a majority in the primary election. If no majority is attained, the top two vote getters face off in the runoff election, with the winner requiring a plurality of the votes. City commissioners are elected citywide and serve two-year terms.

Given the growing Asian American population in Sugar Land and the dispersed characteristics of the Asian American community, it is not surprising that the two Asian Americans elected to its city council were from the at-large districts. This served as an impetus for former city council member Daniel Wong's unprecedented 2008 mayoral campaign, and provided another example of tipping point politics in an Asian-influenced suburb, as seen in the Cupertino case study in Chapter 5.

Asian American Political Mobilization and Incorporation Efforts in Sugar Land

In less than a decade, Asian Americans have made significant strides in their political incorporation into Sugar Land politics, beginning with elected representation on its city council. Two Asian Americans (Daniel Wong, a Chinese American, and Tom Abraham, an Asian Indian) currently serve on the Sugar Land City Council. Wong vacated his city council seat in order to run for mayor in 2008. Neeta Sane, an Asian Indian, was sworn in as a member of the Houston Community College Board, which represents the Sugar Land area. Sonal Bhuchar, an Asian Indian, was elected to the Fort Bend School Board from the district that covers Sugar Land. Mini Timmaraju, who is also Asian Indian, recently served as the district director for Congressman Nick Lampson, who represents this area.

An Asian American presence on the Sugar Land city commissions and boards is even more prevalent. For example, in 2008, four Asian Americans served on the eleven-person Building and Standard Commission. Two Asian

Americans served on the Sugar Land 4 B Commission, which is a nonprofit organization that attempts to "promote, assist and enhance economic development activities and quality of life opportunities within the City of Sugar Land" (City of Sugar Land 2008). And three Asian Americans, including the chair, Bridget Yeung, were on the high-profile Planning and Zoning Commission. This Asian American political presence on city commissions and boards is stronger than in many of the suburbs I describe in this book, including California suburbs like Daly City, the largest Asian American–majority city in the continental United States. Their appointments were due to the influence of the two Asian Americans, Tom Abraham and Daniel Wong, on their fellow city council members.

The first Asian American elected official in Sugar Land was Naomi Lam, a Chinese American immigrant from Taiwan, who won a three-way race for trustee of the Fort Bend Independent School District in 2001. In 2002, Thomas Abraham, an Asian Indian immigrant, ran unsuccessfully for the Sugar Land City Council at-large position 1, losing to James Thompson, who received 55 percent of the vote. That same year, Daniel Wong, a Chinese American immigrant, defeated Karyn Dean by receiving 52 percent of the vote for at-large position 2. Abraham ran again in 2004 against Naomi Lam and Mike Casey, which resulted in the city's most closely contested runoff between Abraham and Casey for the at-large seat in its history. Abraham prevailed by a mere two votes. Wong was unopposed that year. Two Asian American immigrants, Wong and Abraham, were able to win seats on the six-member Sugar Land City Council in a historically white and Republican suburb.

Candidate-Centered Mobilization Among Asian American Contributors

Daniel Wong emigrated from Hong Kong in the 1980s to attend the University of Houston, where he earned both his undergraduate and PhD in engineering. Like many Asian American immigrants of his generation and before, Wong was attracted by the economic and educational opportunities in the United States. He eventually began his own successful engineering firm, which worked on major construction projects in Houston and Sugar Land. His personal success led Wong to run for Sugar Land City Council to give back to the larger community. According to Wong: "A lot of Whites in Sugar Land tell me that Asian Americans have done so well economically and educationally in the area but none give back to the larger community. I wanted to change this perception."[6] Wong's entrepreneurial spirit, which allowed him to succeed in the economic arena, served as a personal impetus for running for local political office in a traditionally white Republican suburb. Wong first ran for the at-large position 2 seat on the Sugar Land City Council in 2002. Wong defeated Karyn

Dean by 52 percent to 48 percent, making him the city's first Asian American city council member. In 2004 and 2006, Wong ran unopposed and was re-elected for a second and a third term.

As Table 9.1 shows, Daniel Wong's inaugural 2002 city council campaign had a great impact on the political mobilization of Asian American contributors, especially with regard to the Chinese American community, which contributed the largest amount ($11,750, or nearly 95 percent) of total Asian American contributions. This is expected given Wong's Chinese ethnic background, as Chinese Americans represent the largest Asian American ethnic group in Houston and Sugar Land. As with all candidates, a majority of the initial seed money for Asian American candidates came from those within the candidate's immediate personal networks. Interestingly, non–Asian American contributors accounted for the largest total amount ($18,650) among all racial groups. The significance of this finding suggests that Wong, like many Asian American candidates, must pursue cross-racial coalitions with white voters and contributors to be successful while targeting Asian American contributors. Wong received more than half of his total contributions from non-Asian contributors, which refutes the perception that Asian American candidates can rely only on Asian American contributions.

Table 9.2 shows the geographic locations of Daniel Wong's 2002 Sugar Land City Council campaign contributors by race and ethnicity. Among Wong's Chinese American contributors, an overwhelming majority came from within Sugar Land (thirty-nine, or 61 percent), with the second largest from Houston (eighteen, or 28 percent). Many of these Chinese American contributors were likely from Wong's personal and professional networks that he developed in both cities. The same is true for Wong's non-Asian contributors from Houston, which accounted for the largest amount (twenty-eight, or 57 percent) of the total non-Asian contributions.

The large number and percentage of Chinese American and non-Asian contributors from Houston also suggest that strong political linkages existed between the large city of Houston and the medium-sized suburb of Sugar Land during Wong's 2002 campaign. In particular, as I have argued above, Houston has always served as the political cog for Asian American local political

Table 9.1 Daniel Wong's Sugar Land City Council Campaign Contributions by Racial and Ethnic Group, 2002 Primary Election

Racial and Ethnic Group	Total Amount ($)
Asian Americans	12,400
Chinese Americans	200
Non-Asian contributors	18,650

Table 9.2 Daniel Wong's Sugar Land City Council Racial and Ethnic Campaign Contributors by Geographic Location, 2002 Primary Election

Racial and Ethnic Group	Houston	Sugar Land	Other (within state)	Outside of State
Chinese Americans	18	39	5	2
Asian Indians	1	2	0	0
Vietnamese Americans	0	1	0	0
Non-Asian	28	11	10	0

mobilization efforts in its surrounding suburbs such as Sugar Land, Stafford, and Fort Bend. This political symbiosis is true vice versa, as demonstrated by Gordon Quan's Houston City Council campaign, for which, he said, the majority of Chinese American contributions came from Sugar Land. For many of these Chinese American contributors, the importance of supporting Asian American candidates' campaigns outweighs the political boundaries that separate them, and an inherent relationship exists between Houston and Sugar Land, as many Chinese Americans who own businesses in Houston live in Sugar Land.

In 2004, Tom Abraham was elected in his second try for the Sugar Land City Council (at-large position 1) to become the city's first Asian Indian elected official. Abraham, a longtime resident of Sugar Land, focused on a two-tier strategy to win his 2004 election over Mike Casey by 40 percent to 33 percent. Concern during this election among Houston Asian American community leaders, such as Rogene Gee Calvert, was raised when former trustee of the Houston Independent School District Naomi Lam declared her intention to run for the same district seat. Lam received approximately 27 percent of the total votes, finishing a distant third. Given that no exit poll was conducted, it is unclear whether ethnic polarized voting occurred in which the Chinese American vote went to Lam while the Asian Indian vote went to Abraham, splitting the potential bloc vote to allow a second Asian American to join Daniel Wong on the Sugar Land City Council.

Table 9.3 shows the two-tiered campaign contribution strategy pursued by Tom Abraham. While Abraham relied less on non-Asian contributions than Wong did in his 2002 inaugural campaign, non-Asians contributed a significant portion to Abraham's 2004 campaign with $16,250, or 39 percent of Abraham's total contributions. Asian American contributors accounted for $25,350 in contributions, or 61 percent of Abraham's total contributions, with Asian Indians accounting for $19,400, or approximately 77 percent of his total Asian American contributions. Pakistani Americans were next, with $5,250, or nearly 21

Table 9.3 Tom Abraham's Sugar Land City Council Campaign Contributions by Racial and Ethnic Group, 2004 Primary Election

Racial and Ethnic Group	Total Amount ($)
Asian Americans	25,350
Asian Indians	19,400
Pakistani Americans	5,250
Other Asians	700
Non-Asian	16,250

percent of the total Asian American contributions. Two significant trends can be concluded from these findings. First, the contributions reflect Abraham's personal and professional networks, particularly those among the Asian Indian community. Second, the significant percentage of Pakistani American contributors to Abraham's campaign suggests that panethnic alliances were at least sought between these two historically antagonistic Asian ethnic groups. Without a doubt these homeland tensions are alive and well in Sugar Land and Houston between these groups, but Abraham was still able to receive strong support and public endorsements from key Pakastani American leaders such as Houston City Council member M. J. Khan and Texas state Democratic executive committeeman A. J. Duranni.

Table 9.4 reflects the geographic breakdown among Tom Abraham's 2004 Sugar Land City Council election contributions by racial and ethnic group. It is clear that his primary campaign strategy was to focus on Asian Indian and non-Asian (particularly white) contributors in Sugar Land. Among Abraham's Asian Indian contributors, his largest Asian American ethnic contributors, a majority came from Sugar Land (forty-two contributors, or 65 percent of the total Asian Indian contributors). This finding makes sense given that Abraham is a longtime resident of Sugar Land and that many of his personal networks within the growing Asian Indian community in Sugar Land were likely followed by Houston. The largest geographic representation for Pakistani American contributors to Abraham's campaign also came from Sugar Land, where an emerging community is taking shape. Non-Asian contributors in Sugar Land factored strongly in Abraham's total contributions with thirty-seven contributors, or 57 percent of the total non-Asian contributors.

The overall findings for the successful inaugural elections of Daniel Wong in 2002 and Tom Abraham in 2004 suggest that Asian American elected representation can be sustained and built on in Sugar Land. Both Asian American candidates had a positive mobilizing effect not only in their respective Asian American ethnic communities, but also in other communities, particularly non-Asian communities, which suggests the importance of cross-racial coalitions. This axiom has rung and will ring true for past, present, and future Asian

**Table 9.4 Tom Abraham's Sugar Land City Council Racial and
Ethnic Campaign Contributors by Geographic Location,
2004 Primary Election**

Racial and Ethnic Group	Houston	Sugar Land	Other (within state)	Outside of State
Asian Indians	20	42	3	0
Pakistani Americans	5	15	1	0
Other Asians	4	0	0	0
Non-Asian	12	37	7	2

American candidates running in biracial communities where whites represent the majority racial voting base despite large percentages of Asian American immigrant groups. With increased naturalization and immigration to Sugar Land by Asian Americans, the white majority will likely be challenged, which in turn may create a potential group threat scenario among white residents, as illustrated in the Cupertino case study in Chapter 5. The first major test for whether this was to be the case in Sugar Land would come with the 2008 city elections.

Tipping Point Politics Revisited

On May 10, 2008, Sugar Land voters had the opportunity to determine whether three Asian Americans would serve on the six-member Sugar Land City Council. Daniel Wong opted to leave his at-large seat, which covers the Sugar Land and Galveston area, to run for mayor of Sugar Land against another former Sugar Land City Council member, James Thompson. In Wong's former district, two Asian Americans, S. B. Gaddi, an Asian Indian, and Adnand Siddiqui, a Pakistani American, declared to run. Siddiqui later withdrew from the election. City council member Tom Abraham ran unopposed. If Wong and Gaddi or Siddiqui were elected, this would give the emerging Asian American community of Sugar Land half of the six city council seats.

The most important question in the May 2008 mayoral election was whether white residents of Sugar Land were ready and willing to have three Asian Americans on the city council, including the mayor. Many longtime Asian American political leaders in Houston, particularly the political pioneer Martha Wong, believe that there may be white retrenchment brewing in Sugar Land. Wong stated: "I've been hearing from my close political contacts out there that there [are] growing and quiet concerns from white contributors in Sugar Land about the election. Things are happening too fast in the Asian American community that they're not comfortable with."[7] This belief is echoed by Sugar Land resident and first Asian American local elected official Naomi Lam, who stated: "I'm concerned that there is a white backlash among voters in this election, which is why I felt it wasn't the right time to run again for city council."[8]

The success or failure of the three Asian American candidates rested on whether the proper coalitions could be constructed during the election. Respected Houston-area political consultant Mustafa Tameez, a Pakistani American who has helped elect minorities from Daniel Wong in Sugar Land to Lee Brown of Houston, the city's first African American mayor, was of the belief that regardless of white retrenchment in Sugar Land, the three Asian Americans could win if the proper political coalitions could be constructed to offset the majority white Republican base. According to Tameez:

> We [Daniel Wong] can win in Sugar Land because we have 35 percent of the population as Asian, but what makes it difficult to win is if that South Asian and East Asian coalition does not form. I don't think necessarily that can happen unless a catalyst, such as a political operative or an established Asian American elected official, from the outside comes in and shows how it is done. The first generation guys who are running find it very difficult [to form panethnic coalitions] because there are multiple factions within their respective ethnic communities.[9]

In short, Tameez's primary political strategy, on one hand, was to construct a pan–Asian American coalition among Chinese Americans, Asian Indians, and Pakistani Americans that would be naturally mobilizing around the three Asian American candidates running in the May 2008 city elections. And on the other hand, the strategy was also to construct a cross-racial coalition among progressive to moderate white Democrats who were more likely to gravitate to the three Asian American candidates as opposed to their conservative counterparts.

Tameez attempted to achieve this coalition through a series of concentrated mailers during the last month before the election that were specifically and ethnically sensitive to the Chinese American, Asian Indian, and Pakistani American communities, which featured all three Asian Americans on a political slate. For example, a handwritten form letter endorsing a particular Asian American candidate was attached to the doors of all identified Asian American registered voters of the same ethnicity. Political mailers sent to registered white Democrats in Sugar Land focused on Democratic Party ideology while endorsing the three Asian American candidates and creating political contrast with their Republican counterparts. As in many cities, the Sugar Land City Council and mayoral races are nonpartisan, but the reality is that political ideology is still very important among its voters. Tameez, a well-respected veteran political operative, realized this, but he also understood the importance of targeting the emerging Asian Americans who are sensitive to their respective ethnic groups.

The theoretical model that I propose in this book espouses the importance of common interests, common ideology, and strong leadership to allow for Asian American–led coalitions to seek and attain political incorporation in suburbs, beginning with descriptive representation. The campaign strategy of Tameez illustrates this belief that all are important and that political strategy in attaining such coalitions should not be underestimated and underappreciated. When such coalitions emerge around Asian American candidates, they must be able to articulate and construct both cross-ethnic and cross-racial political alliances if they are to have any chance of electoral success regardless of the size of the Asian American community. This campaign strategy was to be tested in the May 2008 election.

As illustrated in Table 9.5, the primary election results indicated a two-candidate race between former Sugar Land City Council members Daniel Wong and James Thompson, in which neither received the required majority percentage of the votes. This forced a June 21, 2008, general election. With only 17 percent of the Sugar Land registered voters voting in the primary election, Wong's largest number of votes came from absentee votes prior to the May 10 election. A large majority of these votes likely came from the Asian American community in Sugar Land because this was one of the key campaign strategies that Wong's campaign consultants utilized given the proclivity and preference of many Asian American immigrant voters to vote absentee. Wong was the only candidate among the three who received more absentee votes than votes on election day, which further indicates the strong voter support that he received from the Asian American community. However, Wong also focused on a two-tiered strategy that sought to gain support from moderate white Democrats against the more conservative Thompson. This strategy likely did not work because moderate Democrats either were not drawn to the polls en masse or did not overwhelmingly support Wong. Conservative voters were clearly drawn to Thompson.

As a general runoff election between Wong and Thompson became certain, the Sugar Land Chinese American community, with the assistance of the

Table 9.5 Results of the Sugar Land Mayoral Primary Election, 2008

Mayoral Candidate	Early Votes	Election Day Votes	Total Votes (percentage)	
Russell Jones	765	845	1,610	(19.9)
Daniel Wong	1,434	1,390	2,824	(34.9)
James Thompson	1,619	2,033	3,652	(45.1)

Source: Sugar Land City Secretary's Office. 2008b. "2008 Sugar Land Mayoral Primary Election Results."

Houston 80-20 Asian American Political Action Committee, intensified their mobilization around Wong's campaign through several efforts. The first effort was to mobilize the Chinese American and South Asian communities to vote during the city's early voting period, which was June 9 to 16. The get-out-the-early-vote drive was facilitated by the formal campaign website, www.vote danielwong.com, paid for by the Daniel Wong for Mayor of Sugar Land Committee. The website provided all the necessary dates and locations for the early voting. For those who were not likely to vote early, the home page of the website reminded viewers of the general election date, June 21, 2008, from 7 a.m. to 7 p.m. and stated that "you MUST go to your own precinct location."

In many ways, the message on the website focused on mobilizing the largely immigrant and professional Asian American community in Sugar Land, which is unfamiliar with the formal process of a general election when a candidate does not win a majority of votes in the primary election. Like all formal candidate websites, Daniel Wong's also served as an important medium for communicating with mainstream voters about his political career and endorsements to show that he was a mainstream candidate for the entire Sugar Land community. This perspective is illustrated by the website's link "What's Done," which emphatically declare: "At-Large Councilman, representing ALL of Sugar Land, since 2002." The second form of mobilization by the Sugar Land Asian American community was to hold several rallies to support Wong's candidacy to further solidify the broader community. This was evident prior to the May 2008 primary election in two separate rallies held in the preceding two months.

The end result of these grassroots mobilization efforts was a panethnic coalition of Asian American voters that numbered nearly 2,500, which is the largest number of Asian Americans to vote in a Sugar Land election. A majority of these Asian American voters were mobilized over an eight-week period and led by Wong's campaign and community-based organizations such as the Houston 80-20 Asian American Political Action Committee. The question was whether it would be enough to offset the tipping point politics that would occur during the days leading up to the 2008 general election.

According to Table 9.6, Wong was unable to overcome the primary vote gap that Thompson had going into the 2008 Sugar Land mayoral general election. Since no exit poll was conducted, it is uncertain whether racially polarized voting occurred for the two mayoral candidates. However, the primary and general election results raise the salient question of whether tipping point politics is occurring in Sugar Land, as seen in other suburbs, most notably in the Cupertino case study in Chapter 5.

Several examples of tipping point politics from the perspective of the mainstream white establishments are evident in print and spoken words leading up to the May 2008 primary election and the June 21 general election in Sugar Land. The first example occurred three days before the primary election

Table 9.6 Results of the Sugar Land Mayoral General Election, 2008

Mayoral Candidate	Early Votes	Election Day Votes	Total Votes (percentage)
Daniel Wong	1,452	1,646	3,098 (39.4)
James Thompson	2,352	2,402	4,754 (60.6)

Source: Sugar Land City Secretary's Office. 2008a. "2008 Sugar Land Mayoral General Election Results."

on May 7, 2008, in a column by Beverly K. Carter, who owns the *Fort Bend Star,* the major local newspaper in Fort Bend County. In this column, Carter opines the following based on a letter:

> Everything hasn't been sweeter. . . . In Sugar Land, where a new mayor and new city council person are on the ballot, the public contest has been something Fort Bend County has seldom seen—overt racism . . . of the Asian kind. I received a letter from a writer with a supposed Chinese surname, Ahmed Zhiang. Since no telephone number was on the letter and I couldn't verify the writer, I didn't run it. However, Mr. Zhiang sounds like he is well-connected in the Asian community. He claims that since Sugar Land has 30% Asian population, and the city government likes to color itself as "diverse" and "multicultural," it is ripe for the election of an Asian mayor. Mr. Zhiang calls it a conspiracy because its goal is race-based. A.J. Durrani, who chairs the [Houston 80-20 Asian American Political Action Committee] PAC Endorsement Committee, denies any conspiracy, but admits that the group rarely endorses a candidate based on his qualifications, but instead looks only at his racial background. If the candidate is Asian, he gets the endorsement. Mr. Zhiang says that the conspiracy has entered into religious institutions of the Asian community, including Buddhist and Hindu temples, Islamic Mosques and even Christian churches where Asians predominate where classes are given in the worship centers on how to go about voting for only Asians. He says instructions are given on how to register to vote, without regard to citizenship. According to Mr. Zhiang, a Chinese man named Fong, whose head is shaven to make him look like a Buddhist monk, is a central figure in the conspiracy. In addition to serving on the 80-20 endorsement committee, he spends virtually full-time in teaching Asians to vote a race-based ticket. A major supporter of Hubert Vo, a state legislator who was recently in the news because of his ownership of slum-like apartments in Houston, Fong readily admitted that his only goal in politics is to achieve election results based upon race. Fong and another conspirator, known only as Mustafa, regularly address the Asian community groups urging them to vote solely upon the issue of race. (Carter 2008, 1)

The above editorial commentary reflects the form of white resentment that has historically fueled white flight to the suburbs as urban centers changed in racial composition and the issue of racial representation became the central focus. The differences are now the suburban context and the racial group in question that is seeking greater political representation in local government. Carter's editorial blatantly seeks to frame the issue of Wong's candidacy in readers' minds, particularly white readers' minds, that Asian Americans care only about themselves and seek to overtake Sugar Land local government, as opposed to the belief that he represents the entire community. The editorial had no critical commentary on Wong's leadership credentials. Using Ahmed Zhiang as a scapegoat to raise the political innuendoes of race-based politics to mobilize white voters is clearly one of the strategies and results of the editorial. By associating the image of "conspirator" with the person "known only as Mustafa" (Wong's campaign consultant, Mustafa Tameez, one of the most respected political operatives in Houston), the editorial expresses an us-versus-them mentality that clearly is not part of the primary message and motives that underlay Wong's mayoral campaign.

The collateral damage of the above editorial was clearly felt by Daniel Wong's campaign, as the Houston 80-20 Asian American Political Action Committee, which was instrumental in providing support to his campaign, was forced to respond to these unwarranted charges. Mustafa Tameez took a back-seat in the public arena during the crucial period leading up to the June 21 general election. Cecil Wong, president of the Houston 80-20 Asian American Political Action Committee, wrote the following response, which appeared in the May 21, 2008, letters section:

> Dear Bev,
> I am writing this letter in response to your column on May 7, 2008 in the *Ford Bend/Southwest Star*. I am deeply disappointed that you decided to print a letter from a clearly unverifiable character named Ahmed Zhiang whose sole purpose is to slander the reputation of Houston 80-20 and the Asian American community. Houston 80-20 is in fact the Houston chapter of 80-20 Initiative, a national, nonpartisan, Political Action Committee dedicated to the promotion of Asian American participation in the American political process. . . . Your quoted statements about the Houston 80-20 board members Durrani and Fong were all unfounded, untrue and unfitting, and they were never contacted to confirm the statements attributed to them. We strongly refute the assertion that Houston 80-20 endorsement is solely race based and regardless of qualification. . . . We strongly refute the assertion that Houston 80-20 gave classes on how to vote for only Asian Americans and without regard to citizenship, at any Asian American religious institutions in Sugar Land or otherwise. . . . Forming a PAC is the right of all Americans interested in supporting our electoral system, so attacking Houston 80-20 goes against the core of our American values. If we truly value diversity, active participation by all sub-groups including Asian Americans is essential in order to tap the strength of diversity for the benefit of the greater community. (Wong 2008, 1)

The second example of subtle white resistance to Daniel Wong's mayoral campaign allegedly occurred in words spoken by the former Sugar Land mayor

David Wallace and Wong's mayoral opponent James Thompson. According to Jonathan Wong, Daniel Wong's campaign advisor:

> Our election was lost because the current mayor and Daniel's opponent used the phrase "we must elect the best person to be the face and voice of our city." The quote was heard by some of our constituents. I also heard James Thompson say it himself. So did Daniel. . . . The current mayor [David Wallace] won the first diversity award from the Anti-Defamation League several years ago. It is highly alarming that this man lacked the integrity to stand by his values in a city with 40 percent minorities. . . . Despite Daniel being more qualified, more respected, and more hardworking than his opponent, people came out to vote against him in record numbers. The single reason we can chalk this up to is lingering prejudice with regard to Asian Americans holding executive level positions in public office.[10]

Such statements by both the former and current mayor using innocuous terms like "best person" and "face and voice of our city" are not racially polarizing on the surface. But they can be used to create a sense of us-versus-them among the majority white voters who underlie tipping point politics in suburbs like Sugar Land that are undergoing both rapid demographic and political transformations. Such statements in a public forum were likely to have an impact on white voters in Sugar Land who felt that Asian Americans were gaining too much political power too quickly.

Given the above political climate, the data strongly suggest that James Thompson received a large percentage of his additional 1,100 votes in the general election from supporters of Tom Jones, the third candidate in the primary election. Whatever the reasons for this shift, in many ways this result was expected given the political undercurrent that many Asian American community activists in Sugar Land and Houston had felt was taking shape prior to the primary election. This belief is further compounded by the at-large position 2 election, which also took place on May 10, 2008, in which S. B. Gaddi finished a distant second to Jacquie Chaumette with 30.5 percent and 69.4 percent of the votes, respectively, in Daniel Wong's vacated district. Since Tom Abraham ran unopposed for the at-large position 1 seat in this election cycle, he remains the sole Asian American city council member.

There is another important question raised in the June 2008 general election results regarding Asian American political incorporation efforts in Sugar Land. Is it a setback to Asian American political incorporation efforts that they have gone from a political scenario of two city council members with a possible third to the stark reality of only one member after the June 2008 general election? Tipping point politics has become a natural part of the trajectory of Asian American immigrant Transformed suburbs during the critical stage of Asian American political mobilization in which this group is seeking close to or a majority of representation on the city councils. This is one of the key lessons drawn from both the Cupertino (Chapter 5) and Sugar

Land suburb case studies because they are relatively ahead of similar suburbs in the area of descriptive representation. Perception is reality in local politics, especially when the majority racial group begins to feel threatened that an emerging and competing racial group is seeking to gain political power.

The tipping point in Sugar Land local politics likely arose from the perspective of white conservative residents on Daniel Wong's decision to vacate his at-large city council position for the most powerful and visible elected office in the city, just as it was in Cupertino with the prospect of longtime white residents voting for an Asian American candidate in the 2008 Cupertino City Council special election.

As in Cupertino, it is likely that Asian American candidates in Sugar Land will overcome tipping point politics and the perceived group threat of white voters as future Asian American candidates emerge because of the success of Tom Abraham, Daniel Wong, and others in both Sugar Land and nearby suburbs in Fort Bend. There are many highly educated and professionally established Asian Americans who are likely to run in future city council and school board elections, the type of residents that suburbs attract. However, a caveat must be raised because, as I argue in this book's theoretical model, such a candidate must build cross-racial coalitions in the form of the two-tiered strategy. Without this ability, such Asian American candidates in Sugar Land or any suburb, for that matter, will not be competitive.

Another important element that will determine the success of Asian American candidates in Sugar Land is political parties. While many local elections are nonpartisan, political parties can play an important role in such elections by supporting Asian American candidates and voters who are politically aligned with their interests. In the case of the 2008 Sugar Land mayoral election, the Republican establishment in Sugar Land was vigilant in supporting James Thompson during the general election while Daniel Wong did not receive any Democratic Party support.

The gradual establishment of the necessary community political loci, such as community-based organizations, the ethnic media, and a strong political ideology that is panethnic in Sugar Land, is likely to facilitate political incorporation efforts around future Asian American candidates. Moreover, the strong nexus that exists between the Houston and Sugar Land community-based organizations and leadership is another reason why the 2008 Sugar Land mayoral general election is likely a temporary setback for Asian American political incorporation efforts. The key to establishing strong Asian American political incorporation efforts in the suburbs is the presence of three factors: a large Asian American community, the development of various political loci that have access to this community, and the establishment of a strong panethnic ideology to guide this community. The first factor is likely to increase while the other two factors are likely to develop gradually as both the Asian American community in Sugar Land and Houston mature demographically and politically.

Asian American political incorporation efforts are likely to extend beyond the Houston–Sugar Land area. Political change is currently taking shape outside of Sugar Land as suburbs throughout Harris County have been sites of similar Asian American political mobilization activities. In the nearby suburbs of Fort Bend and Stafford, Asian Americans have successfully mobilized around various Asian American candidates for local office. In Fort Bend, Neeta Sane, an Asian Indian woman, became the city's first Asian American to be elected to the Houston Community City College Board, which covers Stafford to Sugar Land. A similar feat was achieved by Ken Mathew, an Asian Indian, who became the first Asian American to be elected to the Stafford City Council. In many ways, the success of Houston city politics has set the tone for Sugar Land and other suburbs as to how Asian American political incorporation can occur in a predominantly conservative region that happens to be in the southwestern region of the United States.

Notes

1. Gordon Quan, former Houston City Council member, interviewed by the author, Houston, Texas, March 26, 2008.

2. Martha Wong, former Houston City Council member, interviewed by the author, Houston, Texas, March 25, 2008.

3. Rogene Calvert, board member of the Houston 80-20 Asian American PAC, interviewed by the author, Houston, Texas, March 25, 2008.

4. M. J. Khan, Houston City Council member, interviewed by the author, Houston, Texas, March 25, 2008.

5. Mini Timmaraju, director of field operations for Congressman Nick Lampson, interviewed by the author, Sugar Land, Texas, March 27, 2008.

6. Daniel Wong, former Sugar Land City Council member, interviewed by the author, Sugar Land, Texas, March 26, 2008.

7. Martha Wong, former Houston City Council member, interviewed by the author, Houston, Texas, March 25, 2008.

8. Naomi Lam, Fort Bend Independent School District trustee, personal communication with the author, April 1, 2008.

9. Mustafa Tameez, political consultant, interviewed by the author, Houston, Texas, March 26, 2008.

10. Jonathan Fong, political consultant, personal communication with the author, July 7, 2008.

10

Bellevue, Washington: Asian American Politics in a Pacific Northwest Suburb

The gateway city of Seattle, known internationally as the Emerald City, is a political anomaly given its long and rich history of pan–Asian American and cross-racial coalition building that has culminated in arguably the most successful level of Asian American political incorporation of any major city in the continental United States. Since the 1880s, Seattle has served as an entryway for Asian contract laborers to the continental United States from Hawaii, Asia, and Alaska (Chan 1991). From then on, the Emerald City has seen an ethnically diverse Asian American community flourish and highlight several social and political movements that have affected both the local Seattle and national Asian American community.

As illustrated in Map 10.1, King County, the nation's twelfth largest county in population, is located in the state of Washington and contains the largest Asian American community of any county in the Pacific Northwest. King County encompasses all or part of sixty-six cities, the largest city being Seattle, where over two-thirds of its residents live in the suburbs. In 2000, Asian Americans accounted for 11.2 percent of the total King County population with 195,352 residents of Asian or Pacific Islander descent (US Census 2006j). This is the second largest racial group behind whites at 73.4 percent, but ahead of Latinos and African Americans at 5.5 percent and 5.3 percent, respectively. At the city level, Asian Americans have made their presence felt in the Seattle suburbs, where they represented approximately 13 percent of the citywide population in 2000, the second largest group after whites. In King County, Asian Americans represent approximately 11 percent of the total county population, with the largest Asian ethnic groups being Chinese at 2.6 percent, Filipino at 1.9 percent, Vietnamese at 1.6 percent, Japanese and Korean at 1.2 percent each, and Asian Indian at 0.9 percent (American FactFinder 2000).

161

Map 10.1 Asian American Population Distribution in King County, 2000

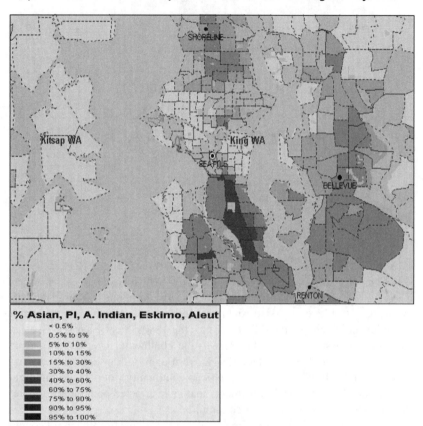

% Asian, PI, A. Indian, Eskimo, Aleut
- < 0.5%
- 0.5% to 5%
- 5% to 10%
- 10% to 15%
- 15% to 30%
- 30% to 40%
- 40% to 60%
- 60% to 75%
- 75% to 90%
- 90% to 95%
- 95% to 100%

Source: Reprinted with permission from the University of Washington, Seattle Civil Rights and Labor History Project. Map produced by Socialexplorer.com.

The political mobilization in Seattle is historically unmatched by any other similar gateway city because Seattle has elected over twenty Asian Americans to its school boards, city councils, courts, Washington state Senate, Washington House of Representatives, and governor's mansion. Indeed, Seattle's long history of Asian American descriptive representation at all levels of government contradicts one of the primary theses in this book: that Asian Americans struggle for political incorporation in large gateway cities. In short, Seattle remains a political anomaly for Asian American political representation in comparison to similar cities with large Asian American populations. In 2008, one Asian American (Bruce Harrell) was elected to the Seattle City Council, District 3, seat with 61 percent of the vote. At the state level, three Asian Americans (State Senator Paull Shin, State Representative Bob Hasegawa, and State

Representative Sharon Tomiko Santos) currently serve in the Washington State Legislature, with only Senator Shin being elected from outside of Seattle (Lai and Nakanishi 2007). All of these local- and state-level Asian American elected officials are Democrats.

In Seattle, Asian American political incorporation, beginning with descriptive representation, is attributed to the presence of strong community-based organizations, strong and experienced leaders who seek both cross-racial and panethnic coalitions, and a strong political ideology to guide its community politics. All three of these elements have been present in Seattle's racial minority communities since the 1970s. One of the key community-based organizations that has promoted cross-racial political coalitions at the citywide level is the Minority Executive Directors Commission (MEDC), which consists of executive directors and program directors who are persons of color working in private, nonprofit human service and community development agencies in Seattle and King County. MEDC was founded in 1981 by Bernie Whitebear, Roberto Maestas, Bob Santos, and Larry Gossett, who had the broad vision of building alliances among the city's Asian Pacific American, African American, Native American, and Chicano Latino communities regarding advocacy and public policies. According to its website:

> MEDC is recognized for its success in sustaining a diverse multi-racial coalition of individuals who work together to inform, educate, influence and empower our diverse constituencies in an effort to work toward social, political and economic equity and justice for communities of color in King County. (Minority Executive Directors Coalition 2009)

MEDC set the tone for minority politics in Seattle in seeking cross-racial support rather than competition in city elections around descriptive candidates, which has plagued larger cities such as Los Angeles, as I showed in the 1993 Los Angeles mayoral case study in Chapter 4.

Another reason for the unprecedented political success of Asian American candidates in Seattle is the early establishment of a panethnic ideology in the political arena within the Seattle Asian American community by organizations such as Asian Pacific American Community Action (APACA) during the late 1970s. APACA has a history of political mobilization around Asian American candidates through activities such as hosting panethnic candidate forums. According to Martha Choe, a second-generation Korean American who was elected to both the Seattle City Council and the Washington State Legislature: "These early organizations help bridge the gap between Asian Americans and other racial groups in Seattle. Groups such as APACA stressed that it's OK to be different, but that we have more commonalities."[1]

The final piece of the puzzle for Asian American political success is the presence of strong leadership within its community. One of the first leaders was Wing Luke, who broke the glass ceiling and paved the way for future Asian

American candidates by making Asian American candidacies for city and state-wide positions in Seattle and Washington State acceptable. According to former Washington governor Gary Locke:

> Asian American representatives starting with Wing Luke to Ruby Chow to me to Martha Choe have allowed the Asian American community to build upon the idea that Asian American candidates are acceptable. This idea has permeated to outside of Seattle for local and statewide elections in the suburbs where more Asian Americans are getting elected.[2]

Luke's strong leadership and vision as Seattle's first Asian American city council member in 1962 made him a champion of civil rights for all people, which helped establish a cross-racial and panethnic vision in Seattle's Asian American community among its elected leadership. Indeed, the political success of the Asian American community with regard to the three important elements (strong leadership, panethnic and cross-racial ideology, and the presence of common interests that bind such coalitions) begets future success of this community in the area of political activism.

Early Forms of Asian American Political Activism

Historically, the Asian American community in Seattle has been a politically active community that extends beyond traditional forms of political participation. Beginning in the 1930s when antimiscegenation laws were in full effect throughout the western part of the United States and when Asian Americans were barred from US naturalization, Filipino immigrants, mostly cannery laborers, were able to form the Filipino Labor Union (FLU) in Seattle, which fought for greater wages and rights for its union members. During the 1970s, the Seattle chapter of the Japanese American Citizens League was instrumental in the first stages of the mobilization efforts seeking redress and reparations for the 110,000 Japanese Americans who were unconstitutionally incarcerated during World War II. This ultimately culminated in the American Civil Liberties Act of 1988.

At the same time, from 1960 to 1970, Asian American ethnic groups in Seattle were instrumental in forging multiracial alliances with African Americans, Latinos, and white progressives in seeking greater civil rights for Asian Americans during the Asian American movement. For instance, in 1969, Mineo Katigiri formed the Asian Coalition for Equality (ACE), and student activists, some of whom were part of the ACE, formed the Oriental Student Union (OSU) at Seattle Central Community College. University of Washington Asian American students formed the Asian American Student Coalition (ASC) soon after (Seattle Civil Rights and Labor History Project 2009). All of these Asian American student groups promoted a pan-Asian identity that galvanized the Asian American movement and lay the foundation for local politics in Seattle.

Early Asian American Descriptive Representation in Seattle

As mentioned above, the first Asian American elected to the Seattle City Council was Wing Luke, a first-generation Chinese American, in 1962. Luke was the first Chinese American elected official in any large city in the continental United States. Luke had served as the state assistant attorney general from 1957 to 1962, when he decided to run for an open city council seat. Mobilizing a cross-racial alliance of 1,000 supporters, Luke won the seat by 30,000 votes (Seattle Civil Rights and Labor History Project 2009).

Luke's promising political career ended when he was killed in a plane crash in 1965. The loss of Luke resulted in the creation of the Wing Luke Museum, located in Seattle's historic International District, which honors not only Luke but many of the early Asian American pioneers in Seattle and the Northwest. It is the only pan–Asian American museum of its kind. In June 2008, through the financial support of the city, private corporations, community groups, and other donors in the amount of $23.2 million, a new Wing Luke Museum building opened to the public. It includes historic immersion tours, which allow patrons to go back to the early 1900s when the first wave of Asian Americans began to arrive in Seattle (Broom 2008). Despite the tragic loss of Luke, he inspired a future generation of Asian Americans, such as Cheryl Chow and Gary Locke, who were protégés of Luke, to run for the Seattle City Council and other elected positions (Yu and Yuan 2001).

Asian American elected representation on the Seattle City Council through panethnic alliances would extend three decades after Luke. Another Asian American elected to the Seattle City Council is John Eng, who was elected in 1973 and served until 1981. Eng served the latter part of his tenure with Dolores Sibonga, who was appointed in 1978 (giving Asian Americans two council members from 1978 to 1981) and served until 1991. Cheryl Chow, the daughter of Ruby Chow who was the first Asian American to be elected to the King County Council, sat on the Seattle City Council from 1990 to 1998. During this entire period, no more than two Asian Americans were elected to the nine-member Seattle City Council. This changed with the watershed period beginning in 1996, when three Asian Americans (Martha Choe, Charlie Chong, and Cheryl Chow) served on the city council.

Perhaps the monumental figure for Asian American descriptive representation in Seattle is Gary Locke, a second-generation Chinese American who was nominated as US secretary of commerce in 2009 by President Barack Obama. Born in South Seattle, Locke, a graduate of Yale University and Boston University Law School, had long cultivated his political career in his home district. He first won a bid to the Washington State House of Representatives in 1982, serving in the legislature for eleven years and chairing the influential House Appropriations Committee, where he earned a reputation as a financial wizard and coalition builder. In 1993, Locke became the first Chinese American to be elected as King County executive by defeating incumbent Tim Hill with a cross-racial

alliance of voters representing over 70 percent of the vote. Locke's rise to political prominence as Washington governor began with the experience and networks gained through his elected position as King County executive, the
highest elected position in the county and one of the highest elected positions
in the state (Yu and Yuan 2001).

Political experience, cultivation of multiracial coalitions, a gradual public
acceptance of Asian Americans by mainstream voters, and a panethnic strategy
that focused on local and national Asian American contributors and voters were
key to Locke's historic 1996 victory as the first Asian American governor of a
major state in the continental United States. He served two terms as governor
before leaving the public sector. In 1996, a watershed moment had been reached
for the Washington State Asian American community as five Asian Americans
(Velma Veloria, Stan Fleming, Gary Locke, Paull Shin, and Art Wang) held
seats in the Washington State Legislature, the largest number of statewide representatives for any state in the continental United States at the time. The significance of this is that Washington State voters and contributors were primed
and ready for Asian American elected representation beyond the Seattle City
Council. Locke declared to run for governor that same year.

Locke focused on a two-tiered strategy that involved a multiracial alliance
with mainstream voters throughout the state and strong panethnic support
among the Asian American community. Locke held national fund-raisers in
Asian American communities throughout the United States, such as San Francisco, Los Angeles, and Washington, DC. In combination with this national
campaign fund-raising strategy that established Locke as a national figure in
the Asian American community, Locke's campaign strategists also targeted the
ethnic media, both in the United States and abroad. It has been estimated that,
among the $2.2 million raised by the Locke campaign during the primary and
general elections, about 18 percent ($396,000) was contributed by donors living
outside of Washington State. Approximately 37 percent of those out-of-state
contributions were from California (Yu and Yuan 2001). Many of these contributors were likely Asian Americans.

One of my major theoretical arguments in this book is that Asian American candidates can play a central role in mobilizing both new and old Asian
American voters and contributors who are within and outside their political
districts. This candidate-centered approach to understanding Asian American
political mobilization is not new, as other racial groups have demonstrated, but
what is unique is the importance of a two-tiered strategy that is necessary for
Asian Americans to win elected representation regardless of the population
base in their respective districts. Locke illustrates this political axiom for Asian
American candidates because his political experience in the Washington State
Legislature and as King County executive gave him the political exposure and
networks in the mainstream and, at the same time, the recognition that would
allow him to be successful. However, unlike prior Asian American candidates

in Washington, Locke realized that Asian Americans (local, state, and national) could play an important role, and he utilized key Asian American political loci (community organizations and networks, the Asian ethnic print media) to his political advantage.

When Locke became the first Asian American to be elected governor of a major state in the continental United States, his victory was felt by Asian Americans in Seattle and across the nation. In his famous inaugural speech on January 15, 1997, "A Hundred Year Journey: From Houseboy to the Governor's Mansion," Locke tells the tale of his Chinese immigrant ancestors:

> My grandfather came to America to work as a "house boy" for the Yeager family, who lived in a house that's still standing, less than a mile from here. . . . His purpose was to get an education, and so the Yeager family agreed to teach him English in return for his work. Like everyone else in our family, my grandfather studied and worked hard, and he eventually became the head chef at Virginia Mason Hospital in Seattle. So although I may be standing less than a mile from where our family started its life in America, we've come a long way. . . . And our journey was successful because the Locke family embraces three values: Get a good education, work hard and take care of each other. Our family history is more the norm than the exception. There is Governor Rosellini, this state's first Italian-American governor, whose parents migrated to America at the beginning of this century. There is Representative Paul Zellinsky, whose grandfather was a Russian sea captain. There is Senator Dan McDonald, whose ancestors were among the pioneer families of this state. And there is Senator Rosa Franklin, whose family rose from slavery in South Carolina to civic leadership in Tacoma. There are millions of families like mine, and millions of people like me—people whose ancestors dreamed the American Dream and worked hard to make it come true. And today, on Martin Luther King's birthday, we are taking another step toward that dream. (Locke 1997, 1)

Locke's inaugural speech also highlights the racial and ethnic transformations of King County during the past century. Beginning with Wing Luke, Asian Americans have reached a level of descriptive representation and incorporation that is unrivaled by any major city in the continental United States. Even without a presence on the Seattle City Council, Asian Americans are part of the discussion of important public policies. The development and persistence of Seattle community-based organizations like the Asian Pacific American Coalition of Washington and leadership such as Ruth Woo, widely considered in the Seattle community as a political matriarch, ensure that Asian Americans are not forgotten in city hall.

As the Asian American community, in particular, transformed both ethnically and politically due to post-1965 immigration that represented a broader spectrum of Asian immigrants than the previous generation, the suburbs surrounding Seattle began to develop into potential Asian American enclaves. Bellevue is one suburb that has undergone dramatic Asian American transformations and has witnessed increased Asian American representation.

A Political Shift to the Suburbs

While Seattle represents the antithesis of Asian American candidates' struggle to win elected representation in large cities, Asian American political growth with regard to descriptive representation is happening at a more rapid pace in Asian American–influenced suburbs. For example, in 2008, six Asian Americans served on city councils in five suburbs outside of Seattle. All of them have as many as or more Asian American city council members than Seattle. They are the following: Bellevue City Council (Conrad Lee and Patsy Bonincontri), Federal Way (Michael Park, mayor), Shoreline (Cindy Ryu, mayor), Oak Harbor (Michael Paggao, mayor pro tem) and Issaquah (S. Russell Joe, city council member). In Seattle, Bruce Harrell, who is half Asian American, was able to replace another Asian American city council member (David Della) in 2007.

Seattle, as the model city in the Northwest for Asian American elected representation, may be gradually shifting to its nearby suburbs, as shown in the recent inability of the Asian America community to gain more than one city council member since the watershed 1993, when three Asian Americans served on the city council simultaneously. To the credit of the Asian American community's efforts in Seattle, they have been able to maintain Asian American descriptive representation during this period, but the community has struggled to build on this, unlike the small- to medium-sized suburbs I have examined thus far, Cupertino (Chapter 5), Garden Grove and Westminster (Chapter 6), and Gardena (Chapter 7).

In the past decade, the suburbs have emerged as potential beacons for Asian American elected representation at the local level. In 2008, suburbs such as Federal Way (Mike Park), Shoreline (John Chang, Cheryl Lee, and Cindy Ryu), and Bellevue (Conrad Lee and Patsy Bonincontri) have elected or appointed multiple Asian Americans to their respective city councils.

As in other similar suburbs, gravitational migration due to the presence of ethnic networks and businesses, along with good public schools and safe neighborhoods, has facilitated Asian American community formation in these cities over the past decade. No such suburb has seen a greater growth of its foreign-born population than Bellevue, which has surpassed Seattle's.

Asian American Political Mobilization in a Seattle Suburb

As illustrated in the inset of Map 10.2, the upscale, high-tech suburb of Bellevue, located approximately eight miles east of Seattle across Lake Washington, contains a significantly large Asian American population. Change is in the air beyond the many cranes and new buildings that dot the skyline of downtown Bellevue, as Asian Americans have been making it their home for the past twenty years. Bellevue, which means "beautiful view," was named by its

Map 10.2 Chinese and Taiwanese American Population Distribution in Bellevue, 2000

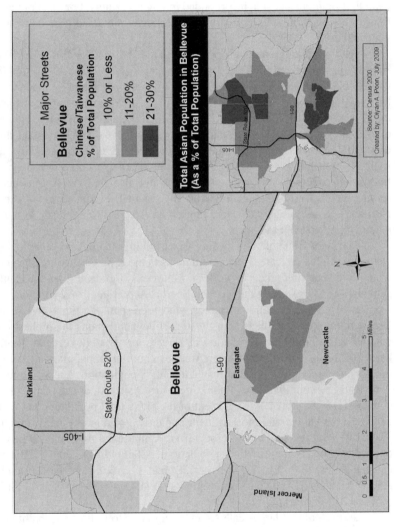

French settlers, who began arriving after 1882 (University of Washington Library 2010). Asian immigrants, particularly Japanese American immigrants, started to arrive in Bellevue in 1894. Many of these immigrants worked in the logging industry and cleared land for farming. In 1910, the US Census showed that 1,500 residents lived in the Bellevue area (Bagley 1929). It was not until 1953 that Bellevue became incorporated into King County. For most of the period following World War II until 1980, Bellevue remained a predominantly white suburb.

The city's demographics changed during the 1980s and 1990s, when Asian Americans constituted the fastest-growing racial group in Bellevue. In 1980, the Asian American population in Bellevue was approximately 3.8 percent of the total population. In 1990 and 2000, the Asian American population increased to 9.9 percent and 18 percent, respectively. In 2000, approximately 57 percent of all Bellevue's foreign-born residents were born in Asia. While racial shifts do occur in the city, many Asian Americans there are more conservative and Republican than those in Seattle. This is exemplified by Conrad Lee, the city's first Asian American city council member and also its longest consecutive serving member. Although the Bellevue City Council, as in many cities, is nonpartisan, Lee has publicly declared himself a registered Republican, as have a majority of the seven members.

The city of Bellevue is a medium-sized suburb that has become the bellwether for highly educated Asian immigrants in the King County area, many of whom have been recruited to work on Bellevue's high-tech industry satellite campuses of Microsoft, Nintendo, and Boeing. According to Washington State representative Sharon Tamiko Santos, who represents the most diverse and largest immigrant state district in Seattle, Bellevue contains the highest non-naturalized foreign-born population in King County.[3] Bellevue, like Seattle, has a long history of a diverse Asian American immigrant population where no one Asian ethnic group has dominated the city's population. According to the American Community Survey 2006, single-race Asian Americans (28,849) accounted for approximately 25 percent of the city's total population (114,748) and were the largest and most affluent population of any city in Washington State. The largest Asian ethnic groups were Chinese (11,464, or 40.0 percent of the city's total Asian American population), Asian Indian (5,909, or 20.5 percent), Japanese (3,800, or 13.0 percent), Korean (3,593, or 12.5 percent), other Asian (2,229, or 7.7 percent), Vietnamese (1,194, or 4.1 percent), and Filipino (660, or 2.2 percent).

The result of this large-scale Asian immigration to Bellevue is that it is the first city in King County history to have more nonwhites as a percentage of the city's population than Seattle (Bach 2006). In 2000, approximately one-third of Bellevue's residents were foreign born, up from one-quarter five years before (Bach 2006). Bellevue has the highest percentage of foreign-born residents among major cities in the state, in which 32 percent of residents are nonwhite.

The largest immigrant communities, which began to arrive in the 1990s, came from China, India, Russia, and Mexico. Many of these immigrants were attracted to Bellevue because of its business and high-tech jobs, manual labor jobs, quality schools, and public safety. Many Asian Americans have been drawn to Bellevue from the late 1980s to the present due to gravitational networks that have developed there. Asian American political incorporation in Bellevue has followed.

Local Government Structure and Asian American Descriptive Representation in Bellevue

Like many small- to medium-sized suburbs, Bellevue employs the structure of a city council and manager. The city council consists of seven part-time members who are elected citywide, which has allowed local mobilization efforts centered on Asian American candidates to be parlayed into descriptive representation. A primary election is held if multiple candidates emerge, and the top two candidates run in the general election. The top vote getter in the general election wins the seat. Each member serves a four-year term with no term limits, and elections are staggered. If a member resigns during his or her term, the council solicits applications from the public. Each council member interviews and votes among the pool of candidates. A simple majority is required to fill the vacancy. The candidate confirmed has to run for reelection the next election cycle. Among the seven council members, two are nominated by the council to serve as deputy mayor and mayor by a nomination-and-election process that requires a simple majority vote for both. Applications for city commissions are taken by a city council member who acts as a liaison to the entire council by interviewing and suggesting a candidate. All commissioners serve a four-year term with a limit of two consecutive terms.

Two Asian Americans, Conrad Lee and Patsy Bonincontri (who is of Chinese descent), currently serve on the Bellevue City Council among the seven members. Lee first ran for the Bellevue City Council in 1992 as a Democrat, but lost in this city, which has a large mainstream Republican voting base. Lee consulted Congresswoman Jennifer Dunn, a Republican, who advised him to switch parties. Lee ran again in 1994 and won as a Republican (Ng 2005). Lee is serving the longest consecutive terms (four) of any council member in the city's history.

The Immigrant Entrepreneurial Candidate

Conrad Lee, like many immigrants who arrived in the 1960s, was drawn to the United States because of its educational opportunities. Lee, who emigrated from Hong Kong in 1958 to attend the University of Michigan, has lived in Bellevue for over forty years, and is currently an engineer and small-businessman in the area aside from his part-time position on the city council. The reason that Lee first ran in 1992 for the Bellevue City Council was to give back to the community and to serve as a role model for Asian Americans. A December 2007 editorial commentary in the *Northwest Asian Weekly,* the pan–Asian American newspaper of Seattle, declares that Lee represents "the new face of Bellevue" in a city that has 30 percent immigrants, of which Asian Americans are the largest racial group at nearly 17 percent of the city's population ("Conrad Lee" 2007). In this light, Lee reflects the immigrant entrepreneurial candidate who has quickly emerged from the suburbs to run for and win elected positions in city government. As Lee states: "My family and I were always forward thinking. When we fled the communists in mainland China when I was a child and settled in Hong Kong for a better economic and political life, even then I was looking forward to coming to the United States to study."[4]

Conrad Lee is currently entering his fourteenth year on the city council, the longest period for anyone who has served on the Bellevue City Council. A registered Republican, Lee embodies the classic immigrant entrepreneurial candidate. He is a successful professional and his primary motivations for running stem from his realization that Asian Americans need to be represented in a community in which they have become a vital part in other ways. Arriving in one of the initial waves of highly educated and professional Asian Americans to settle in Bellevue, as opposed to the metropolitan Seattle area, Lee has witnessed firsthand the dramatic demographic shifts occurring in Bellevue. While Asians represent one of the largest new immigrant groups over the past decade, their socioeconomic backgrounds are similar to those of earlier Bellevue residents. According to Lee:

> when I first arrived in Bellevue nearly thirty years [ago], it was the same type of professionals that lived here, only they were Boeing engineers. Today, we have a similar highly educated, professional class with the establishment of the Microsoft campus in Bellevue and our highly rated public schools, especially Bellevue High School, which was rated by one national magazine as one of the top 100 public high schools in the nation.[5]

Lee has been the city's sole immigrant face on the Bellevue City Council for the past fourteen years. During this time, Lee has been the key political catalyst in mobilizing both new and old members of Bellevue's immigrant Chinese American population into the political arena, particularly in the area of campaign contributions.

Table 10.1 shows Conrad Lee's campaign contributions in 2005, the year of his most recent reelection campaign, in which he raised a total of $59,510. It is important to examine the 2005 campaign because it was one of Lee's most competitive bids for reelection. In the past, such as in 2001, Lee often ran un-

Table 10.1 Conrad Lee's Bellevue City Council Campaign Contributions, 2005 Primary Election

Racial and Ethnic Group	Within Bellevue ($)	Within Washington State ($)	Outside Washington State ($)
Chinese Americans	13,210	14,260	5,200
Other Asian Americans	1,725	1,270	0
Non-Asian	10,530	13,065	250
Total	25,465	28,595	5,450

Source: Author's coded findings from the Public Disclosure Commission, King County.

opposed. But in the 2005 election, Lee ran against Vicki Orrico and won by a slim majority of 51.7 percent to 48 percent, with the remaining percentage being write-in candidates. Orrico had hired a professional political consultant, which tested the extent to which Lee was able to mobilize both the non-Asian and Asian American communities in Bellevue and King County.

Two major trends are evident from Conrad Lee's 2005 campaign contributions. First, Lee pursued a two-tiered campaign strategy of courting Asian Americans, particularly Chinese Americans, and non-Asians. Asian Americans contributed approximately 46.1 percent of Lee's total 2005 contributions, with the remaining 53.9 percent being from non-Asians. Again, this reflects a common trend among successful Asian American candidates who realize the importance of developing political networks both inside and outside of the Asian American community.

Conrad Lee continues to mobilize Asian American contributors around his campaigns, particularly Chinese Americans, who live both within and outside of Bellevue. Chinese Americans who live within Washington State (outside of Bellevue) represented the largest sector of Lee's campaign contributions at $14,260, or 24 percent of Lee's total contributions. Nearly half of these Chinese Americans were from small- to medium-sized suburbs outside of Seattle, such as Mercer Island, Redmond, Medina, and Kirkland. Chinese Americans who live within Bellevue contributed $13,210, or 22 percent of Lee's total contributions, the second largest group of contributors. All viable Asian American candidates must build cross-racial coalitions in the area of contributions and votes. Non-Asian contributors also played a significant role in Lee's 2005 Bellevue City Council campaign, as those living within Washington State (outside of Bellevue) contributed $13,065, or approximately 22 percent, the third largest group of contributors. Like Asian Americans in this geographic category, nearly half of these contributors were from small- to medium-sized suburbs outside of Seattle. And finally, non-Asian contributors from within Bellevue contributed $10,530, or 17.7 percent.

The significance of Lee's 2005 Asian American contributions is that Asian American candidates can mobilize both new and old members of the Asian American community in Bellevue and other cities in the political process. This has not always been the case with other Asian American political organizations in the Seattle area. An example of such struggles is the Northwest Coalition of Asian Pacific Americans (NCAPA), a nonpartisan federal PAC established in 2008 that seeks to bring Asian American communities together and empower them by providing access and representation in local and statewide politics. One of the major priorities of NCAPA is fund-raising for its priority membership ($1,000 to $5,000) and basic membership ($100 to $1,000). According to Albert Shen, the president of NCAPA:

> Asian Americans typically don't want to give the type of money that buys you access to big fundraisers for candidates like Hillary Clinton or Barack Obama. While many can afford it, they need to be educated about why it is important to them. Even in the suburbs, I've found it difficult to raise contributions and political awareness among the growing Asian American populations.[6]

For this reason alone, it is important to examine Asian American political mobilization in local politics through a theoretical framework that places Asian American candidates at the center of this process, as I argue in this book, because they have the ability to galvanize the largely foreign-born Asian American community members through their campaigns. Asian Americans, both those who are old and new to American politics, understand the universal truth that Asian Americans are politically underrepresented at all levels of government. There is no need for Asian American candidates to sell the importance of why Asian Americans must be involved as both contributors and voters to support their campaigns. But crafting such a message to mobilize Asian Americans to give money for political causes from a nonpartisan organization perspective is more difficult.

Backdoor Politics

Council member Patsy Bonincontri was nominated and confirmed by a majority of the city council in March 2008 after having served on the Bellevue Planning Commission. Bonincontri's March 2008 appointment by the city council was historic because it finally gave the Bellevue Asian American community a council member in addition to Conrad Lee. The role that Lee played demonstrates the significance of initial descriptive representatives who can influence the nomination process with their city council colleagues. Bonincontri's road to the city council was unique because it was to fill the seat that was vacated by Connie Marshall, who resigned in January 2008. As discussed above, the Bellevue City Council historically calls for an open application process from

Bellevue community members to apply for the position. Each applicant is then interviewed by the council, followed by a council vote that requires a simple majority.

The main factors that led to Patsy Bonincontri's decision to run in this special election process were her experience and interest in developing city planning policy. As Bonincontri states:

> I have been involved with City planning through the planning commission for the last 10 years and the experience has been very positive, both in terms of the work that was accomplished and the relationship that was built with the community and city staff. When the opportunity came up to serve on the City Council, I made an evaluation of my personal life and decided it would be a good fit at this time to increase my contribution to the city.[7]

With regard to the question of whether the Bellevue Asian American community had any influence on her decision to run, Bonincontri answers:

> Honestly, the Bellevue Asian American Community did not influence my decision that much. I'm an "issue oriented" person and really did not pay too much attention to the race and gender factor. Although I'm well aware that this is very much on a lot of folks' minds. . . . Having said that, since I have been appointed, many people have come up and told me that it is great that I am a role model for minority youth [for] which I'm really glad. Any positive influence that I can have on our youth I'm happy to provide. I intend to carry out my duties as a councilmember to the best of my ability and that would serve both the Asian Community as well as the general community.[8]

Patsy Bonincontri was eventually selected over twenty-one other candidates by a slim majority of four members of the Bellevue City Council. According to Conrad Lee: "This is a historical breakthrough for our city. . . . Government is finally catching up with reality. The Eastside, including Bellevue, has become very diverse and international. Over a third of its population was born outside of the country" (E. Lee 2008, 1).

In many ways, Patsy Bonincontri's appointment reflects the influence of descriptive representatives in city government and the growing symbolic influence that the Asian American community is having on key city decisions regarding elected representation. Three separate meetings took place over a three-week span among the six Bellevue City Council members to decide on a replacement. During the first meeting, Bonincontri received three votes (Conrad Lee, Mayor Grant Degginger, and Deputy Mayor Claudia Balducci) and former council member Mike Creighton received two votes (Phil Noble and Don Davidson). Jennifer Robertson, who was serving on the Planning Commission, received one vote (John Chelminiak).

Because the four majority votes necessary were not obtained during the first meeting, a second meeting was held. Patsy Bonincontri again received three votes (Conrad Lee, Mayor Grant Degginger, and Deputy Mayor Claudia Balducci),

Michael Creighton received three votes (Phil Noble, Don Davidson, and Degginger), and Jennifer Robertson received two votes (John Chelminiak and Degginger). The political divisiveness on the city council regarding the candidate was clear. Degginger's decision to vote for each of the three candidates was an attempt to avoid choosing a particular candidate camp because he felt all three were worthy when he initially supported only Bonincontri during the first meeting.

As public criticism grew toward the city council and its inability to choose a replacement after the first two meetings, the third and final meeting became crucial. Patsy Bonincontri received the elusive fourth vote when John Chelminiak sensed his candidate, Jennifer Robertson, would not be able to garner more than two votes. Therefore, Chelminiak became the crucial swing vote to determine the outcome. It is likely that Bonincontri's gender played an important role in her selection because the fact that the outgoing council member was a woman had been defined as a major concern among the council members during their discussions. However, race likely played an equal if not more important role due to Conrad Lee's presence during the entire process. According to Lee:

> I made sure that I was advocating to all the members why another Asian American, who also happens to be a woman, were the most important criteria [*sic*]. Despite resistance from several city council members such as "she's not political enough," I advocated for her because she possessed the professional background and political experience as a two time chair of the Planning Commission.[9]

The presence of Conrad Lee, the only minority and immigrant council member in a city with a nearly 30 percent immigrant population, was invaluable in influencing his city council colleagues. When Lee had attempted but failed to gain the appointment as mayor from his colleagues earlier in 2008, his determination to alter the political culture of the Bellevue City Council to better reflect the city's changing demographics became stronger when Connie Marshall resigned in January 2008. Lee's constant advocacy to his colleagues for a more diverse city government is reflected in Deputy Mayor Claudia Balducci's following statement to the *Northwest Asian Weekly* after she voted for another council member for mayor: "We have made an effort to put more of them [minorities] on city boards and commissions. I very much support that" (Tabafunda and Lee 2008, 1).

The importance of both the Asian American political loci, such as Asian American elected officials like Conrad Lee and the Asian American ethnic media, cannot be undervalued as they play an important role in advocating Asian American elected leadership in Bellevue. When Lee sought the appointment as mayor in 2008, the *Northwest Asian Weekly* stated in an editorial entitled "Conrad Lee: The New Face of Bellevue":

> On Jan. 7, 2008, the seven members of the Bellevue City Council will elect a new mayor by choosing one of their own. This is a largely ceremonial role,

as the decision-making power lies with the council. This doesn't mean, however, that the position is unimportant. Conrad Lee certainly doesn't think so, and he is very eager to receive the appointment of mayor of Bellevue. . . . He is also the only person of color and only immigrant. As Bellevue becomes increasingly diverse—30 percent of the city's population is made up of immigrants—it needs a mayor who reflects that trend. ("Conrad Lee" 2007)

When Patsy Bonincontri was appointed, the same Asian American newspaper ran another editorial, "Bonincontri Is a Boon for Bellevue," which stated:

It is gratifying that Bellevue, known for its old boys' network, understands the need for diversity and is taking steps to promote it, especially at the top levels of civic office. . . . Just two years ago in 2006, when the Seattle City Council had a vacancy, five of six finalists were women of color, including three Asian Americans. The appointment went to the only Caucasian finalist, Sally Clark. That Bellevue would prove to be a more progressive city than Seattle was truly surprising and inspiring. ("Bonicontri Is a Boon" 2008)

As Bellevue's city council leadership begins to diversify, Asian Americans will be able to achieve influence in city government beyond descriptive representation on the council. As I argued in Chapter 2, descriptive representation is the key for any minority group to gain greater local political incorporation by transforming the political institutions from within. Conrad Lee has attempted to influence the city government by nominating and advocating for other Asian Americans on key city commissions. In some cases, he has been successful and, in others, he has not. Regardless, Lee remains an insider advocate for Asian Americans on city commissions because they are often the pipeline for future Asian American candidates. A snapshot of 2007 revealed that two Asian Americans were serving on the two highest profile of Bellevue's eight city commissions: Planning Commission (William Lai, one Asian American, or 14 percent representation) and Transportation Commission (Tom Tanaka, one Asian American, or 14 percent representation). On the city's Youth Link Board, four of twelve Asian Americans were serving, or 33 percent representation. The potential for future Asian American candidates to run for city council from these commission positions is good, as with former city planning commissioner Patsy Bonincontri. Overall, Asian Americans are still underrepresented in the city of Bellevue's local government (city council and city commissions) in proportion to their citywide population, but they are gradually making inroads.

Potential Barriers to Political Incorporation: The Downtown Business Elites and the Asian American Community

There is a saying among Bellevue locals that the city's power brokers are the city council, the city manager, and the "Emperor," a nickname given to Kemper

Freeman Jr., who is arguably the most influential and wealthiest resident of Bellevue. Freeman is CEO of Kemper Development Company, a family real estate business started by his father, which develops and owns major portions of downtown Bellevue, including the city's posh Bellevue Square and movie theater. In 2005, Freeman was the mastermind of a $1 billion facelift plan for downtown Bellevue that required a majority vote from the Bellevue City Council (Bolt and Cook 2005). What makes Freeman's relationship to city government so unusual is that he is a resident of Bellevue, where a great deal of his investments and developments are located. What has resulted from this relationship is what has been termed by Conrad Lee a "win-win situation" for both Freeman and the residents of Bellevue.[10] To do otherwise would be the analogy of biting the hand that feeds you. The city of Bellevue receives a major tax base from the downtown business, which benefits the residents with respect to their property tax base and public services, including the city's schools. *Newsweek* named five of Bellevue's public schools among the top 100 schools in the nation based on the number of advanced placement tests taken (Long 2010). Lee was instrumental in changing the policy allocations of downtown from revenue based to needs based, which allowed for greater city funding of the general services.

The extent of Kemper Freeman Jr.'s actual influence in Bellevue politics is debatable. In the opinion of Conrad Lee, Freeman has to "get in line with the others" when it comes to influencing the Bellevue City Council.[11] An example of this is that the city of Bellevue has held several public deliberations around a proposed light rail system that would run eighteen miles from downtown Seattle to downtown Bellevue and on to Redmond ("Residents Give Input" 2007). An exploratory committee has been commissioned by the city council to examine the feasibility and impact of similar light rail systems in other cities, in order to avoid the common pitfalls. The findings were presented to the public at a city council meeting on May 20, 2008. Freeman has voiced his concerns to the Bellevue City Council regarding a Bellevue light rail system because he wants to maintain the revenue from those who park their cars at his malls and theater, along with the overall aesthetics of the downtown business corridor.

Others in the Asian American community believe Freeman does exert great political influence and that the Bellevue City Council members implicitly understand the political consequences if they disagree with him. Assunta Ng, the publisher of the *Northwest Asian Weekly,* who has met with Freeman, states: "Kemper Freeman has a cadre of attorneys who attend the Bellevue City Council meetings when an important issue comes up who meet and lobby the Bellevue City Council. They [council members] know his influence and that he can try to circumvent them."[12]

Other Asian American community leaders are more concerned with whether Freeman and the downtown business elite will be sensitive to immigrant issues as the city changes. According to Alaric Bien, executive director of the Chinese Information Service Center (CISC) and a Bellevue resident:

> I am uncomfortable with how much of what goes on in the city is dictated by Kemper Freeman et al. When he and his pals go to the city council and demand $10 million to build a performing arts center while the few human service providers are there asking that the city not cut our paltry service contracts, there is something wrong. I don't know if it has so much to do with Asian American interests or more that some of us see other needs and issues that are not even on the radar screen of the downtown types.[13]

While Freeman's political presence in Bellevue is undeniable given his role in redeveloping its downtown, perhaps the greatest impact is the malaise that it has created among its residents. Indeed, many of the residents of Bellevue, including Asian Americans, have grown accustomed and politically apathetic to local issues because they have reached a level of contentment. Bellevue provides all the necessities that are wanted by many of its residents who moved there either recently or well before the suburban transformation: rising house values, low crime rate, low tax base, and great public schools. For example, during the past decade, the average single-family house price rose 137 percent in Bellevue, compared to King County at 122 percent. Because the city of Bellevue's infrastructure is relatively new, it requires low maintenance, which allows more funding for other public amenities, such as newly paved and wider roads and public parks. It is this "golden egg" that Conrad Lee refers to that has resulted in a sense of complacency that made it sometimes difficult to mobilize and discern group interests.[14] For Asian Americans, both US citizens and recent immigrants who live in Bellevue, the challenge may not be Freeman, or any of the other Bellevue business elites such as the Bellevue Chamber of Commerce, but rather trying to find and articulate the key Asian American issues within the community so political mobilization can occur around them. These issues are beginning to emerge and have found Asian American interests aligned with Latino and Russian immigrant interests.

Finding Common Ground: Mobilizing Bellevue's Asian American and Latino Communities

Galvanizing issues are beginning to emerge among the large Eastside immigrant communities (Asian American and Latino) in Bellevue around common immigrant issues such as the city's English as a second language (ESL) program. On July 30, 2003, a coalition of immigrant community leaders packed the meeting chambers of the Bellevue School District to voice their concerns about drastic changes to the district's existing ESL program. The broad coalition consisted of the Japanese American Citizens League, the Eastside Latino

Leadership Forum, and the Circle of Friends. The coalition initially raised concerns about the program when a beloved Korean American ESL teacher, Grace Seo, a Korean-born graduate of the Bellevue School District, was let go after having taught at the Stevenson Elementary School for two and one-half years amidst allegations that she spoke with an accent (Solomon 2003).

The intent of the Bellevue School District's restructuring was outlined by ESL director Fred Cogswell in an internal memo referred to as a "vision statement" that had received input from district officials and a few parents. Two of the most controversial proposals that immigrant parents felt they should have been consulted on were the following: (1) ESL students at elementary schools where ESL enrollment was low would be bused to other schools with larger enrollments; and (2) certified ESL teachers would be employed only at schools with larger ESL enrollments, which explains why Seo was released. Many immigrant parents in the coalition felt that ESL is much more than speaking flawless English because teachers like Seo are role models to immigrant children. According to Anthony Ruiz, a member of the Eastside Latino Leadership Forum: "Kids need the . . . Grace Seos to connect with them on a cultural level and spur them on" (Solomon 2003, 1). Two of the demands made by the coalition were the rehiring of Seo and the replacement of Cogswell as ESL director. In the end, Seo settled her lawsuit with the city and moved to Maryland, and Cogswell was replaced.

In many ways, Grace Seo and the ESL restructuring show the potential of an Eastside immigrant coalition in Bellevue, and how the city's leaders are seemingly out of touch. The vision statement is a primary example. Although it was meant to be an internal memo (a draft, as Cogswell stated), many immigrant families were unsure about the fate of their ESL children a few months before the beginning of the 2004–2005 school year. This example also illustrates how Asian Americans in Bellevue are only beginning to obtain access to and influence on key decisionmaking in its local schools, despite their high enrollment rates. Eastside Asian Pacific Islander organization leader Nadine Shiroma was able to meet with the superintendent during the Seo lawsuit, which resulted in the formation of the Asian Parent Advisory Committee, a group that works with the superintendent on a variety of policy-related issues and concerns. According to Shiroma:

> Grace Seo's case was a defining moment for me in my many years of grassroots activism on the Eastside because we were able to mobilize so many Asian American and Mexican American parents on such short notice. I see the area of education, in regard to immigrant concerns, as a future political battleground in Bellevue.[15]

The area of education impacts all communities, particularly immigrants who choose to live in Bellevue primarily for its outstanding public schools and its ESL programs. One Bellevue public school even has a Spanish immersion program. For Asian American and Latino parents, education policy is likely to be the major galvanizing issue that will bring these communities together to work in alliance, spearheaded by community-based groups like the Eastside Asian Pacific Islander organization, founded in 1999 to promote dialogue and civic participation within Bellevue's Asian Pacific Islander community, and the Eastside Latino Leadership Forum.

Another area within the Bellevue School District that will likely be a battleground for future Asian American political mobilization is its school board, particularly due to the lack of Asian American and Latino representation on it. As a central focus for Asian American and Latino immigrant communities becomes making education policies representative of all their community members' concerns and interests, the likelihood of future Asian American candidates running for the school board is great. The ability of such candidates to mobilize both a panethnic and cross-racial coalition will be key to their success.

Despite the potential collaborations between Asian Americans and Latinos, future challenges exist in constructing a coalition between these communities around common interests. While a majority of Asian American immigrants who have arrived in the past five years are mostly high-tech workers recruited by companies like Microsoft, the majority of Latino immigrants are undocumented and work in the service-based industries of Bellevue, as exemplified by their large presence in the Service Employees International Union (SEIU) Local 6 (Hipple 2003). Because a majority of the Eastside janitors are undocumented immigrants from Mexico and Central America, many fear deportation and choose not to participate in any political activities, including joining the local union. It is estimated that only 47 percent of Latino janitors on the Eastside are unionized, compared to nearly 85 percent of Latino janitors in Seattle (Hipple 2003). These socioeconomic differences between the Bellevue Asian American and Latino immigrant communities pose difficult, but not insurmountable, challenges in finding common issues that will mobilize both communities.

Future common interests will likely stem from bilingual education issues, as seen with the Asian American and Latino coalition against the ESL program reform and Seo's firing, and other social justice issues such as police brutality. With regard to the latter issue, the Asian American and Latino communities joined together after the tragic shooting during a domestic violence call involving an unarmed twenty-four-year-old Guatemalan immigrant, Nelson Martinez, by a white Bellevue police officer, Michael Hetle, in August 2001. Hetle had a history of public complaints about racial harassment. The shooting led to a multiracial march and rally of an estimated 100 protestors at the Bellevue city hall that included Asian American members from the Japanese American Citizens League and the Eastside Asian Pacific Islanders organization. Many felt it was necessary to mobilize for Latinos in Bellevue. One Guatemalan immigrant at the rally stated: "We need to form a Latino organization in Bellevue that will fight for us. Without one, we can't do anything" (Olson 2001, 1). The Eastside Latino Leadership Forum was the organization created after the Martinez shooting with the encouragement and help of the city of Bellevue. Hetle left the Bellevue police force two years after the shooting through a legal settlement with the city.

It is within the social justice context that various Asian American political loci, such as community-based organizations and Eastside Asian American leaders like Nadine Shiroma and James Arima, can play integral roles in mobilizing the recent Asian American immigrant population, who did not experience and understand the importance of multiracial coalitions taught by the civil rights movement. Asian American descriptive representatives, should they choose to do so, can also play an important role in mobilizing both the large Asian American and Latino immigrant communities. Conrad Lee, along with the majority of his city council colleagues, did not speak publicly about the Nelson Martinez shooting, much to the disappointment of Seattle and Eastside Asian American community leaders. As discussed earlier, the challenge for these various Asian American political loci will be waking up recent Asian American immigrants to the political malaise that has limited their civic participation in recent years. The key to achieving this goal will be descriptive representatives like Conrad Lee and Patsy Bonincontri serving as catalysts for Asian American political mobilization efforts in conjunction with established and emerging Asian American political loci in Bellevue and Seattle. Without such a community-based strategy to integrate all the various political loci that are necessary for successful group political mobilization in Seattle and its surrounding Asian American suburbs, Asian American political efforts will remain limited. As I show in the next section, such a political synergy is slowly emerging.

A Political Synergy Between the Emerald City and Bellevue

Unlike the Houston and Sugar Land case study in Chapter 9, limited political synergy exists between Seattle and its crescent suburbs on the other side of Lake Washington, such as Shoreline, Federal Way, and Bellevue. A primary reason for this limited political synergy is geopolitics. Many of Seattle's Asian American community-based organizations are limited in their geographic scope as well as by the physical barriers of crossing Lake Washington to reach the Eastside to participate in candidate and community events. As an Eastside member joked: "Some Asian American Seattle leaders think that Lake Washington is the Pacific Ocean."[16] Although many of these organizations' leaders may live in suburbs like Bellevue and work in Seattle, the geographic politics of constituent services and funding takes precedence. One such leader is Alaric Bien, executive director of the CISC located in Seattle's International District that works primarily with the Chinese and Asian American immigrant communities of Seattle, who resides in Bellevue. According to Bien:

> For me personally, I like the fact that we have good schools, low crime. The main reason most Asian families move to Bellevue is for the schools. But even in the schools, as long as parents feel that their children are getting the best education possible, we don't see a lot of participation there either. I think it is when the next generation comes up and more American born Asians move in then we will start to see more interest in political activity.[17]

With the appeal of its strong public schools, low crime rate, and ethnic networks, it is likely that other Asian American service-based organization leaders with growing families will follow the same path to Bellevue. And as the immigrant population in Bellevue continues to outpace Seattle, there is an inevitable potential for satellites of immigrant service organizations based in Seattle, like the CISC, to expand to the Eastside.

Another reason for the disconnect between Seattle and Bellevue political mobilization efforts among its respective Asian American leadership is the perception that exists among Seattle's Democratic Asian American leadership that Bellevue represents a Republican suburb, which makes it difficult to build political relationships around ideology and interests. According to Grace Yuan, a Seattle attorney and community activist: "I'm not going to attend a fundraiser for a local Asian American candidate who happens to be Republican like Conrad Lee, because I don't have a personal relationship with him that allows me to overlook those political ideological differences."[18] James Arima, who lives on the Eastside and is a state Democratic Party insider, offers a more pragmatic view of this dichotomy: "The Asian American leadership in Seattle will support us, but they are not going to build the infrastructure for the Eastside community. That's up to us."[19]

These major barriers are likely to be overcome in the near future, as the Washington State congressional districts that have been a Republican stronghold are shifting to the Democratic Party due to changing demographics of the suburbs. Over time, as these social networks mature, the linkage between the urban core and its suburbs will strengthen, which will benefit future Asian American candidates during group political mobilization in Bellevue and other Seattle suburbs.

Recent developments have given hope for a potential political collaboration between the Asian American communities in Seattle and Bellevue. One of the most important events to illustrate this was the "Asian Pacific Islander Political Leadership Training in Bellevue," which took place on March 29, 2008, at the city hall. This represented the first attempt by a Seattle-based organization to make one of its suburbs, in this case Bellevue, the site for Asian American political mobilization and candidate training efforts. The one-day event was sponsored by the Seattle-based nonprofit organization the Progressive Majority, and featured many Seattle and suburban Asian American elected officials who spoke to a group of aspiring candidates from the state of Washington. The purposes of the leadership training were (1) to learn the basics behind running for office; (2) to find out how to work on campaigns; (3) to engage in roundtable discussions with elected officials and campaign workers; (4) to support current, past, and upcoming Asian Pacific Islander leaders; and (5) to launch the NCAPA PAC. Among the Asian American elected officials speaking at the various roundtables were Cindy Ryu and Michael Park, Korean American mayors of Shoreline and Federal Way, respectively. Both cities are medium-sized suburbs that are undergoing demographic transformations and political incorporation efforts similar to those of Bellevue.

The significance of the Asian American leadership training seminar in Bellevue is that it reflects the trajectory of where future Asian American candidates are likely to arise: the suburbs surrounding Seattle. If a political synergy can be established between the exceptional Asian American political infrastructure and leadership in Seattle and those in its nearby suburbs like Bellevue, it will be a positive sign for future local political incorporation efforts throughout the suburbs of King County. Bellevue stands as the Asian-influenced suburb that can lead the charge and serve as an exemplary case for how this can be done. However, as shown in this chapter, whether the Bellevue Asian American community can overcome the various and unique socioeconomic challenges in this Pacific Northwest suburb will depend largely on the emergence of a growing and strong Asian American elected leadership. This must be combined with strong community and organizational support as well as a common ideology established and articulated around key issues that span across ethnic and racial lines.

Notes

1. Martha Choe, former Seattle City Council member, interviewed by the author, Seattle, Washington, May 20, 2008.

2. Gary Locke, former Washington governor, interviewed by the author, Seattle, Washington, May 21, 2008.

3. Sharon Tamiko Santos, Washington state representative, personal communication with the author, May 22, 2008.

4. Conrad Lee, Bellevue City Council member, interviewed by the author, Bellevue, Washington, May 21, 2008.

5. Conrad Lee, Bellevue City Council member, interviewed by the author, Bellevue, Washington, May 21, 2008.

6. Albert Shen, president of the Northwest Coalition of Asian Pacific Americans, interviewed by the author, Seattle, Washington, May 22, 2008.

7. Patsy Bonincontri, Bellevue City Council member, personal communication with the author, June 5, 2008.

8. Patsy Bonincontri, Bellevue City Council member, personal communication with the author, June 5, 2008.

9. Conrad Lee, Bellevue City Council member, interviewed by the author, Bellevue, Washington, May 20, 2008.

10. Conrad Lee, Bellevue City Council member, interviewed by the author, Bellevue, Washington, May 21, 2008.

11. Conrad Lee, Bellevue City Council member, interviewed by the author, Bellevue, Washington, May 21, 2008.

12. Assunta Ng, publisher, *Northwest Asian American Weekly,* interviewed by the author, Seattle, Washington, May 21, 2008.

13. Alaric Bien, executive director of the Chinese Information Service Center, personal communication with the author, June 2, 2008.

14. Conrad Lee, Bellevue City Council member, interviewed by the author, Bellevue, Washington, May 20, 2008.

15. Nadine Shiroma, founding member of Raising Our Asian Pacific American Representation, personal communication with the author, May 30, 2008.

16. James Arima, president of the Asian Pacific American Caucus of Washington, interviewed by the author, Bellevue, Washington, May 20, 2008.

17. Alaric Bien, executive director of the Chinatown Information and Service Center, interviewed by the author, Bellevue, Washington, May 20, 2008.

18. Grace Yuan, attorney, interviewed by the author, Seattle, Washington, May 19, 2008.

19. James Arima, president of the Asian Pacific American Caucus of Washington, interviewed by the author, Bellevue, Washington, May 20, 2008.

11

Daly City, California:
The Barriers to Filipino American
Political Incorporation

Daly City is the largest Asian American majority city in the continental United States, with Asian Americans constituting approximately 51 percent of the city's total population of 103,621 (US Census 2006k). Often referred to as the "Pinoy Capital of the United States," Daly City is also home to the largest Filipino American community. This community is the city's largest Asian ethnic group at 32 percent, followed by Chinese Americans at approximately 14 percent. Daly City also holds a foreign-born population of 53.2 percent, which makes it one of the top six US cities with a total population of over 100,000 to have a majority of foreign-born residents (Estrella 2003).

Given the demographic characteristics as captured in Map 11.1, one might logically assume that Daly City is classified as an Asian American Transformed I suburb with its large Filipino American population. However, it is important to reiterate that the size of a city's Asian American population is not a sole guarantee for local political incorporation, but merely a precursor. Other political loci must be present in the Asian American community; namely, solid community-based organizations and the presence of a strong ideology to guide local political incorporation efforts. Without both of these political loci in the local Asian American communities, even cities with majority Asian American populations face challenges in achieving local political incorporation that begins with descriptive representation. Therefore, Daly City is instead a primary example of an Asian American Delayed I suburb because it contains a large Asian American population, but lacks the presence of those two necessary community political loci, which has resulted in limited political incorporation that has frustrated the community.

Daly City, a medium-sized suburb located less than five miles south of San Francisco, sprang from humble beginnings in 1868 when a farm worker named John Daly invested in farmland there. Over a period of time, this once-bedroom

Map 11.1 Filipino American Population Distribution in Daly City, 2000

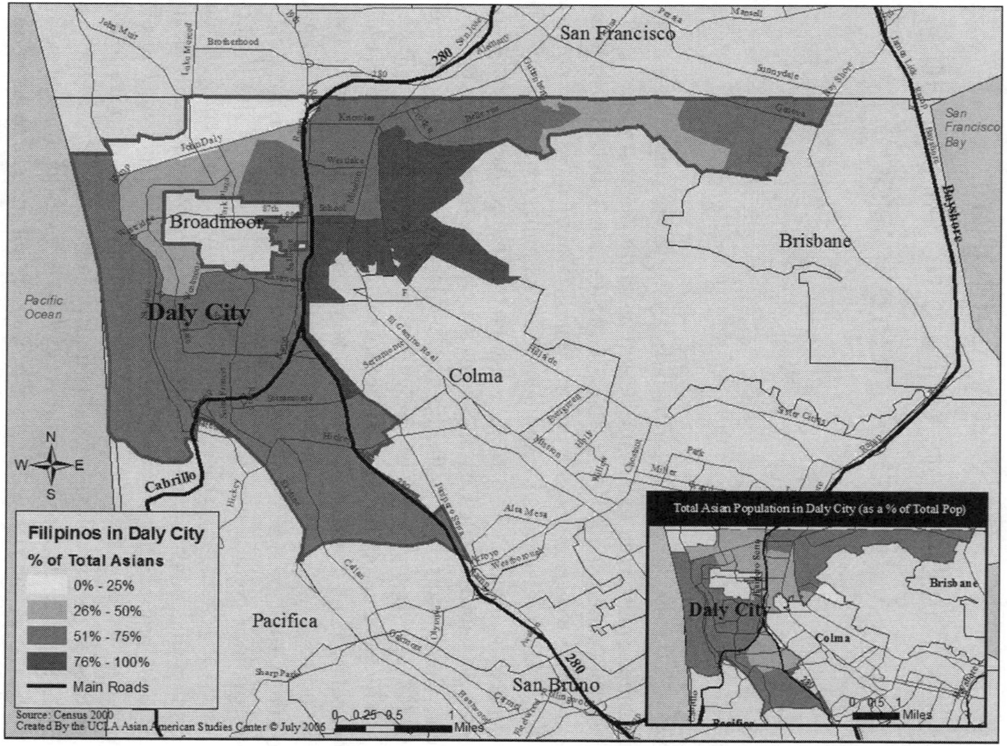

Filipinos in Daly City
% of Total Asians

0% - 25%
26% - 50%
51% - 75%
76% - 100%
Main Roads

Source: Census 2000
Created By the UCLA Asian American Studies Center © July 2006

community with an Italian American majority has flourished and transformed itself into the largest Asian American–majority city in the continental United States. During the past thirty years, Filipino and Chinese Americans have been drawn to the area because of the social and cultural networks established by the first wave of immigrants who settled there after the Immigration and Nationality Act of 1965 and, most recently, also because of the affordability of the homes. Many of the immigrants from the Philippines were a mixture of professionals and blue-collar workers who were attracted to the economic opportunities of San Francisco along with the more affordable housing of Daly City.

The influences of Filipino Americans and other Asian Americans can be seen throughout the central public areas of Daly City in the many businesses and their patrons, including Serramonte Mall, the city's largest shopping center; the presence of a Manila corporation's fast-food restaurant, Jollibee; and the city's annual adobo cook-off.[1] In 2009, Daly City, the sister city of Quezon City in the Philippines, celebrated its fifteenth Filipino American Friendship Celebration, which is a two-day cultural celebration that features Philippine dignitaries and local leaders. Official sponsors of the event range from the city of Daly City to Comcast to Wells Fargo Bank. Indeed, such events have transformed the once-sleepy suburb of South San Francisco into a mainstream event that has firmly embedded Filipino Americans in the city's cultural and political landscapes.

Local Government Structure and the Glass Ceiling

The city council of Daly City consists of five part-time members who are elected citywide for four years with no term limits. Each year, members of the local government (city council and mayor) meet to nominate and vote on the vice mayor and mayor. All local elected officials must be US residents (naturalized or US born). City commissioners are nominated by a council member to be voted on and approved by a majority of the city council.

Despite the strong Filipino American presence in both businesses and residences in Daly City, this ethnic group has lacked historical descriptive representation in city government. As the city's largest Asian ethnic community, Filipino American leaders in Daly City and the Bay Area began to set their sights on gaining local representation in the 1980s. But the dozen or so Filipino Americans who set their sights on the city council since this time all saw their campaigns fail despite the large Filipino American population. The question of when and who would be the breakthrough Filipino American candidate came from the unlikeliest of candidates and, ironically, one who was not embraced by the established Filipino American leadership due to generational and cultural issues.

All of the Filipino American candidates who ran during the 1980s focused solely on mobilizing the Daly City Filipino American community. But as discussed in Chapter 2, large Asian American populations are not enough to guarantee descriptive representation. Asian American candidates must pursue a two-tiered campaign strategy that seeks to mobilize Asian American voters through panethnic strategies and to foster cross-racial alliances. Many of these Filipino American candidates did neither, which explains this historical lack of descriptive representation despite the large population of Filipino Americans in Daly City. Ironically, it was not until 1993 that Michael Guingona became the city's first Filipino American city council member despite not being publicly endorsed by the Daly City Filipino American community.

A Historic City Council Campaign

Despite the above-mentioned demographics, Filipino Americans specifically and Asian Americans generally have lacked political representation in city government, most notably on the city council, which has been historically dominated by Italian Americans, the city's former majority group. For nearly twenty years, Filipino American candidates ran unsuccessfully for the city council. Between 1972 and 1992, twelve Filipino Americans ran for city council. Finally, in 1993, Daly City native and attorney Michael Guingona, someone widely considered to be an outsider to the traditional Daly City Filipino American political establishment, became the first and only Filipino American to serve on the city council. Guingona, whose family moved to Daly City from San Francisco in 1965 when he was three years old, attended Daly City's public schools from kindergarten through twelfth grade. During this period, Guingona witnessed the role that Filipino Americans played in the suburban transformation of Daly City. He also realized that the old ethnocentric ways of doing politics in the Filipino American community did not work, and that a two-tiered campaign strategy of building both mainstream and panethnic coalitions was the key to achieving political success in Daly City.

In 1993, when Michael Guingona first ran for the Daly City Council at the age of thirty-one, he understood that he needed to be more than an ethnic candidate who courted only the Filipino American vote. He did not want to follow the pattern of his Filipino American predecessors who focused only on the Filipino American community with their large voting potential but small voter turnout. Guingona realized the key to success was to run as a mainstream candidate who appealed to all the constituents in his community—the established Italian American community as well as the emerging Filipino and Asian American community. And he knew that he also had to build networks with the city's professional associations and labor unions. According to Guingona:

In 1991, five Filipino American candidates ran for three open seats. I came in fourth. I called my opponents and congratulated them. My 1993 campaign started up the next week. I wanted to portray myself as a local kid who went to school with your sons and daughters. I didn't want to wear my ethnicity on my sleeve. . . . I wasn't endorsed by many of the Filipino American community leaders because I couldn't speak their native language [Tagalog] fluently. . . . The Filipino American community's voice does not have to resonate with an accent.[2]

Michael Guingona, who has been reelected two times since 1993, currently serves as city mayor, a position that rotates among the council members. His monumental 1993 candidacy was not endorsed by the Filipino American community leaders. The main reason was that Guingona was perceived as a community outsider among the traditional leadership because he was a relative newcomer to the political arena who did not speak Tagalog. As a result, Guingona decided not to attend the historic 1993 Filipino American community caucus, which was created to endorse a consensus Filipino American candidate among the multiple ethnic candidates running, and instead focused on building multiracial support for his campaign.

According to Alice Bulos, former head of the Filipino American Democratic Caucus and widely considered by community members as the "Grandmother of Filipino American Politics," the attempt was to elect one consensus Filipino American candidate to prevent the splitting of community votes. According to Bulos: "The Filipino American community was frustrated in the years before. We came together to figure out what was the best strategy. We invited the 5 to 6 Filipino American candidates who had declared to run in 1993 to make their plea and to vote on one candidate to endorse publicly."[3] Eventually, at the 1993 Filipino American community caucus, the Filipino American community endorsed a local Filipino American businessman named Mario Panoringan, who at the time was the head of the Daly City Chamber of Commerce. Panoringan had previously run for city council in 1986. However, Michael Guingona finished second among five candidates for three open seats. He credits his 1993 success to the ability to redefine the Filipino American leadership as one that looks out for everyone in the community but also is sensitive to Filipino American concerns. As Guingona explains:

When an issue comes to me on the city council that is ethnic specific, I become a Filipino American advocate. One of my goals is to create an atmosphere on the city council that white council members would not do. It involves fostering a relationship with my white colleagues to make them sensitized to the Filipino American community's concerns not just to be a token brown face.[4]

Despite Guingona's electoral successes since his historic 1993 election, the Daly City Filipino American community is arguably still significantly underrepresented in key political offices citywide. As a community that constitutes 32 percent of the city's population, few Filipinos and other Asian Americans sit on any of the city's key political seats. For example, in 2006, among the twenty-one school board members in Daly City's six unified school districts, only one Asian American holds a position (City of Daly City 2006). The same is true on city commissions, which often serve as a pipeline to the city council, where Filipino Americans hold only three of the seats. Many of these commissioners were appointed by Michael Guingona. Most importantly, no other Filipino American has run for city council other than Guingona and Mario Panoringan since 1993.

Limited Filipino American Political Mobilization

Michael Guingona's 1993 campaign received little coverage among the Filipino American ethnic print media. The focus of the media was on the endorsed Filipino American candidate, Mario Panoringan. The same was true with regard to Guingona's campaign contributions, the majority of which came from non-Asian supporters that Guingona had cultivated through his professional networks. Guingona's successful campaign demonstrates the political weaknesses of the Filipino American community as a voting bloc despite its perceived strength in numbers in Daly City. Filipino American community activist Perry Diaz sums this point up: "Guingona saw an opportunity that would be favorable to his [1993] candidacy. He wooed the non-Filipino, mostly white voters, and got their support. He became the mainstream candidate and beat the Filipino American community's candidate" (Pascual 2004, 1).

Table 11.1 provides the findings of Michael Guingona's campaign contributions received during the period from April 1993 to December 1993. It also reveals his general campaign strategy, which was to focus on his Asian American connections, not necessarily only Filipino American ones, and to build cross-racial support among non-Asian contributors. The following amounts by group contributed to Guingona's groundbreaking campaign: Asian Americans (excluding Filipino Americans) contributed $605 (12 percent), Filipino Americans contributed $1,725 (34 percent), non-Asians contributed $950 (19 percent), and unions and professional associations contributed $1,750 (35 percent). These findings support Guingona's assertion that he made a conscious effort during his second campaign to establish broader support among contributors beyond the Daly City Filipino American community, which had been the strategy of the unsuccessful Filipino American candidates before him. Moreover, Guingona's successful campaign strategy shows that a two-tiered campaign strategy is necessary even in the largest Asian American–majority city in the continental United States. Those two tiers must seek to forge cross-racial alliances with non-Asian voters and contributors while simultaneously building panethnic alliances within the Asian American community.

Table 11.1 Mike Guingona's Daly City Council Campaign Contributions, 1993 Primary Election

Contributors	Amount (percentage)	
Filipino Americans	$1,725	(34)
Other Asian Americans	$605	(12)
Non-Asians	$950	(19)
Unions and professional associations	$1,750	(35)
Total	$5,030	(100)

Moving Beyond One: Filipino American Community Divisions in Daly City Politics

The lack of Filipino American political representation and incorporation in Daly City politics is partially a reflection of its community and the lack of key political loci within it. The presence of a large Asian American population base, combined with the development and maturation of key community loci and ideology, has offered great opportunities for Asian American candidates in mobilizing community political loci, as demonstrated among the Asian American Transformed I suburbs with Cupertino (Chapter 5), Garden Grove and Westminster (Chapter 6), and Gardena (Chapter 7). But this has not been the case for all large Asian American–populated suburbs, as is shown by Daly City. A strong campaign strategy is equally important in Asian American suburbs regardless of their Asian American population size. As Daly City moved from an Italian American majority to an Asian American majority, non-Asian residents began to question whether Asian American candidates would reach out to the former mainstream community. Perry Diaz, a longtime Filipino American community activist in Northern California, states:

> Once a Filipino American candidate highlights his ethnicity, he loses. If a White candidate speaks Tagalog, he will get Filipino votes. If a Filipino American has a political brochure in Tagalog, he will be questioned by the mainstream. The white community will view a Filipino American candidate as a minority candidate only. Guingona got some Filipino American support but did it by keeping it low profile. He ran as a mainstream candidate. Most of the power-brokers in Daly City are of Italian descent and Guingona was able to reach out to them.[5]

Race becomes an important issue for suburban cities that undergo dramatic demographic transformations, particularly among non-Asians. While the demographics may shift, the previous power structure remains entrenched in local politics. Asian American candidates in such suburbs, as in larger cities, must negotiate the racial fault lines that comprise the city's political terrain to have a chance at electoral success. Arguably, the fears and concerns of the former majority are more acute in suburbs because of the relative size of the communities where demographic shifts are more distinct and obvious.

The other barriers that have limited Filipino American political incorporation exist within the Daly City Filipino American community itself. Unlike other suburbs such as Sugar Land (Chapter 9) and Bellevue (Chapter 10) where one Asian American on their respective city councils was viewed as inadequate by their respective Asian American community leaders, the Daly City Filipino American community appears to be content with having one Filipino American among the three city council members. This belief is supported by the fact that no other Filipino American, aside from Michael Guingona, has run since 1993 either to replace Guingona or to build on the Filipino American presence on the council. To Guingona's credit, he has appointed several Filipino Americans to city commissions, with the hope that they will run in the future. According to Guingona:

> One of my goals when elected was to put Filipino Americans into positions to give the community presence in local government. Some of these include Ed Manalang (Personnel Commission), Lloyd Bangolog (Planning Commission), and Ray Cordova (Parks and Recreation Commission). Many of these individuals I appoint were active in my campaign. They all serve on policy-making commissions.[6]

Whether any of these commissioners or others in the future will emerge to replace Guingona remains to be seen, regardless of the fact that Daly City has no term limits for its city council members. One thing is certain: if the Filipino American community is going to realize stronger political incorporation by developing a critical mass in city government, it will need to continue to build off the Guingona legacy in all areas of city government, particularly the city commissions and the school boards. Currently, few Filipino Americans serve in this capacity and this limits the potential for a political pipeline of visible and experienced Filipino American candidates in the future.

A fair and difficult question that must be raised and addressed is why have Asian Americans, particularly Filipino Americans, been unsuccessful in the suburb of Daly City? One of the reasons for the lack of political incorporation of the Daly City Filipino American community stems from two sources that supersede city dynamics. First, as in all majority foreign-born communities, the process for gaining political power takes several steps: immigration, naturalization, voter registration, education, and voter turnout. The Daly City Filipino American community, which is the largest ethnic group among the majority Asian American community, has struggled with both naturalization and voter registration due to its large immigrant population during the past thirty years. Second, as in many recent immigrant communities, many immigrant Filipino Americans are transnational because they retain a strong national and regional identity. Benito Vergara explores this identity among Daly City's Filipino American community in his book *Pinoy Capital: The Filipino Nation in Daly City,* particularly among first-generation Filipino Americans as they endure homesickness with reminders of Filipino culture in the city's newspapers, restaurants, civic groups, and festivals. According to Vergara:

> Community leaders and academics have seized upon the proliferation of Filipino hometown associations and the like in the United States as evidence of the impossibility of political and "national" unity. The evidence points overwhelmingly to the predominance of regional identity over a "national" form. (Vergara 2008, 38)

The result is that these homeland cues remind and enforce, among the first-generation Filipino Americans, the various regional differences that affect Filipino American group consciousness in both the Philippines and the United States. This has made it difficult to mobilize and unite them around common ethnic group interests in Daly City politics (San Juan 1994; Vergara 2008). Such regional factionalism can be transformed into competing and adverse community-based organizations, which are crucial to group political mobilization efforts around Asian American candidates. This factionalism was evident in the lack of consensus support among such Filipino American community-based organizations around Filipino American candidates, including Michael Guingona, as seen in 1983. Moreover, this regionalism has also resulted in fragmented and competing political ideologies that prohibit ethnic solidarity of the city's largest Asian American ethnic community. Without strong leadership within the Daly City Filipino American community, such competing factions and ideologies are likely to curtail future political incorporation efforts in the one suburb where Filipino Americans have the greatest political opportunity to establish themselves.

Intraethnic divisions along cultural and regional lines are nothing new for Asian Americans. Similar regional and dialect differences (Chinese and Taiwanese Americans, in particular) have plagued Asian American political incorporation efforts in cities such as Los Angeles and San Francisco (Hua and Stannard 2007). In other suburbs, such as Cupertino, intraethnic divisions are emerging that curtail panethnic strategies and ideology. However, in Daly City, this issue has been particularly acute and salient in past and present Filipino American political incorporation efforts. As a result, such divisions have limited any potential unifying influence by established Filipino American community leaders and other political loci in Daly City. This finding, combined with the lack of the factors that have allowed for successful Asian American political incorporation in other suburbs (a strong candidate pipeline and the presence of an overarching and unifying political ideology in city politics), has largely contributed to the classification of Daly City as an Asian American Delayed I suburb.

Michael Guingona's initial and sustained electoral success is ironic. Due to its recent immigrant population, generational differences between traditional and acculturated Filipino Americans has become stronger. As mentioned previously, Guingona was viewed as an outsider by the Daly City and South San Francisco Filipino American leadership because of his age (thirty-one years old when he won in 1993) and his limited ability to speak Tagalog, the majority Filipino dialect spoken in Daly City. In short, he was too Americanized for the immigrant Filipino American established leadership, who viewed his cross-racial coalition as counter to their ethnic-specific political interests that had guided the community's politics for two decades. These reasons led Guingona to skip the Filipino American community caucus in 1993 because he realized that he would never win their endorsement and instead courted the mainstream white vote. Ironically, it was this perceived outsider to the Filipino American community who provided it with the political voice on the city council that it desperately needed.

The history of Asian American political mobilization in Daly City represents a political conundrum in which this Asian American–majority suburb has been culturally changed by the recent influx of Asian American immigrant communities, specifically Filipino Americans. Yet this majority community still has not been able to create a pipeline of Filipino American candidates to replace Michael Guingona before or after November 2010, when he must leave office. Whether Filipino Americans can construct such a candidate pipeline and attain future sustained descriptive representation in the post-Guingona era will largely determine the future political trajectory of this community. Ultimately, its ability to achieve both will primarily rest on transcending internal ethnic divisions and establishing coalitions among the many Filipino American community-based organizations that currently exist by changing the focus away from regional cultural and support groups to those that promote panethnic unity.

Michael Guingona represents the type of candidate who is both panethnic and mainstream, the ideal two-tiered candidate, but one who is not easily replicated in the Daly City Filipino American community, as such characteristics take time to develop. Ideally, such a future candidate will serve on one of the key city commissions. However, none of those Filipino Americans whom Guingona has nominated to the city commissions has taken the next step. As a result, such a Filipino American candidate most likely will exist among the second generation of Filipino Americans in Daly City. The second generation, which is US born and less likely to be tied to regional divisions in the Philippines, is more likely to see the benefits of panethnic and cross-racial coalitions. How long it will take to cultivate such a candidate remains the greatest question for this Asian American–majority city if it is to continue the political trajectory that Guingona began in 1993. Although visible Filipino American community leaders have attempted to mitigate these divisions at the community level, it is nonetheless difficult to mobilize as an ethnic bloc around common Filipino American candidates without the two-tiered approach that has been absent among past ethnic candidates outside of Guingona. For the Daly City Filipino American community that accidentally elected such a two-tiered Filipino American candidate as Mike Guingona, the major question is whether it can find and cohesively support another Filipino American candidate to sustain descriptive representation for the city's largest ethnic group.

Notes

1. Adobo is a popular slow-cooked dish in the Philippines that usually consists of the following: soy sauce, vinegar, garlic, and pork or chicken.

2. Michael Guingona, Daly City Council member, interviewed by the author, Daly City, California, July 7, 2005.

3. Alice Bulos, former regional chair of the National Filipino American Women's Network, personal communication with the author, July 21, 2005.

4. Michael Guingona, Daly City Council member, interviewed by the author, Daly City, California, July 7, 2005.

5. Perry Diaz, columnist for FilAmNation.com, personal communication with the author, June 17, 2005.

6. Michael Guingona, Daly City Council member, interviewed by the author, Daly City, California, July 7, 2005.

12

Eau Claire, Wisconsin: The Political Rise of the Hmong American Community

The metropolitan region of Minneapolis and St. Paul in Minnesota, known as the Twin Cities, currently contains the nation's largest Hmong American community, but surprisingly it is not the site for the greatest electoral gains of Hmong Americans in the Midwest. This honor goes to the medium-sized city of Eau Claire, which contains a total population of approximately 62,000 and is located in central Wisconsin. Among Wisconsin's Asian American population in 2000, Hmong Americans accounted for approximately 33 percent, which is twice the size of the second (Asian Indian) and third (Chinese) Asian American ethnic populations combined in Wisconsin. Wisconsin ranks third among states with the largest Hmong population, trailing only California and Minnesota. The Hmong American population (1,599 in 2000) in Eau Claire is about 5 percent of the county's total population, the city's largest Asian American ethnic group and largest minority group. Map 12.1 shows that Hmong Americans are the major Asian American ethnic group in Eau Claire.

The city of Eau Claire is neither a suburb nor an exurb. The nearest large city is Minneapolis, which is approximately an hour and a half drive away. However, while it does not fit the classical suburban definition, Eau Claire is a medium-sized city. I chose to study Eau Claire because of this size characteristic along with the unprecedented electoral success of an understudied Asian ethnic refugee group, the Hmong Americans. This group, which began to arrive directly in Eau Claire in the late 1970s, has subsequently transformed the general community and its civic institutions.

The socioeconomic plight of Hmong Americans is similar to that of other refugees in that they left their homeland primarily to avoid political persecution. The Hmong American community fled to the United States from Laos after being recruited by the Central Intelligence Agency to fight against the Vietnamese Communist forces (Yang 2001). With the promise of a future

Map 12.1 Hmong Population Distribution in Eau Claire, 2000

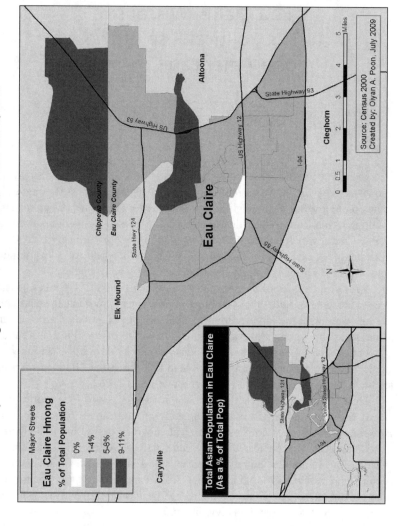

homeland if their country fell, a majority of Hmong Americans have settled and created a concentrated presence in cities such as Fresno, the Twin Cities, and Eau Claire. Many of them have economically struggled since entering the United States. According to the 2000 US Census, 38 percent of Hmong Americans in the United States live in poverty (Pfeifer and Lee 2004). This national statistic indicates the at-risk characteristic of the Hmong American community, which is facing different socioeconomic challenges than a majority of the Vietnamese Americans in Orange County, California's Little Saigon (Chapter 6).

The first wave of Hmong refugees entering the United States began in May 1975 with the fall of Saigon and Laos to Communist forces. In 1985 nearly 27,000 Hmong refugees were admitted to the United States, and there is currently a community of more than 200,000 nationally. During the 1970s and 1980s, voluntary resettlement agencies attempted to disperse the Hmong American community nationally in such cities as Providence, Rhode Island, and Des Moines, Iowa. The medium-sized city of Fresno, California, became a primary destination for many Hmong American refugees between 1977 and 1993. Prior to 1977, only one Hmong American family lived in Fresno, compared to 35,000 in 1993 (Pfeifer 2003). The desire for family reunification among Hmong American refugees was one of the primary reasons for this growth. As economic conditions worsened in Fresno in the mid-1990s, secondary and tertiary migration of Hmong Americans occurred to the Midwest, mostly to the Twin Cities region in Minnesota, which would supplant Fresno as the "Hmong American Capital," but also to small- to medium-sized cities throughout Wisconsin, as seen in Eau Claire from the mid-1990s to the present.

Local Government Structure

The city of Eau Claire has a city council of eleven part-time members, six of them from at-large districts and five from alderman districts. Each serves a three-year term with no term limits. The president of the city council is elected citywide and also serves a three-year term with no term limits. The vice president is appointed by the council, with a majority required. Positions on city commissions are determined by application and a majority vote by the council with terms varying by commission.

While Eau Claire may not have as great a total population of Hmong Americans as metropolises such as the Twin Cities, this community undoubtedly has a presence and recognition among the majority white community because it is the largest minority community. The size of the Hmong American community, along with the existence of at-large districts, has allowed Hmong American candidates to politically mobilize citywide in Eau Claire as well as to utilize out-of-state Hmong American networks to achieve an unprecedented string of electoral wins on the Eau Claire City Council. Underlying this political mobilization are strong community leadership and a guiding ideology that focuses on biracial coalitions with white voters and local civic groups.

The Hmong American Community and Its Civic Consciousness in Eau Claire

The history of Hmong Americans in Eau Claire began in 1976 when the family of Yong Kay Moua, current executive director of the Hmong Mutual Association, arrived under the sponsorship of the Trinity Lutheran Church. Moua's family was the first to arrive directly from Laos. At the time of the family's arrival, Vietnamese Americans were already present in Eau Claire. Like many political refugees who are displaced without much warning, Moua arrived with few social and economic resources.[1] From 1976 to 1979, four Hmong families arrived in Eau Claire, with many of the young men and women seeking education at local technical colleges with the hopes of developing a trade profession. Toward the end of 1979, a secondary migration occurred when other Hmong American families began to move to Eau Claire from gateway cities such as Chicago, the Twin Cities, and Milwaukee. According to Moua: "The Hmong community in Eau Claire was big enough to attract them. Many of these families wanted to participate in the local public education system and sought greater job opportunities and social support."[2] At the same time that the Hmong American community started to develop with this secondary migration, the Vietnamese American community began to move from Eau Claire to the West and Southwest regions as their ethnic networks developed in those areas from 1980 to 1982.

The development of the Eau Claire Hmong American community as it took shape in the early 1980s also resulted in cultural misunderstandings with the majority white community. It was during this time that some Hmong American families were allegedly reported to be eating dogs in the neighborhoods. This stereotype was facilitated by the cultural practice of Vietnamese in Vietnam. Such false accusations based on cultural misunderstandings and racial lumping eventually provided the impetus for local political mobilization and coalition-building efforts by the Hmong American community. As Moua explained:

> At this time, I was a student at a technical college when I asked one of my professors: How can we clear this issue? He suggested that we call a meeting of understanding with the city council, county agencies, the police and fire departments so we could clear the misconceptions of who we are, so we could get to know city leaders so that they can learn that we are here to stay.[3]

Indeed, the Hmong American community was here to stay in Eau Claire. And in order for this to be successful, both the Hmong American community and the white community needed to break down the cultural barriers and misunderstandings that had occurred. Moreover, since the Hmong American community intended to remain in Eau Claire, it was absolutely essential that it be more visible in local government, especially given its heavy reliance on social services.

The above goals were achieved through two local political mobilization efforts by the Hmong American community. First, the Hmong American community leadership began to work with city and county agencies to establish two-year internships with local businesses that were willing to hire and train Hmong Americans with the hope that they would be retained after the internship. If they were not, at least these interns would have marketable skills to work in other similar businesses. Second, in 1989, after an unrelated shooting in the Twin Cities of two Hmong American youths by a white police officer, the Eau Claire Hmong community leaders and the Eau Claire police chief decided to create an annual public forum to improve community relations with the Hmong American community.

The two goals of breaking down cultural barriers and increasing visibility of Hmong Americans in city government came to fruition in the form of an annual Hmong Community Fellowship Banquet. Community sponsors of the dinner included the Hmong Mutual Association, the University of Wisconsin at Eau Claire, the Eau Claire Police and Fire Departments, various CEOs of businesses in the private sector, the Chamber of Commerce, and nonprofit organizations. The banquet grew from 30 people in its inaugural year of 1989 to nearly 300 people during its twentieth year in 2009, with a majority of the attendees being from the mainstream civic organizations and the community. While the size of the event has changed, the primary goals and objectives of the banquet have remained the same: to inform Hmong Americans where they can get assistance from various social agencies, to acquaint Hmong Americans and civic leaders, and to convey the message to the mainstream that Hmong Americans want to give back to the general community.

The significance of the Hmong Community Fellowship Banquet and its primary goals and objectives is that it awakens the civic consciousness of the Eau Claire Hmong American community and it develops leadership within it. An example was the formation of an informal committee of seven Hmong Americans in 1989 that created the foundation for the development of influential community political loci in the form of community-based organizations such as the Hmong Mutual Association. The committee also established a guiding political ideology that focused on group empowerment of Hmong Americans in local government.

The seven Hmong Americans on this informal committee who were instrumental in working on and establishing a strong relationship between white civic leaders and the Hmong American community were Yong Kay Moua, Charles Vue, Saidang Xiong, Thao Yang, Chou Lee, Kao Xiong, and Kou Xiong. Most of these individuals still reside in Eau Claire and continue to serve as community representatives in different capacities. With this critical leadership, the focus shifted to descriptive representation in political institutions. The committee examined local political institutions like the school board and city council so as to understand how they worked and the roles of their members. Soon, the committee began to encourage well-qualified members of the Hmong American community, including members of the committee, to seek local political office.

The ability of Hmong Americans to develop a strong political locus in the form of community-based organizations, combined with a unifying ideology focused on greater political empowerment and visibility in civic affairs, served as the impetus for a sustained electoral success in Eau Claire at the city council level that is unmatched in other communities with significant or larger Hmong American communities. For example, the Twin Cities region and its suburbs have yet to elect a Hmong American city council member despite several attempts.

Perhaps the most visible Hmong American community-based organizations are mutual associations created to address the specific and unique needs of this refugee community. For example, the Eau Claire Area Hmong Mutual Assistance Association (ECAHMAA) is a nonprofit organization that is funded by federal, state, and local grants. According to the ECAHMAA's Mission Statement: "[It] strives to actively assist Southeast Asian families to become socially and economically self-sufficient by: accessing educational opportunities, teaching job skills, strengthening family relationships, and promoting and preserving traditional customs" (Eau Claire Area Hmong Mutual Assistance Association 2006). True to its mission, the ECAHMAA provides multiple forms of assistance, such as a twenty-four-hour translation service for legal, medical, and other needs; a food pantry; college scholarships for Hmong American high school students; and public workshops at the local Hmong Community Center on a variety of socially related topics ranging from cultural activities to voter registration and information.

Early Hmong American Political Mobilization

Given the socioeconomic struggles that Hmong American refugees face in the United States, their political participation rates are below those of other racial and ethnic groups. Previous studies have suggested that low socioeconomic status is the single most predictive variable for low political participation rates, particularly among racial minority groups with large immigrant populations (Wolfinger and Rosenstone 1980; Flanigan and Zingale 1998). It is without a doubt that Hmong Americans face linguistic and cultural barriers that are more acute because of their refugee status than do most immigrant groups, including other Asian Americans. An informal poll in 2001 found that only 21 percent of its Hmong American respondents voted that year (Doherty 2007). Despite their low voter turnout rates, Hmong Americans in Eau Claire have defied the assumption that a largely refugee community with low socioeconomic status is not only likely to vote, but is even more likely to participate when it comes to later stages of political incorporation, such as running for elected office. Since 1993, as many as ten Hmong Americans have run for elected positions in Wisconsin. In Eau Claire, four Hmong Americans have run for city council from 1996 to the present, all of them winning.

Table 12.1 illustrates the large number and success of Hmong American candidates running for the Eau Claire City Council. Some of this can certainly be attributed to Joe Bee Xiong's ability to break the political representative glass ceiling for Hmong Americans in Eau Claire. But other factors for the string of wins for Hmong American candidates include transplanted cultural norms that are congruent with public service and the need for a political voice in local affairs that is particularly acute for a refugee group struggling to find its place in a new country. Many Hmong American observers in Eau Claire believe that the Hmong American community possesses a strong group consciousness and unity.[4] According to Hmong American community leader Yong Kay Moua, the Hmong in Laos during the pre-Communist era often served as public servants to the monarchy and were the mediators of the sixty-four ethnic groups in Laotian society.[5]

Two primary reasons help to explain the exceptional political mobilization of the Hmong American community in Eau Claire. The first reason is that it is a community that overwhelmingly relies on government social services, which puts this community in direct contact with local-, state-, county-, and federal-level agencies. As a result, there is a heightened awareness of the importance of being involved in civic affairs and institutions, on one hand, and the socioeconomic fate of one's community, on the other hand. This important relationship provided the impetus for the urgency of descriptive representation so that Hmong American interests could be represented. The second reason for Hmong American political mobilization in Eau Claire is that Asian Americans

Table 12.1 Hmong Americans Elected to the Eau Claire City Council

Hmong American City Council Member	Years Served (number of terms)
Joe Bee Xiong	1996–2000 (2 terms)
Neng Lee	2000–2002 (1 term)
Saidang Xiong	2002–2004 (1 term)
Thomas Vue	2006 to present (2 terms)

are the second largest racial group in the city, unlike in St. Paul, where Hmong Americans are the largest and the highest-profile Asian American ethnic group. As a result, Hmong Americans do not have to compete with other racial groups for limited political resources such as elective office and social services. Moreover, given this high profile, whites in Eau Claire understand the importance of supporting Hmong American candidates for city council and other local elected positions as a positive step for their overall integration into the general community.

From the Hmong candidate perspective, all of those who have been elected to the city council have expressed no interest in seeking future political office.[6] For example, Joe Bee Xiong stepped down from the city council in order to spend more time with his family, and Saidan Xiong, the third Hmong American elected, after only serving one term due to the need to focus on his full-time business. If political power is not the sole objective of Hmong American candidates in Eau Claire, why do they run? The reasons offered by each of the four Hmong American city council members are the following: (1) to provide a stimulus for Hmong Americans to involve themselves in electoral participation, (2) to create a greater recognition of the Hmong-American community and Hmong issues among the general populace, and (3) to provide some group representation for Hmong-Americans in relation to government policies that influence Hmong Americans.[7] These motives contradict traditional studies of candidate motives for elected office.

The ability of Hmong Americans to maintain at least one Hmong American on the city council since 1993, despite relatively low Hmong voter turnout, illustrates their level of local political incorporation and ability to form coalitions with white voters. This is a necessary strategy for all Asian American candidates in suburbs, regardless of the Asian American population size. But the important question as it pertains to this book is, how did this political mobilization begin? True to my theoretical model, the three major elements—a significant Asian American population, strong community loci, and a strong ideology—have been planted and nurtured in the Hmong American community.

Campaign Contribution Findings in Eau Claire City Council Elections

As shown in previous suburb case studies of Cupertino (Chapter 5), Garden Grove and Westminster (Chapter 6), Sugar Land (Chapter 9), and Bellevue (Chapter 10), Asian American candidates can effectively mobilize both old and new Asian Americans into the political process extending beyond traditional forms of political participation, such as voting to include campaign contributions and volunteering. Asian American candidates who are wise in their campaign strategies will target such political support, as did the last three Hmong American city council members (Neng Lee, Saidang Xiong, and Thomas Vue).

All three of these candidates' city council campaigns were able to mobilize Hmong Americans (locally, statewide, and nationally) in the specifically targeted area of campaign contributions.

Table 12.2 shows how Neng Lee and Saidang Xiong were able to mobilize Hmong Americans in the city of Eau Claire, the state of Wisconsin, and nationally. The total amounts received by Lee and Xiong do not reflect the degree of mobilization within the Hmong American community because the amounts of individual contributions from Hmong Americans typically ranged from $5 to $50, which is much lower than other Asian Americans typically contribute as individuals. Much of this can be attributed to class issues.

Both Neng Lee and Saidang Xiong focused on a two-tiered track in which Hmong Americans served as an important base for funding their respective campaigns while also targeting mainstream white contributors. Lee relied more heavily on white contribution support (over 51 percent of his total contributions) than on Hmong American support (21.2 percent) in Eau Claire. For Xiong, Hmong Americans in Eau Claire represented the largest percentage of contributors to his campaign at 43 percent, compared to the city's whites at 11.2 percent.

Neng Lee's and Saidang Xiong's campaigns were effective in mobilizing Hmong Americans beyond the city of Eau Claire. For Lee, Hmong Americans in Wisconsin (outside of Eau Claire) contributed 14.9 percent of total contributions. Six Wisconsin cities were represented among Lee's individual contributors in this category. Hmong Americans outside of Wisconsin contributed 4 percent of Lee's total contributions, mostly from the Twin Cities region. For Xiong, similar trends exist in which Hmong Americans in Wisconsin (outside of Eau Claire) contributed 28.3 percent of his total contributions, the second largest group of contributors. Eight cities in Wisconsin were in this category. Hmong

Table 12.2 Neng Lee's and Saidang Xiong's Campaign Contributions, 2000 and 2002 (percentage of total in parentheses)

	Neng Lee, 2000		Saidang Xiong, 2002	
Amount received from Hmong Americans				
In Eau Claire	$1,067	(21.2)	$2,180	(43.0)
Outside of Eau Claire within Wisconsin	$750	(14.9)	$1,435	(28.3)
Outside of Wisconsin	$200	(4.0)	$780	(15.4)
Amount received from whites				
In Eau Claire	$2,577	(51.1)	$570	(11.2)
Outside of Eau Claire within Wisconsin	$450	(8.9)	$85	(1.7)
Outside of Wisconsin	0		$20	(0.4)
Total amount raised	$5,044		$5,070	

American contributors outside of Wisconsin represented 15.4 percent of Xiong's total contributions, also from the Twin Cities. The Hmong American contributions outside of Eau Claire demonstrate the symbolic nature of Lee's and Xiong's respective campaigns to many Hmong Americans in the Midwest. Many of the out-of-district Hmong American contributions received by Lee and Xiong were the result of social networks established through Hmong American mutual associations in these cities, and the proactive campaign strategies of both candidates to solicit their help. According to Saidang Xiong:

> I basically sent campaign letters to other states like Minnesota asking for money if they can't vote for me. I had no fund-raisers in these states. I'm proud to say that I received the highest amount of contributions for all the candidates running in 2002. Everyone in the [Midwest] Hmong community knows me after the election.[8]

Thomas Vue, the current Hmong American serving on the Eau Claire City Council, utilized a fund-raiser approach to reach out to the Hmong American community in Minnesota and in other parts of Wisconsin. Vue recalls:

> During my first campaign, I contacted the President of the Laos Family Community organization in [St. Paul] Minnesota and asked him to contact people who he knew so that I could make a presentation to them and get their monetary support. In my first presentation in the Twin Cities, I received close to $3,500. I then contacted the president of the La Crosse Hmong Association, who I went to school with, and was able to raise $4,000. Overall, during my first campaign, I raised more than $10,000 from Hmong Americans in Minnesota and Wisconsin [outside of Eau Claire].[9]

The overall Hmong American campaign contribution findings show that the symbolic nature of the need for Hmong American candidates in Minnesota and Wisconsin is well understood among the general Hmong American community in both states. Why else would they give money to candidates who do not represent them per se in local civic affairs? Nevertheless, the benefits of descriptive representation for Asian Americans go well beyond the symbolic to a substantive impact on the lives of those who are part of this community. An example is Eau Claire City Council member Thomas Vue and his multiple roles with the city's Hmong American community. One clear role is to represent the general community and the specific interests of the city's largest minority group on the city council. But another role is to educate Hmong Americans on the key issues coming up in the city council and to encourage them to participate politically. As Vue states:

> I try to conduct a monthly meeting at the Eau Claire Area Hmong Mutual Association to tell members of the Hmong community about issues that influence them. For example, at the last meeting, I told them about a public tax vote that was coming up in the city council and how it would result in a 2 to 3

percent increase in their city taxes. I encouraged all of them to attend the city council public hearing on it before the council votes on the resolution.[10]

This example and the overall contribution findings support previous studies that find ethnic representatives serve multiple roles in mobilizing and incorporating their respective communities into the political process (Mansbridge 1999). For Hmong Americans in Eau Claire, such issues remain at a premature stage because this community seeks to gain greater political incorporation in other civic institutions.

Creating and Sustaining a Hmong American Political Pipeline in Eau Claire Politics

A sustained candidate pipeline, which Asian Americans are finally achieving in the suburban context, is an essential component that needs to be created and nurtured in order to sustain group political incorporation efforts. In Eau Claire, despite the relative success of Hmong American city council candidates, much work needs to be done to address the lack of representation in other civic institutions. The Eau Claire Area Hmong Mutual Assistance Association and the Partnership for Strong Hmong Families, two of the most visible Hmong American community-based organizations in Eau Claire, have attempted to address this void within the community through the two-year Hmong Leaderships for Eau Claire Program. The program was initiated in 2007 after a 2006 community-based forum, which also involved the Minority Affairs Office in Wausau and the Children's Service Society of Wisconsin, invited Hmong American clan leaders throughout Wisconsin to join community discussions regarding future leadership in the Hmong American community. Out of the discussions, it became clear that there was a need for leadership training from within the Hmong American community and that a void remained in local civic institutions. The findings of the 2006 forum included the following:

> At least 10 local agencies in Eau Claire [are] searching for diverse representation to fill vacancies in their boards and committees that includes nonprofits, neighborhood associations, the technical college, and the City of Eau Claire. . . . In the past 25 years, the Leadership–Eau Claire Program run by the Chamber of Commerce has had only four Hmong graduates, out of a population of nearly 3,000 Hmong in the Eau Claire area. Hmong-Americans in our community are not stepping into the leadership roles for various reasons. Some reasons may be: mainstream organizations have not successfully mentored and supported emerging leaders; the high cost of leadership development programs; long work hours and family responsibilities; unfamiliarity with the "how-to's" of civic engagement; language and/or cultural barriers; and a generation gap in Hmong-American understandings of leadership and community involvement. As a result, there is a very, very small pool of Hmong individuals who are trying to represent their community on multiple boards,

councils and committees. . . . The greater Eau Claire community continues to be ignorant of many issues affecting a significant portion of the minority population. Often, boards and stakeholder groups are composed of middle-class, Euro-American professionals. The perspectives of the Hmong community are not evident in many key discussions about important issues such as school budgets, urban development, and human services. One or two visible and recognized Hmong leaders serve on a score of boards, community groups and service organizations. When community groups do request Hmong participation, there is a shortage of candidates. (Eau Claire Area Hmong Mutual Assistance Association and Partnership for Strong Hmong Families 2006, 13)

With the above concerns, the Eau Claire Area Hmong Mutual Assistance Association and the Partnership for Strong Hmong Families initated the Hmong Leadership for Eau Claire Program. The program sought to rectify the leadership deficiencies by recruiting and training emerging Hmong American leaders through the establishment of scholarships and encouraging and recruiting Hmong participants to join established leadership development programs (Eau Claire Area Hmong Mutual Assistance Association and Partnership for Strong Hmong Families 2006). The initial class began in 2007 with twelve participants (five women and seven men) and in April 2008, nine of them graduated. Among these graduates, three had college degrees, one was an entrepreneur, and another was a Hmong clan leader.

The leadership program consists of seven monthly evening sessions that include guest speakers and fellowship among the participants to promote opportunities for social networking. For example, the first session included the Eau Claire City Council president, a member of the Eau Claire County Board of Supervisors, and a Hmong member of the Eau Claire City Council. Participants engaged in a leadership exercise and also prioritized their interests in areas of civic life for future sessions. Another session involved attending a public city council meeting. All of these sessions are designed to achieve the mission, goals, and objectives for enhancing the participants' knowledge of the complex web of community institutions, their confidence in their own leadership capacities, and their motivation to serve the community. The sessions provide participants with an introduction to fundamental government, nonprofit, and business practices through presentations by local leaders and observation of civic leaders in action. Armed with this civic understanding and social networks, it is hoped, participants will take the next step and take on a leadership role in the larger Eau Claire and Hmong American communities.

A Tale of Two Cities: The Need to Expand
Descriptive Representation to the Eau Claire School Board

In the Midwest, the two cities with the largest number of Hmong American elected officials are St. Paul and Eau Claire. On the surface level, the differences between these two cities are like night and day. The former is one of the largest cities in Minnesota, with the largest number of Hmong Americans in the nation; the latter is a medium-sized city with an agriculturally based economy. The pathways to political incorporation are also distinctly different between the two cities. In St. Paul, Hmong Americans have been able to achieve elected sustainability that is limited to the school board. Five Hmong Americans have been elected to the St. Paul School Board, yet no Hmong American has been able to get elected to the St. Paul City Council. The most recent attempt was on November 27, 2007, when Pakou Hang, a student working on his PhD at the University of Minnesota and a well-respected community political activist, finished 365 votes behind longtime incumbent Dan Bostrom for a council seat with the highest concentration of Hmong Americans in the city (Moua 2007). Hang, a first-time candidate, received nearly $47,000 in contributions, a substantial portion of it coming from the Hmong American community throughout Minnesota and the Midwest. By way of contrast, in Eau Claire, Hmong Americans have clearly demonstrated the ability to attain elected sustainability on the city council during the past decade, but have failed to elect a Hmong American to the school board.

Why are there differences in entry levels for Hmong American political incorporation between St. Paul and Eau Claire? One answer is that, despite these different entryways into the political system, one major commonality binds the two cities, and that is the importance of local context, such as a city's size, in determining the success of political incorporation. Eau Claire is a medium-sized city (61,704 total population) compared to the large city of St. Paul (287,151 total population), according to the 2000 US Census (Pfeifer and Lee 2004). Hmong Americans are the largest minority group in Eau Claire, despite representing only 5 percent of the total population, and, as a result, they remain in the consciousness of the mainstream community, as discussed above, with the proactive attempts by various mainstream civic leaders to build relationships between the two communities. In St. Paul, Hmong Americans and other Asian American ethnic groups must compete with other racial groups, including whites, Latinos, and African Americans, for limited local elected positions. Such is not the case in Eau Claire, where Hmong American city council candidates and community leaders have established intergroup relations with mainstream civic leaders. Another reason for the difference is that the available seats on the city councils are fewer than those on city school boards, which make the former arguably more competitive than the latter, as demonstrated by the fact that city council candidates must raise more money and their campaigns are often more expensive than school board campaigns.

In order to achieve full political incorporation, Hmong Americans in Eau Claire must attain elected representation in other key local civic institutions besides the city council. Education issues that pertain specifically to the Hmong American youth are acute, as many Southeast Asian refugee groups continue to struggle to reach comparative levels with whites in regard to graduation rates. The city council's influence on primary, secondary, and tertiary education policy is limited compared to the school board's influence on education policy issues. As mentioned earlier, the first and last Hmong American to run for the Eau Claire School Board was Charles Vue in 1993, nearly twenty years ago. This must change, and hopefully it will change, as qualified Hmong American candidates are recruited and encouraged to run for such elected positions by both the Hmong American and mainstream civic leadership. Programs like the Hmong Leadership for Eau Claire Program are likely to facilitate a potential candidate pipeline that will extend beyond the city council.

Notes

1. Yong Kay Moua, executive director of the Hmong Mutual Association, interviewed by the author, Eau Claire, Wisconsin, July 22, 2008.

2. Yong Kay Moua, executive director of the Hmong Mutual Association, interviewed by the author, Eau Claire, Wisconsin, July 22, 2008.

3. Yong Kay Moua, executive director of the Hmong Mutual Association, interviewed by the author, Eau Claire, Wisconsin, July 22, 2008.

4. Yong Kay Moua, executive director of the Hmong Mutual Association, interviewed by the author, Eau Claire, Wisconsin, July 22, 2008.

5. Yong Kay Moua, executive director of the Hmong Mutual Association, interviewed by the author, Eau Claire, Wisconsin, July 22, 2008.

6. Yong Kay Moua, executive director of the Hmong Mutual Association, interviewed by the author, Eau Claire, Wisconsin, July 22, 2008.

7. Yong Kay Moua, executive director of the Hmong Mutual Association, interviewed by the author, Eau Claire, Wisconsin, July 22, 2008.

8. Saidang Xiong, former Eau Claire City Council member, interviewed by the author, Eau Claire, Wisconsin, July 22, 2008.

9. Saidang Xiong, former Eau Claire City Council member, interviewed by the author, Eau Claire, Wisconsin, July 22, 2008.

10. Saidang Xiong, former Eau Claire City Council member, interviewed by the author, Eau Claire, Wisconsin, July 22, 2008.

13

Fitchburg, Massachusetts:
The Political Incorporation of
Asian Americans in a Boston Suburb

Over 250 years old, the city of Fitchburg, Massachusetts, is the oldest suburb among the suburbs that I examined in this book. Located about thirty-five miles outside of the Boston city limits, Fitchburg began as one of New England's industrial centers during the eighteenth century. Granite and paper were the primary resources for the industries. The city is named after John Fitch, who was one of the city's first settlers in 1748. Situated between the Nashua River and the Fitchburg Railroad line, the city was the hub between Boston and Albany, New York. The economy of Fitchburg during its heyday was driven by the industrial mills powered by the Nashua River, which helped produce machinery, tools, paper, clothing, and firearms (City of Fitchburg 2008). Today these mills are still visible along Water Drive, some having been converted to other industries and some serving as historic sites to remind the residents of Fitchburg's industrial past. Today, as illustrated in Map 13.1, Fitchburg is home to a small but thriving Southeast Asian population that is gradually changing both the demographic and political culture of this industrial Boston suburb.

Fitchburg reached its economic peak during 1850–1920 as dramatic developments were made in water power to propel its cotton mills, which produced paper and clothing.[1] However, these golden years ended as deindustrialization negatively impacted the city's reliance on its local economies, along with environmental pollution concerns about mills along the Nashua River.

Fitchburg was a polyethnic city that drew many immigrants from all over the world during its industrial period from the mid-1800s to the early 1900s. German, French, and Irish immigrants found work in the granite quarries and textile mills. Many of the current white residents of Fitchburg can trace their ancestry from these ethnic groups. However, Southern and Central Europeans were not the only immigrants to arrive in Fitchburg during the industrial period.

Map 13.1 Southeast Asian Population Distribution in Fitchburg, 2000

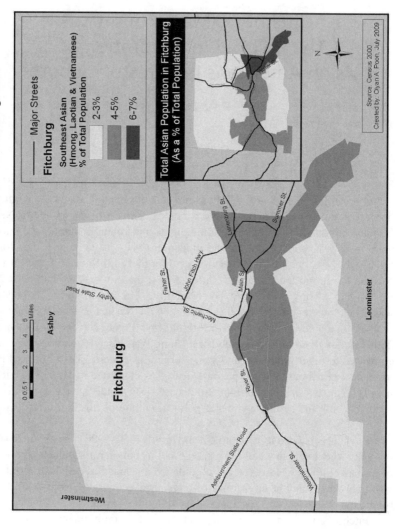

Immigrants from Asia, particularly China, also formed part of the pre-1965 Asian American community.

The Pre-1965 Formation of the Asian American Community in Fitchburg

The pre-1965 Asian American community in Fitchburg was indeed small, but not necessarily invisible from the mainstream. Many of the city's pre-1965 Chinese immigrants who came to Fitchburg from the western states were originally from the Canton region of southern China, making Fitchburg their new home as early as 1880. By 1888, public documents indicate, Fitchburg had five Chinese American–owned laundry businesses and one restaurant (Kilpatrick 1975). The first publicly recorded Asian American birth was on August 19, 1929, that of Thomas Donovan Tuck Wong, the firstborn son of Mary Ann Wong and John Wong, and the grandson of John Fong Ying, who owned the city's first Chinese restaurant, the Canton Restaurant. As Doris Kilpatrick, the official historian of Fitchburg, writes:

> The Canton Restaurant in the Park Building in Depot Square displayed a festive appearance lavishly decorated with Chinese and American flags and great bowls of roses on the banquet tables. It was August 19, 1929 and a number of city and state notables had gathered to celebrate an event hitherto unknown in Fitchburg—the christening of Fitchburg's first Chinese native son. (Kilpatrick 1975, 269)

The early twentieth-century Chinese American community formation in Fitchburg was begun by the John Fong Ying family, the first Chinese American family to settle permanently in Fitchburg. As indicated in the quotation above, the family was well liked by the mainstream residents and leadership in Fitchburg due to their public visibility with the restaurant. While most states in the American West, particularly California, were in the midst of "The Chinese Must Go" movement during this period, Fitchburg was known to be more hospitable to racial movements. On May 18, 1893, the city's newspaper, the *Sentinel,* printed the following: "Someone said the Chinese must go, but we noticed John [in reference to the caricature 'John Chinamen'] hard at work as usual this morning, and he wore the same complacent smile. Now, suppose China decided that all Americans must leave China! Yet, few people take the Mongolian's side" (Kilpatrick 1975, 273). While racial tensions did exist between whites and the newly arriving Chinese, for the most part Fitchburg was a liberal city that was openly receptive to them.

Chinese Americans were not the only Asian American residents of Fitchburg prior to 1965, because Japanese and Korean Americans found their way to the city as war brides of white former military servicemen who served in

Japan and Korea (Kilpatrick 1975). For example, Japanese war brides such as Hanako Kimura and Michiko Hazebuchi were among those who helped to establish the pre-1965 Japanese American community. Both gave birth to several biracial children who grew up to further develop the Japanese American community.

Post-1965 Asian American Community Formation in Fitchburg

The post-1965 immigration of Asian Americans to the continental United States included a large percentage of professionals and highly educated immigrants from throughout Asia. This brain drain from Asia also affected the Asian American community in Fitchburg. Korean Americans came to Fitchburg to live and to practice their professions. For example, in the 1970s, two Korean American doctors established their practice in Fitchburg. By 2000, Fitchburg had a total population of 39,102, with the following racial groups: whites (81.9 percent), Latinos (15 percent), Asian Americans (4.3 percent), and Native Americans (0.4 percent).

Asian Americans, the city's third largest racial group, are becoming more visible in civic life, from its schools to its local government. Most noticeable are the Hmong Americans, who make up the city's largest Asian American community. This community has gradually transformed itself from a quiet refugee community seeking to survive to one that attempts to mobilize around both ethnic and racial issues that impact their community.

In 1978, the United States' involvement in its clandestine war against Vietnamese Communist forces in Southeast Asian countries like Laos resulted in the arrival of Fitchburg's first Hmong American families in the following decades. Similar to the Eau Claire, Wisconsin, case study in Chapter 12, the Hmong American community in Fitchburg began with compassion. Sponsored by several families in Fitchburg, Hmong Americans in Thailand refugee camps relocated directly to this city and eventually were followed by other Hmong American families from states such as Connecticut, Rhode Island, Wisconsin, Minnesota, and California. It is estimated by Kao Yang, president of the Hmong-Lao Foundation and board member of the United Hmong of Massachusetts, Inc., that nearly 600 Hmong Americans currently reside in Fitchburg.[2]

Local Governmental Structure and the Emergence of a Hmong American Political Consciousness

The Fitchburg City Council has five part-time members, all from at-large districts. Each member is elected for a two-year term with no term limits. Elections are held every two years. A primary election is held if more than ten candidates file, in order to bring the pool down to ten so that only two candidates are running for an open seat each year. The top five vote getters fill the seats. The mayor is also elected citywide for a two-year term with no term limits. If more than two candidates file to run for mayor, a primary election takes the top two vote getters. The plurality winner in the general election becomes mayor. All members for the various city commissions are appointed by the mayor and confirmed by the council committee on appointments.

An unprecedented two Asian Americans occupy elected seats: Dean Tran, a Vietnamese American immigrant, is a city council member and Lisa Wong, a second-generation Chinese American, is mayor. Both candidates relied heavily on the Hmong American community for support, which signaled the gradual emergence of a panethnic Asian American political consciousness.

The first political awakening of the Hmong American community in Fitchburg occurred in 1982 when the community began to seek assistance from local, state, and federal agencies to address their socioeconomic needs through social welfare programs. Given their refugee status, many Hmong Americans relied heavily on governmental assistance, from food stamps to welfare. The Hmong American leadership worked with city and state officials to design programs to assist Hmong Americans and help them adjust. The Hmong-Lao Foundation attempted to build a cultural bridge with Fitchburg's residents and its civic institutions. Examples of its activities include cultural exchanges in city parades and the city's formal establishment of the Hmong New Year Celebration, which takes place annually in late August.

A second political awakening of the Hmong American community took shape in 1997 when funding for many of the city's programs ended due to the Personal Responsibility Work Opportunity Reconciliation Act (PRWORA) of 1996, which terminated federal food stamp benefits for legal immigrants and refugees (Fujiwara 2005). This was a difficult period that left many Hmong Americans to struggle until 2007, when funding resumed. In 2007, a new leadership emerged in the Hmong-Lao Foundation with the election of Kao Yang and Choua Der Vang as president and vice president, respectively. Their top priority, according to both Yang and Vang, is to secure back payment for the Hmong American community that they believe was rightfully owed to them during the twenty-year period from 1987 to 2007.[3]

Since their election, Yang and Vang have met several times with members of the Fitchburg City Council and the mayor to discuss this issue. They remain hopeful that the monies will be secured in the near future for individual Hmong Americans and then used for the creation of a Hmong American Cultural Center, their second goal, to provide cultural programs. These programs will include Hmong language classes for the Hmong American youth, who are rapidly losing their culture, and senior services for its rapidly aging Hmong American population. In order to achieve these goals, the Hmong American community has understood the importance of Asian American descriptive representation and incorporation in local government. Now it only needed Asian American candidates to run, and this finally occurred with the inaugural candidacies of Dean Tran and Lisa Wong in 2005 and 2007, respectively.

One might think that Fitchburg, with its small Asian American population base, would not be a contemporary suburb to examine as an emerging site of Asian American political incorporation. This is precisely why Asian American population size does not determine political incorporation, but only serves as a precursor among many factors. Yet despite its relatively small population base of Asian Americans, Fitchburg currently has two Asian Americans, Dean Tran and Lisa Wong, who hold elected positions in city government. This represents the largest number of Asian American elected officials in any Massachusetts city, including Boston. Tran is the city council vice president and one of five at-large council members after being elected in 2005 with the second highest vote count. Lisa Wong, the city's first minority mayor, was elected in November 2007. Wong's election made national headlines because she was a first-time candidate who defeated a three-term incumbent by winning over 70 percent of the vote. In many ways, the elections of Tran and Wong demonstrate that Asian American descriptive representation is occurring faster in small- to medium-sized suburbs than in large gateway cities such as Boston, which elected its first Asian American city council member, Sam Yoon, in 2005. Although Boston has the largest Asian American aggregate population in Massachusetts, it has struggled to elect an Asian American to any local office.

Community Locus in Action: The Hmong-Lao Foundation

The Hmong American community began to form its own civic institutions to address the specific concerns of community members. In 1982, key leaders of the Hmong American community established the Hmong-Lao Foundation, a nonprofit organization that provides interpretive and translation services to assist the low- to moderate-income Hmong and other Asian populations in Fitchburg through information and referral, employment, housing, health education, and public assistance. Its initial goal was to act as an intermediary between the Fitchburg Hmong American community and city and state elected officials and institutions in the area of social services, which this community relies on heavily given their refugee status, and to serve as translators for the general community.[4] Since this time, the foundation has become a key community-based organization that serves multifaceted roles for the Hmong American community by expanding its services to include political advocacy, naturalization assistance, and voter registration.

In addition to providing essential social services support to the emerging Hmong American population, the Hmong-Lao Foundation works to strengthen cultural ties for its growing second generation, which is far and long removed from the killing fields of Laos. In the modest building that houses the Hmong-Lao Foundation on Pritchard Street in downtown Fitchburg, courses are offered to teach the younger generation to read and write Hmong.

Realizing the importance of connecting with the local political structure in order to gain awareness and support of their social, economic, and political conditions, the Hmong-Lao Foundation from 1995 on has organized and promoted, with other Hmong American organizations throughout central Massachusetts, perhaps the most visible yearly event in this community—the Hmong New Year Parade, which takes place in Saima Park every September. This weekend event has given a high profile to Fitchburg's Hmong American community among the city's mainstream residents and leaders. Although this visibility and interaction with the local mainstream is necessary, it simply is not enough. A political consciousness also had to be developed to mobilize around future city council candidates who would inherently understand the social needs. The Hmong American community found such an Asian American candidate in Dean Tran, a refugee whose family fled Vietnam and relocated in Fitchburg.

Return of the Native Son

The resettlement of Dean Tran's family in Fitchburg was a long journey that embodies the early Vietnamese American refugee experience in the United States. This journey began in Saigon when his family fled the Communist forces of Ho Chi Minh. According to Tran: "My father served for twenty-five years in the South Vietnamese Army as a lieutenant. We fled Vietnam and relocated in a Cambodian camp. It was later when we were sponsored by a Catholic priest in Clinton, Massachusetts, in 1980 where we first located in the United States."[5] In 1985 when he was six years old, Tran's family moved to the city of Fitchburg. The second youngest of six children, Tran endured the challenges that many Asian American youth encounter, which involve trying to fit in and becoming part of the mainstream. Tran recalls: "As a youth in school, I realized that my peers who came from important families in the city were often treated different than me."[6]

Dean Tran, who holds an MBA from Brandeis University in Waltham, Massachusetts, thrived in school. Soon after earning his degree, Tran married and the first of two daughters was born. At that point, an important question hit him: where do you want to raise a family? Given his own experiences in Fitchburg, Tran realized that it would be an ideal city to raise his daughter. He explains: "I had a vested interest in the city, of course. I wanted to create a better environment for my daughter, the school system that she was in, and for its citizens that reflected the diversity of the city. . . . I seriously believe that racism exists unless someone makes a dent in the political system."[7]

Motivated by the goal of change for the better, Dean Tran's interest in the city council peaked, but with cautious optimism. Tran knew both the importance and the challenges of running as a minority candidate in Fitchburg. Prior to Tran, only one minority candidate (Willie "Jay Jay" Johnson, an African American) had run for a Fitchburg City Council seat, but he had failed. As one of the few Vietnamese Americans in Fitchburg, Tran noticed a common theme among all successful minority candidates: their ability to build biracial coalitions between the majority white and Asian American constituents. Although Tran believes that "race was never a factor" during either of his campaigns, he effectively employed this biracial coalition strategy in winning his inaugural election in 2005 and reelection in 2007, largely with the support of white residents coupled with the support of the Hmong American community, the city's largest Asian American ethnic group. This two-tiered strategy is common for Asian American candidates regardless of their suburb's Asian American population. Approximately 99 percent of Tran's votes in both elections came from whites, which is understandable given the demographics of the city. The remaining 1 percent of Tran's supporters came mostly from Hmong American community-based organizations and their members in Fitchburg, such as the United Hmong of Massachusetts. According to its president Kao Yang: "The Hmong community is very supportive of Hmong or any Asian candidate. We would encourage our members to put up lawn signs and encourage their family and friends to support Tran."[8]

The support of Dean Tran's campaigns by the Hmong American community, even though they do not share the ethnicity of the Vietnamese American Tran, demonstrated the potential for building panethnic alliances in suburban settings where common interests are likely to similarly allow for the transcending of divisive ethnic politics often associated with larger cities. Class variation is also less likely in the suburban context than in large cities, which typically are more economically stratified. If ethnic differences within the Asian American community can be overcome through the actions and rhetoric of respective ethnic community leadership, political mobilization is likely to occur along panethnic lines. In Fitchburg, under the strong leadership of Kao Yang, the United Hmong of Massachusetts followed its leader's rhetoric and actions in calling for the community to support Tran's historic campaign in myriad ways.

Dean Tran focused on a grassroots campaign that emphasized his qualifications. No contribution data were available for either of Tran's campaigns given that a majority of his funds were self-financed with some help from family. Tran did no fund-raisers and did everything on a grassroots level with the main support of his wife and two daughters. Tran states: "Grassroots is needed if you have no name recognition. The goal of my campaign was to tie my name to the qualifications. I went out walking the precincts from door to door to let them know who I am."[9] Part of these qualifications included Tran's appointment to the City Planning Commission, which represents one of the key commission springboards to city council. In his inaugural 2005 election, Tran finished as the third highest vote getter (2,705 votes) for three open seats on the Fitchburg City Council, becoming the city's first minority elected official (Fitchburg City Clerk's Office). Since this time, Tran has become a veteran of local politics and his name recognition is strong among the community. At the same time, Tran became the face of the newly emerging and changing demographics of Fitchburg. He was not the lone Asian American candidate in 2007, as another political precedent for the Asian American community then occurred.

The Perfect Political Storm

The city of Fitchburg was ripe for political change due to the economic struggles to revitalize its local economy and the perceived lack of vision among its political establishment, which allowed for the opportunity of a political outsider such as Lisa Wong, age twenty-eight, to make electoral history in the 253-year-old city. From 2001 to 2005, Fitchburg had lost nearly 1,100 jobs. Although Wong, the daughter of Chinese immigrants, may be seen by most observers as a political outsider to the Fitchburg mayor's office, she is not a political neophyte. Having served on the planning committee and holding a master's degree in urban planning, Wong represented the perfect candidate with the right credentials and one who could serve as a panacea for the mainstream white voters of Fitchburg. Young and charismatic, she embodied hope for a new economic vision among Fitchburg's younger voters, who formed a large portion of her campaign volunteer base.

Lisa Wong's challenger for the mayoral seat was conservative, four-time-elected Fitchburg City Council member Tom Donnelly, who accused Wong of being an "interloper" who was half his age and trying to use the city election as a stepping-stone to higher office (Moskowitz and Sacchetti 2007). Donnelly attempted to paint Wong as too politically inexperienced to lead Fitchburg out of its financial doldrums, but failed, as Wong easily won the general election by 5,863 to 1,948 votes (Moskowitz and Sacchetti 2007). After the election, Wong declared at a public gathering of over 100 people that her election represented a call for transformation of the postindustrial Boston suburb to a city economy of technology firms, young professionals, restored mansions, and public recreation on the once-polluted Nashua River. According to Wong: "The voters of Fitchburg voted for change. . . . The citizens of Fitchburg voted for energized leadership. . . . It's about time. Fitchburg has always been a diverse city" (Moskowitz and Sacchetti 2007, 1).

The campaign contributions for Lisa Wong's 2007 mayoral campaign reflect her biracial coalition of mostly whites, with the remaining contributions coming from Asian Americans. As shown in Table 13.1, the total contributions that Wong received were $12,575, with an overwhelming majority ($10,075,

Table 13.1 Lisa Wong's Fitchburg Mayoral Campaign Contributions, 2007 Primary Election

Racial and Ethnic Group	Total Amount (percentage of contributions)	
Non-Asians	$10,075	(80.1)
Asian Americans	$2,500	(19.9)
Total	$12,575	(100.0)

or 80.1 percent) coming from non-Asians, primarily whites. A significant 20 percent of Wong's total contributions came from six Asian American donors who represented four different states (California, Massachusetts, Virginia, and North Carolina).

Lisa Wong had a key ally on the Fitchburg City Council in Dean Tran. Tran decided to embrace his newfound title as the first "minority" on the city council and take his goals of making the city's government more diverse and reflective of its community a step further with his active support of Wong. According to Tran:

> Prior to the election of Lisa, I was the only elected minority in city government. I can't change my identity. I want the Cambodian, the Hmong community to feel comfortable with me. I spoke to Sam Yoon [the first Asian American city council member] in Boston after I was elected about my situation. He said, "Be proud of that title." I took it a step further. I put Lisa Wong in contact with several key prominent Asian American community leaders in Boston that help mobilize her mayoral campaign and get her name recognition. I felt that she was a good change for the city. She was qualified and the fact that we never had a minority mayor was another important reason I supported her. I was the only Fitchburg City Council member that openly supported Lisa because she ran against a fellow city council member.[10]

Wong's emergence as a candidate in the 2007 mayoral election was a culmination of the frustrations that many longtime and recent voters of Fitchburg felt with regard to the conditions and direction of the city.

Among Fitchburg voters, the Hmong American community mobilized their support for Lisa Wong's mayoral campaign as they had done for Dean Tran's inaugural and reelection city council campaigns. Kao Pang states that another Asian American elected official "will bring help and better communication."[11] Pang and other United Hmong of Massachusetts leaders urged members of their community to display yard signs and communicate through phones, work, and public spaces their support of Wong, as they had done for Tran. Pang estimates that in 1997 nearly half of the community events that his community-based organization sponsored were to promote Wong's campaign and the general welfare of the Asian American community in Fitchburg aside from Hmong American interests.

The successful mayoral election of Lisa Wong provided the United Hmong of Massachusetts with another Asian American elected official who they felt would understand and be an advocate for their community concerns. With their support of Wong's mayoral campaign, one of the biggest issues that Kao Pang and others felt needed to be addressed is the impact of the 1996 PRWORA, as part of the Republican-led Contract with America. The PRWORA essentially altered the delivery and goals of federal assistance to the poor, who include many refugees who are at risk in the following ways: (1) ending welfare as an entitlement program, (2) requiring recipients to work after two years of receiving benefits, (3) placing a lifetime limit of five years on benefits paid by federal funds, and (4) curbing federal reliance by encouraging two-parent families (Fujiwara 2005, 122). The Hmong American community was an unfortunate victim of the political battle in Washington, DC, between the Republican-controlled Congress and the Democrats. As noted above, much of their reliance on federal and state assistance is not due to out-of-wedlock births or single-parent families, but the social and psychological disruption and transition of their refugee experience along with a lack of adequate social services, such as job training, that would allow many of the adult refugees to earn adequate economic livelihoods. No such refugee provision was provided in the PRWORA, which would adversely impact them. Given this condition, President Pang and his vice president made it a personal goal to meet several times with Mayor Wong to discuss their situation and to seek retroactive funds since the PRWORA went into effect in 1997. This goal continues to this day.

Finding Ties That Bind in an Emergent II Suburb

The panethnic perspective of the United Hmong of Massachusetts demonstrates two key points: first, that small- to medium-sized suburbs can transcend ethnic divisions that often limit panethnic coalitions in metropolitan areas that are more socially and economically stratified; and, second, the important role that community-based organizations like the United Hmong of Massachusetts and its key leadership play in facilitating panethnic support around Asian American candidates' campaigns during group political mobilization. Rarely does the literature on Asian American political behavior discuss the second point in the context of Asian American refugee groups, particularly the Hmong American community, during local elections. In the suburbs, class issues are not as acute and the ethnic differences can be downplayed during group political mobilization around Asian American candidates. In the context of small- and medium-sized suburbs, common interests are more likely to be formed among Asian Americans, regardless of their ethnicities and population size, as long as strong leaders in the form of candidates and community-based organization leadership exist to promote such strategies. In Fitchburg, the beacon of leadership began and is fostered by city council member Dean Tran and key community-based organization leaders such as Kao Yang who understood both the necessity for diversity on the Fitchburg City Council and the role that they can play in breaking the initial political glass ceiling.

Mayor Lisa Wong is likely to continue fostering the diversity perspective that Dean Tran began with his election in balance with the general interests of the Fitchburg constituency to transform the political culture of the city government. This overall finding bodes well for other Emergent II suburbs that are similar to Fitchburg if Asian Americans are able to continue to make inroads in suburbs where the Asian American population is small. More importantly, it illustrates that Asian American political incorporation, beginning with descriptive representation, can be attained in such contexts and that political power (as measured by the group's ability to attain descriptive representation in local governments), such as Wong's mayoral election and Tran's reelection, can be replicated. While descriptive representation is merely the first step in the continuum of political incorporation, it nevertheless demonstrates an important feature of Asian American political behavior in the new gateway suburbs, such as Fitchburg, for various Asian American ethnic groups—immigrant and refugee—that has not been historically demonstrated in large cities.

Notes

1. Susan M. Roetzer, director of the Fitchburg Historical Society, interviewed by the author, Fitchburg, Massachusetts, August 25, 2008.

2. Kao Yang, president of the Hmong-Lao Foundation, interviewed by the author, Fitchburg, Massachusetts, August 27, 2008.

3. Kao Yang and Choua Der Vang, president and vice president of the Hmong-Lao Foundation, interviewed by the author, Fitchburg, Massachusetts, August 27, 2008.

4. Kao Yang and Choua Der Vang, president and vice president of the Hmong-Lao Foundation, interviewed by the author, Fitchburg, Massachusetts, August 27, 2008.

5. Dean Tran, Fitchburg City Council member, interviewed by the author, Fitchburg, Massachusetts, August 28, 2008.

6. Dean Tran, Fitchburg City Council member, interviewed by the author, Fitchburg, Massachusetts, August 28, 2008.

7. Dean Tran, Fitchburg City Council member, interviewed by the author, Fitchburg, Massachusetts, August 28, 2008.

8. Kao Yang, president of the Hmong-Lao Foundation, interviewed by the author, Fitchburg, Massachusetts, August 27, 2008.

9. Dean Tran, Fitchburg City Council member, interviewed by the author, Fitchburg, Massachusetts, August 28, 2008.

10. Dean Tran, Fitchburg City Council member, interviewed by the author, Fitchburg, Massachusetts, August 28, 2008.

11. Dean Tran, Fitchburg City Council member, interviewed by the author, Fitchburg, Massachusetts, August 28, 2008.

14

Forging Ahead:
The Future Political Trajectories
of Asian Americans

Asian American–influenced suburbs represent "political incubators" that have allowed this community to develop political pipelines of candidates, beginning with local elected offices and leading to higher levels, including state legislatures and the US Congress. Within such political incubator suburbs, characterized as Transformed (I and II) and Emergent (I and II) typologies, Asian American political organizations, the ethnic media, and other important political loci are developing to address the emerging population and its needs. Such political loci are influential during group political mobilization around Asian American candidate campaigns in these suburbs, and can serve as important political allies in achieving descriptive representation in local governments. Perhaps even more importantly, these political incubator suburbs have proven that Asian Americans can replicate and build on elected representation, which has not been demonstrated in American politics outside of the state of Hawaii. In some cases, such as the Transformed I suburbs of Westminster and Monterey Park, California, Asian Americans have taken the majority of positions on city councils.

Many scholars who study immigrant political incorporation in the continental United States have witnessed a dearth of Asian American elected representation in twentieth-century gateway cities, such as Los Angeles and New York City, where Asian American city council members number an underwhelming total of two—former Los Angeles City Council member Michael Woo (District 13) in 1985 and current New York City Council member John Liu (District 20) in 2001. The complex reasons why Asian Americans have not attained descriptive representation even comparable to their total population in such large cities include the following: (1) district elections in large cities that have harmed more than helped Asian American candidates due to a residential dispersion of Asian Americans that has limited substantially populated districts from emerging and mobilizing around Asian American candidates; (2) ethnic competition and the lack of common ideological interests that have limited political mobilization efforts; (3) the existence of entrenched political interests, which have made it more difficult for insurgent immigrant groups like Asian Americans to attain descriptive representation; and (4) the lack of a formal pipeline to allow for the systematic approach to building political power bases that other racial groups have achieved.

The emerging Asian American–influenced suburb has provided a critical mass that has fueled unprecedented local political mobilization efforts. For the first time in the continental United States, majority and plurality Asian American suburbs are emerging in the following areas: Santa Clara County, Los Angeles County, and Orange County, California. In Santa Clara County, a pan-ethnic coalition among the distinct Asian American communities is forming that has contributed to its having the largest number of Asian American elected officials of any county in the continental United States, as seen in Cupertino (Chapter 5). Orange County is fueled by the maturation of the Vietnamese American community, as illustrated in Garden Grove and Westminster (Chapter 6). The political success of Asian American candidates in both Santa Clara and Orange Counties is unprecedented, as their small- to medium-sized suburbs have witnessed majority Asian American city councils along with majority Asian American cities. Historically, the state of Hawaii, which has a majority Asian American population that controls the local and state political institutions, has been the traditional geographic power base for Asian American politics. This axis remains, but no longer stands alone.

For the first time in American politics, Asian American candidates in suburbs in the continental United States are winning, sustaining, and building on Asian American elected representation in their respective local governments, an important measuring stick for group political power. For example, in Transformed I suburbs like Cupertino (Santa Clara County), Gardena (Los Angeles County), and Garden Grove and Westminster (Orange County), where Asian Americans account for 46 percent, 27 percent, and 31 percent of their respective city populations, Asian Americans have achieved a majority or near-majority of city council representatives.

While California leads the charge in the suburbanization of Asian American politics, it is certainly not alone. In Emergent I suburbs throughout the United States, such as Bellevue (outside of Seattle, Washington), Sugar Land (outside of Houston, Texas), and Eau Claire, Wisconsin, Asian American immigrants and refugees are building on elected representation in their respective local governments. In the case of Eau Claire, Hmong Americans, a neglected and understudied Asian American ethnic group, are defying the belief that low socioeconomic status determines low political participation. This Asian American refugee community has elected four different Hmong Americans to its city council over the past decade while larger Hmong American–populated cities like St. Paul and Minneapolis, Minnesota, still have not elected even one Hmong American to their respective city councils.

The suburbanization of Asian American politics in the continental United States has also created a formal pipeline to state-level elected positions. After the June 2008 general elections, a historic eleven Asian Americans served in the California State Legislature, in contrast to the period from 1980 to 1993, when no Asian American served. Many of these Asian American state representatives are from emerging electoral districts in suburbs that include significant Asian American populations, such as California State Assembly member Michael Eng (District 49, which contains large portions of suburbs like Monterey Park, Rosemead, San Marino, and Alhambra), who was elected in November 2006, and California State Assembly member Paul Fong (District 22, which contains large portions of suburbs like Cupertino, Sunnyvale, Milpitas, and Santa Clara), who was elected in November 2008. Both are examples of state-level Asian Americans who rely heavily on their suburban bases to win elections. It is likely that future local Asian American elected officials will follow comparable paths from other similar suburbs.

At the US congressional level, Asian Americans are also emerging from districts that contain large portions of Asian American–influenced suburbs. Nowhere is this more evident than in California, with one example being Congressman Michael Honda (District 15), whose district encompasses large portions of central, northeastern, and southwestern Santa Clara County that consist of suburbs such as Cupertino and Milpitas. Recently elected congresswoman Judy Chu (District 32) represents a district that contains Asian American–influenced suburbs such as Monterey Park, El Monte, and West Covina. As noted in Chapter 6, California State Assembly member Van Tran is attempting to do the same in congressional District 47 in 2010. One important commonality between Honda and Chu is that both have Asian American Transformed I suburbs (Cupertino for Honda, Monterey Park for Chu) in their districts that are instrumental to their respective political successes. Such political incubator suburbs will likely continue to train and provide political opportunities for future state Asian American elected representatives who seek to get elected to the US Congress.

Pursuing Two-Tiered and Toggling Campaign Strategies

In all ten suburbs that I examined in this book, Asian American candidates have been successful by focusing on a two-tiered campaign strategy that includes a mainstream focus (regardless of the city's demographic makeup) while, at the same time, attempting to mobilize a panethnic coalition behind their campaigns. In the latter strategy, the ethnic community to which the Asian American candidate belongs often will provide the political base from which she or he can build. This two-tiered campaign strategy was pursued by nearly every successful Asian American candidate I examined in the ten suburbs. The mechanism that allows Asian American candidates to execute the two-tiered strategy is referred to as toggling, through which Asian American candidates can craft nuanced and linguistically appropriate political campaign messages in the print and electronic media that are tailored specifically to a particular segment of their constituency (Collet 2008).

In the case of Asian American–influenced suburbs where a large immigrant population exists that is catered to by a growing ethnic media, Asian American candidates can focus on issues that relate specifically to ethnic community concerns, which may be completely different from the mainstream's concerns. An example of this can be seen in the two most powerful political suburb bases for Asian Americans in the continental United States, Cupertino and Little Saigon in California. In these suburbs, Asian American candidates have the ability to utilize the ethnic media to craft ethnic-specific messages during group political mobilization that focus on political empowerment (e.g., the need for more descriptive representatives on city councils) and community issues (e.g., more funding for schools that have ESL programs in these suburbs). However, there are times when such strategies can backfire on Asian American candidates, particularly during tipping point politics in these suburbs. An example can be seen in the 2008 Cupertino City Council special election, when Chinese American candidate T. N. Ho tailored his message to a predominantly Chinese American crowd about the need "to form a majority of Chinese-Americans in the city council so as to push for programs favoring the Chinese community," which was quoted in the *Sing Tao* newspaper and eventually made its way to the *San Jose Mercury News* as a hearsay comment by one of its readers (*Cupertino Courier* 2007). Ho later denied the context of his statement in a January 2, 2008, letter to the city newspaper (*Cupertino Courier* 2008).

The significance of the toggling strategy is that, when executed effectively, it can mobilize both new and old Asian American voters into the political process by appealing to them along ethnic and racial lines in nuanced ways that other non-Asian candidates cannot. This strategy adds to the politics literature concerning other minority candidates, particularly African Americans and Latinos, and how they must deracialize their campaigns when they run in local elections (Metz and Tate 1995). For Asian American candidates, deracialization is seen in the form of mainstream strategies that emphasize collective issues involving the city's entire constituency. The toggling method allows Asian American candidates to racialize or ethnicize campaign messages to their ethnic communities in their native languages during group political mobilization (Collet 2008). The effect of this strategy has been political success for Asian American candidates, as seen in Cupertino and Westminster and Garden Grove, California, and Eau Claire, Wisconsin, where large immigrant and refugee populations exist.

Addressing the Multiple Asian American Candidate Scenario

It is understandable that the perception of multiple Asian American candidates running against each other in a local election is, on its surface, a critique of the solidarity of Asian American politics in mature suburbs in major regions of California. However, it is necessary to look beyond the surface level to understand whether there are other significant aspects that can be taken from multiple Asian American candidate scenarios. An example of this issue is, as discussed in Chapter 5, the 2008 California State Assembly, District 22, election in Santa Clara County, which contains Asian-influenced suburbs such as Cupertino, Mountain View, and Sunnyvale.

The popular perception during the 2008 California district primary election was that the Asian American community was divided and politically weak due primarily to the competing candidacies of Kris Wang and Paul Fong. Despite this perception, a closer examination of the political endorsements of Wang and Fong reveals that both candidates received major political endorsements. The following key Asian American political leaders in Cupertino and the Santa Clara County region coendorsed Wang's and Fong's campaigns: Congressman Mike Honda, former Sunnyvale mayor Otto Lee, Saratoga mayor Aileen Kao, former Cupertino City Council member Michael Chang, Cupertino Union School District trustees Pearl Cheng and Ben Liao, and former district California State Assembly member Sally Lieber.

From the above list of coendorsements, it is clear that many of the most influential Asian American elected leaders in Santa Clara County have focused on electing an Asian American representative by supporting both Paul Fong and Kris Wang, rather than publicly choosing a political side. Both Asian American and white political leaders in Cupertino and Santa Clara County attempted to foster a public perception of a unified Asian American community through coendorsements of Fong and Wang despite multiple Asian American candidates running with different special interests behind each of them. Outside the public view, it is also clear that a majority of the Asian American leadership in Cupertino and Santa Clara County supported Fong's campaign, as demonstrated by their strong attendance at his community events and fund-raisers. In contrast, a majority of Wang's supporters came from business and community interest groups that wanted slow and smart growth for Cupertino, which had previously taken public aim at Fong for supporting a controversial condominium development in 2006. For example, in a May 2008 political mailer sent by the Kris Wang for State Assembly campaign, a prominent photo and endorsement that take up half of the front side feature Wang and Edward J. Britt, president of the Concerned Citizens for Cupertino. The endorsement by Britt contained the following revealing passage:

> CCC has worked with Kris Wang for a number of years to keep our community strong, by protecting our schools and communities from over-development. We

have noted that Mayor Wang is especially careful and thoughtful in actually reading financial reports and considering the benefit and impact of proposed projects. She is a true public servant with no ties to special interests. (Concerned Citizens for Cupertino 2008)

This passage is illustrative of one of the primary community interest groups supporting Wang and adds perspective on why two prominent Asian Americans from Cupertino were running for the California State Assembly, District 22, seat, which was due more likely to the differences in Wang's and Fong's stances on the degree and speed of economic growth and development in Cupertino than to divisions within the Asian American community. Although the latter represents the initial reaction, the likely reason for Wang's candidacy was more that she offered a perspective and choice that differed from Fong's on this important issue for white and Asian American voters in the district, especially in Cupertino.

The struggle between two coalitions led by Asian American candidates was likely due more to Kris Wang seeing the opportunity of support from such interest groups that opposed Paul Fong in Cupertino than to the general perception of a politically splintered Asian American community. The results of the 2008 District 22 Democratic primary reveal that an Asian American candidate can be successful despite the presence of multiple Asian American candidates competing against each other.

On one level, the significance of the two competing coalitions led by two Asian American candidates, Paul Fong and Kris Wang, bolsters the argument that Asian Americans in Cupertino specifically, and Santa Clara County generally, are beginning to reach a level of political incorporation in local politics that is unrivaled in any region in the continental United States. This is important for understanding why the multiple-candidate scenario is not as much a threat to future Asian American political incorporation where it is stronger than in many other regions in the form of major party support and endorsements that offset the dilution of Asian American votes. The ability of Asian Americans to attain such a level of political incorporation is a recent phenomenon. In the past, Asian Americans have generally been political outsiders attempting to gain access to the local political institutions primarily through campaign contributions. At the same time, Asian American candidates hoping to break the glass ceiling of elected representation in these cities have primarily focused on their racial and ethnic communities, as seen in Chapter 11 with the Filipino American community in Daly City. This campaign strategy is problematic due to low voter turnout rates among the large immigrant Asian American population even when it constitutes a significant population base. In most cases, this results in limited political incorporation in the form of descriptive representation, a key measuring stick for group political power.

The historic perspective that multiple Asian American candidates running for the same seat will split the votes is no longer necessarily true, particularly when Asian Americans have medium to strong levels of incorporation in a particular city or region. Such a political scenario had been dangerous in the past, especially in cities where Asian American political incorporation was weak. As a result, Asian American candidates tended to rely heavily on Asian American voters without building coalitions with mainstream voters and interest groups. The main reason for this strategy is that they had no political incorporation (e.g., access to mainstream civic institutions and interest groups) and therefore relied exclusively on their Asian American community for political support. However, as Asian Americans achieve greater degrees of political incorporation in other suburbs, they are able to build cross-racial coalitions and receive influential party support for Asian American candidates in local and state district elections. This has allowed many Asian American candidates to build and mobilize, through a two-tiered strategy, a cross-racial coalition at the state level that has worked so well at the local level from the 1990s to the present. As a result, multiple Asian American candidates running for the same seat will split Asian American votes, but this split will inevitably be offset by the Asian American candidates' ability to rely primarily on progressive whites' votes.

In the span of a decade, Asian Americans have become an entrenched part of the political institutions in key regions of California. Competing mainstream interest groups have begun to back Asian American candidates over other candidates, because they see the potential for winning the large Asian American votes in these regions as a political advantage rather than a disadvantage as this group begins to flex its political muscles as contributors and voters. This finding is the result of the gradual political acculturation of this predominantly immigrant-born community. But it also is the result of the local political incorporation efforts occurring in these Asian-influenced suburbs as Asian American candidates have been politically successful in building and mobilizing cross-racial coalitions primarily among white and Asian American voters to gain descriptive representation. With this process of political mobilization have come the political spoils of being sought out and supported by different interest groups, ranging from the Sierra Club to the California Democratic Party, which has resulted in competing political coalitions led by Asian American candidates.

The perspective that multiple Asian American candidates running against each other is a political weakness needs to be challenged and understood as an inevitable growing pain as this group progresses toward full political incorporation. In the Transformed I suburbs that I examined in this book, multiple Asian American candidates running in the same elections have become the norm, as this group has achieved an unprecedented level of electoral success in major regions in Santa Clara County and Orange County, California.[1] What has also become the norm in these Transformed I suburbs is that an Asian American candidate wins in such a situation. As California's Asian-influenced suburbs lead the way in this regard, other Asian-influenced suburbs throughout the continental United States are likely to endure the same growing pains.

Overcoming Tipping Point Politics

Another phenomenon taking shape in Asian-influenced suburbs is tipping point politics, in which the emerging Asian American majority is perceived as a group threat by the outgoing majority white population. This is a natural phenomenon in racially transformed suburbs and represents a significant barrier to the future political incorporation of Asian Americans in the suburbs. Indeed, suburbs experiencing tipping point politics provide a cautionary tale for other suburbs that are likely to undergo similar transformations. Perhaps the most visible suburb with this phenomenon is Cupertino, as seen in the 2007 and 2008 elections. These elections are interlinked because of the rise of Mark Santoro, who is viewed as the anti-Asian vote in Cupertino among long-term white voters, who still represent the majority in the city. In the November 2007 citywide election, Gilbert Wong surprisingly won the second and last open seat over Santoro by thirty-three votes. Santoro was the only non-Asian American candidate running in the entire field and a political neophyte who was able to garner enough votes to warrant a second try in 2008. In the special election in February 2008 to replace Patrick Kwok, Santoro won 54 percent of the city vote, easily outdistancing his two Asian American competitors. Both election results demonstrate the subtle and unique challenges of this suburb and other California suburbs that will follow its demographic trajectory (e.g., Fremont, Sunnyvale, Mountain View, Alhambra, Rosemead, and Westminster and Garden Grove). Even in a city like Cupertino where Asian Americans have had relative success in gaining substantive authority and influence in city politics, a majority Asian American representation on the five-person city council in the near future may elicit racial tensions with white residents and voters. Gilbert Wong's inaugural election and Kris Wang's reelection in November 2007 created the racial makeup of the city council as follows: two Asian Americans, two Caucasians (Orrin Mahoney and Richard Lowenthal), and one Latina (Dolly Sandoval). The perceived group threat among the city's established white voter base contributed to Santoro's near victory in 2007 and carried over to a clear victory in 2008, the election that determined the racial group majority of the city council.

Despite the presence of tipping point politics during the 2007 and 2008 elections in Cupertino, the Asian American community was able to overcome this challenge in the 2009 election, in which Barry Chang finished second among a field of seven candidates (four of whom were Asian American). This allowed Cupertino to have an Asian American–majority city council for the first time in the city's history. Cupertino joins Westminster as the two cities in the continental United States that currently have an Asian American–majority city council. The significance of the 2009 Cupertino election is that tipping point politics is not a permanent barrier and can be overcome in Asian-influenced suburbs.

The concerns of outgoing white majorities in suburbs where Asian Americans are becoming the new majority will likely reveal challenges for future Asian American political incorporation efforts as tipping point politics is likely to emerge among longtime resident white voters who feel their community is changing too quickly and Asian Americans are gaining political power. This issue needs to be taken seriously by Asian American candidates and community leaders, since whites remain the majority voters in many of these suburbs given the low Asian American voter turnout rates. There undoubtedly is a covert feeling of group threat among a majority of longtime white residents, who are witnessing the gradual demographic and cultural shifts occurring in Cupertino and Daly City. For the sake of race relations, it is important that Asian American candidates and community leaders foster and construct important outreach efforts with whites because it is not enough to only articulate the same messages that concern them. One of the key sectors where this can occur is that of professional group organizations with a membership of both Asian Americans and whites. In the case of Mike Guingona and his historic 1993 Daly City Council election (Chapter 11), Guingona was able to draw on his professional networks for cross-racial support. Such professional organizations provide the opportunity for Asian American candidates to build social networks that transcend racial lines and to consolidate socioeconomic interests. In the case of Gardena, California (Chapter 7), it is clear that such social networks were being created within professional organizations by the pioneer Japanese American elected officials, such as Mas Fukai. These paved the way for the only second-generation majority-led Japanese American city council in the continental United States. The same can be seen in more recent immigrant suburbs such as Sugar Land (Chapter 9) and the greater Houston, Texas, area, where Asian American political networks have been built on the two-tiered strategy discussed above.

Tipping point politics in Asian-influenced suburbs is not a new phenomenon, as this same issue took shape during the 1980s in the first suburban Chinatown of the continental United States, Monterey Park, where Asian Americans currently constitute over 60 percent of the city's population. As a result of the demographic shifts, similar tensions arose between Monterey Park's emerging Asian American–majority population and its outgoing majority Caucasian voter base in the form of a citywide law that required the signage of all Asian businesses to be in English. Despite these racial tensions, Monterey Park has had a majority or near-majority Asian American city council from the 1990s to the present. In addition, Asian American political and community leaders have instituted citywide multicultural events that celebrate its diverse Asian, Latino, and European heritages in order to alleviate these racial tensions.

History has shown that urban campaigns can be racialized by white candidates in order to create populist resentment against African American mayoral candidates, as seen with Harold Washington (vs. Richard Daley) in Chicago in 1983 and Tom Bradley (vs. Sam Yorty) in Los Angeles in 1969 and 1973 (Metz and Tate 1995). Most recently, Mexican American candidates such as Los Angeles mayor Antonio Villaraigosa (vs. James Hahn) in 2001 have faced similar issues in large cities in the form of zero-sum politics with African American voters (Drayse and Sonenshein 2005). With the emerging Asian diaspora in US cities along with the suburbanization of Asian American politics, Asian American candidates will face issues similar to those of non-Asian voters but within the small to medium suburban context.

The Sugar Land, Texas, 2008 mayoral election clearly demonstrates anti-Asian resentment among white voters when an emerging population of Asian Americans becomes too powerful, too fast, as symbolized by Daniel Wong's mayoral campaign. With the potential of Asian American candidates to capture a majority of the Sugar Land city government during the 2008 elections, combined with their major population growth in the city, which reached nearly 34 percent in the 2006 census update, the political rhetoric among the areas' political and media establishment became increasingly vitriolic. An example is Beverly K. Carter's commentary that appeared in the *Fort Bend Star* on May 7, 2008 (Carter 2008), which questioned Daniel Wong's mayoral campaign's link to the Houston 80-20 Asian American Political Action Committee and portrayed the relationship as a clandestine attempt to take over Sugar Land's government with only the interests of Asian Americans in mind. The editorial put Wong's mayoral campaign and the Asian American community leadership on the defensive and resulted in the political action committee issuing a public response and rebuttal to the accusations by Carter (2008). Regardless, the political damage had been done and it undermined the potential for biracial coalition building between Asian American and moderate white voters in Sugar Land that was necessary for Wong to win the election.

As a result of tipping point politics, the future success of Asian American candidates in these suburbs depends heavily on their ability to be conscious of group-threat perceptions in these Asian-influenced suburbs by aggressively reaching out to white residents through participating in mainstream community institutions, and making concerted efforts to alleviate tensions and dispel the concerns among skeptical white voters who feel such candidates represent only Asian American interests. It therefore is paramount for Asian American candidates to articulate and pursue a broader vision that understands that Asian American self-interests alone are limited, by making genuinely concerted efforts to build cross-racial coalitions with whites and other racial groups through a two-tiered campaign strategy, regardless of the Asian American population's size. By doing so, in elections where racial attacks occur against Asian American candidates by their opposition candidates who seek such political strategies to mobilize non-Asian voters, charges of racial self-interest can be dispelled by Asian American candidates not only through their rhetoric, but also through a long track record of political action in the broader community. At the same time, city governments must make genuine and sustained efforts to address racial tensions in Asian-influenced suburbs, as seen in Cupertino with the 2003 community forum "A Time to Talk."

Triangulating Key Political Loci in the Asian American Community

As seen in all of the ten suburb case studies, the extent of Asian American political growth and incorporation in small- to medium-sized suburbs is dependent on whether a triangulation can occur among the following three key political loci: Asian American candidates, Asian American community-based organizations, and the emerging and influential Asian American ethnic media. To facilitate this triangulation, common interests and ideology must be identified and articulated, and strong leadership must be groomed. The development of the infrastructure of this political network is occurring at different stages within Asian American–influenced suburbs, and it will likely pay positive dividends for the Asian American community in future local and state elections, particularly in key states where they represent a swing vote in closely contested elections. This triangulation effect is seen most clearly in California, and will likely serve as a blueprint for other states that are following similar political trajectories.

Within the Asian American–influenced suburbs, Asian American community-based organizations represent one of the fastest-growing public service sectors of the past three decades. Almost a decade ago, in 1998, there were over 250 pan–Asian American organizations in Los Angeles and Orange Counties (UCLA Asian American Studies Center 1997). In 2008, over 150 pan–Asian American organizations focused on political advocacy alone (UCLA Asian American Studies Center 2008). Given the weak structure of the Republican and Democratic Parties at the local level in cities like Los Angeles and San Francisco where elections are nonpartisan, community-based organizations represent an important political ally for Asian American elected officials in minority districts. Among all of the Asian American–influenced suburbs that I examined in this book, at least one Asian American community-based organization was heavily involved during group political mobilization around the campaigns of Asian American candidates.

Politically active community-based organizations can play both support-ive and proactive roles in the recruitment of future Asian American elected of-ficials. A supportive role entails helping Asian American elected officials and candidates whose campaign strategies focus on them to gain access to important community resources (e.g., votes, campaign volunteers, and campaign contri-butions). Many of these organizations are nonprofit, nonpartisan organizations that must balance proactive community empowerment efforts with their non-partisan status. The challenge for community-based organizations will be to identify and articulate key issues within the socially and economically diverse Asian American community that can serve as a basis for group identification and mobilization.

The Asian ethnic print media serves as a medium for mobilizing the Asian American community around Asian American candidates during group politi-cal mobilization in small- to medium-sized suburbs. This strategy was evident in historic firsts for Asian American descriptive representation in many of the suburbs that I examined. Two California examples are Kris Wang's 2003 inau-gural city council campaign in Cupertino and Van Tran's 2004 California State Assembly, District 68, campaign. Non-California examples are Daniel Wong's 2002 Sugar Land City Council election and Conrad Lee's 2005 Bellevue City Council election.

As a result of this triangulation, if common interests and a strong ideol-ogy can be found and articulated around salient issues (e.g., descriptive repre-sentation, smart growth, bilingual education in public schools), there is little reason to doubt whether Asian Americans can continue to mobilize effectively in local and state elections in these small- to medium-sized suburbs. New tech-nologies such as Facebook, Twitter, and other Internet social networking sites will also facilitate mobilization efforts among these three Asian American po-litical loci. Whether or not Asian American political mobilization can be done on a consistent basis in the future remains to be seen. However, one thing is certain: if Asian Americans are to attain greater local political incorporation in Transformed suburbs with significant Asian American populations, the ability to triangulate the three Asian American political loci around common interests and ideology will be crucial.

Building Multiracial Coalitions at the Local Level

As suburbs become multiracial, Asian Americans must go beyond group inter-est by finding new ways to build cross-racial coalitions in local, state, and national politics. Figure 14.1 shows the national shift from the traditional para-digm of race relations between blacks and whites to a multiracial paradigm that prominently includes Latinos and Asian Americans. This demographic trend will be reflected in both large cities and small- to medium-sized suburbs

Figure 14.1 Multiracial America, 2007

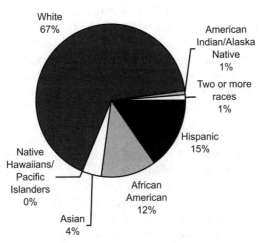

Sources: Kaiser Family Foundation, based on Table 3: Annual Estimates of Population by Sex, Race and Hispanic Origin for the United States: April 1, 2000, to July 1, 2007. Population Division, US Census Bureau.

Notes: Data do not include residents of Puerto Rico, American Samoa, Guam, the US Virgin Islands, or Northern Mariana Islands. Totals do not add up to 100 percent due to rounding. All racial groups and individuals reporting "two or more races" are non-Hispanic.

throughout the nation. President Obama eloquently captured this point during his seminal speech at the 2004 Democratic National Convention in Boston, where he boldly declared: "There is not a black America and white America and Latino America and Asian America—there's the United States of America" (*Washington Post* 2004). It was a timely speech that captured the multiracial face of America, and one that was especially significant for Asian Americans because it put them on the map of America's racial conscience with regard to race relations discourse.

Given the emerging multiracial paradigm in American politics, where do Asian Americans fit within the mosaic? Ideally, when minorities reach a critical mass and whites are no longer the majority of the statewide population, as has occurred in California, the discussion invariably focuses on multiracial coalition building. As is the case for any political coalition, three crucial elements are common interests, common ideology, and strong leadership (Marable 1994; Sonenshein 1993). Common interests cannot alone sustain a coalition. One must have all three elements if coalitions are to be constructed and maintained to achieve their goals, particularly in the ever-shifting political terrain of local politics in both large cities and small- to medium-sized suburbs. Asian Americans have many interests in common with other racial groups. With whites,

Asian Americans generally have similar socioeconomic backgrounds and, therefore, common interests around tangible issues that appeal to both upper- and upper-middle-class voters. This is particularly true in the context of the small- to medium-sized suburbs, as I have shown throughout this book.

Aside from attempting to build panethnic coalitions, many successful Asian American candidates and groups have focused primarily on building interracial coalitions with whites, which I identified earlier in Chapter 1 as the two-tiered campaign strategy that they must employ regardless of Asian American population size. Moreover, because of their broad socioeconomic backgrounds, Asian Americans and whites tend to be broader in their political partisanship and ideology. As seen in Orange County, which traditionally has had a strong conservative Republican power base in California, Vietnamese Americans have emerged as the strongest ideological partners with white conservatives. This partially explains why Little Saigon (Garden Grove and Westminster) has developed into an Asian American Transformed I suburb because the political environment has allowed such coalitions to flourish and Vietnamese Americans are being actively recruited into the Republican Party in Orange County.

In addition to forming political alliances with whites, Asian Americans must identify common interests and ideology with Latinos, as they are often the two largest minority groups in racially commingled suburbs in regions such as San Gabriel Valley (e.g., Monterey Park, Alhambra, Rosemead, Roland Heights), Orange County (e.g., Westminster, Garden Grove, and Irvine), and Santa Clara County (e.g., Sunnyvale, Cupertino, Mountain View). Strong leadership from both communities must work to avoid the natural zero-sum-game politics, which portends that a racial group loses if another racial group wins.

The potential for zero-sum-game politics between the Asian American and Latino communities is taking shape as their populations and descriptive candidates increase in the suburbs. In San Gabriel Valley, Asian American and Latino candidates often run against each other in high-profile state-level elections. In 1994, current congresswoman Judy Chu ran for the California State Assembly against Diane Martinez in an election that resulted in perceived racial tensions between the two communities with regard to political representation in this racially commingled assembly district. Chu lost the Democratic primary. In 1998, Chu ran again for the California State Assembly and faced another Latina in Gloria Romero, with the latter emerging victorious in the Democratic primary. In 2001, Chu ran again in the California State Assembly, District 49, special election after Romero resigned, and won.

As in San Gabriel Valley, competition between Asian American and Latino candidates is emerging in competitive state- and federal-level races in other regions of California. An example of this can be seen in Orange County's June 2006 general election for Congressional District 47, which pitted Vietnamese American refugee Tan D. Nguyen, who had won a heated three-candidate race for the Republican nomination by winning over 55 percent of the vote, against Democrat Loretta Sanchez, a Mexican American who made history in becoming Orange County's first Latino American US representative by changing parties and running against six-term incumbent Republican Bob Dornan in the former Congressional District 46. Sanchez defeated Nguyen in the 2006 general election by winning 62 percent of the vote. Controversy emerged during this election in which Nguyen's campaign was accused of and investigated by federal authorities concerning alleged Latino American voter intimidation in the form of a Spanish-language mailer that stated:

> You are being sent this letter because you were recently registered to vote. If you are a citizen of the United States, we ask that you participate in the democratic process of voting. You are advised that if your residence in this country is illegal or you are an immigrant, voting in a federal election is a crime that could result in imprisonment, and you will be deported for voting without having the right to do so. (Santana 2006)

Although Nguyen was exonerated of voter intimidation by federal investigators, the incident reveals the high stakes that involve both Asian American and Latino American candidates in political districts that are racially commingled, and how they can create electoral competition and racial tensions between these communities. Orange County has witnessed a large demographic shift in its Asian American and Latino American communities and, with these shifts, both communities will naturally seek political representation and influence. As seen in the Little Saigon case study, Vietnamese Americans have attained a medium to strong level of political incorporation in these suburbs, where they are one of the largest racial groups. However, it will be interesting to examine whether Vietnamese Americans can maintain their large political representation in such suburbs as Latinos begin to run their descriptive candidates and mobilize around them.

In Santa Clara County, Asian Americans account for 30.5 percent of the total population, with Latinos at 25.7 percent. As both racial populations continue to grow, the concern is whether they will see themselves as potential allies or adversaries for limited political resources (Marable 1994). As a result, Asian American and Latino community leaders in Santa Clara County have taken on proactive attempts to create opportunities to learn about each community's history in the United States and in Santa Clara County, and to articulate the common interests and ideology by promoting civic participation and coalitions between the communities. Perhaps the most vivid example is the Asian Pacific American Leadership Institute and its civic leadership program, which seeks to target two audiences—politically active college students and professionals who are Asian American and Latinos. This program is the result of a collaboration between two strong leaders—former Cupertino mayor Michael Chang and current East Palo Alto mayor Ruben Abrica—both of whom were the first ethnic candidates in their communities to be elected to their respective city councils. They understood both the political potential and the challenges that Santa Clara County's suburbs pose for their respective communities and that their communities' political destinies are intertwined. Based on their observations of Santa Clara County and its suburbs, Chang and Abrica knew that Asian Americans and Latinos would need to find common ground in the political arena. As a result, the civic leadership program was created as an attempt to foster political cooperation between the groups as various guest speakers provide context for this goal for both communities. It is one of the first leadership programs of its kind in the nation and again emphasizes why strong leadership is important to the success of constructing multiracial coalitions. In 2009, the civic leadership program had over thirty Asian American and Latino participants, who were college students from local universities and junior colleges along with white-collar professionals and local elected officials. They convened on the campus of De Anza College in Cupertino to listen to elected officials and scholars and then broke into smaller groups to discuss solutions to various issues affecting both communities.

Whether common interests can be articulated that result in a Latino–Asian American coalition around public policies such as immigration, public education funding, fair wage, and bilingual education programs remains to be seen. A successful local example can be seen in the Bellevue, Washington, case study (Chapter 10), whereby Asian Americans and Latinos formed a coalition around bilingual education programming in the local school districts. However, this was not the case, as witnessed in the June 1998 election when California voters decided on Proposition 227, which sought to abolish bilingual immersion programs. According to a *Los Angeles Times* and CNN poll, Latinos voted nearly 56 percent against the proposition while 57 percent of Asian Americans voted in favor of it (McLeod and Gaura 1998).

Asian American and African American political alliances in local politics have been few since the 1990s. A factor contributing to this has been the presence of Asian American petite entrepreneurs in historically African American neighborhoods in large cities like Los Angeles, Philadelphia, and New York City. Perhaps the most visible example of this tension was the purported conflicts over Korean American grocery stores in the historic African American community of South Central Los Angeles, which culminated in an estimated $300 million in total damages, half of which were suffered by Korean American small businesses that were strategically looted and burned by both African American and Latino rioters during the 1992 Los Angeles riots, the most expensive and deadliest in US history. Much criticism came from Asian American community leaders with regard to the media's sensationalistic portrayal of the alleged black-Korean conflict and the lack of balanced coverage by the same media with respect to giving Korean American merchants an opportunity to express themselves regarding their socioeconomic situations. As a result, many

Asian American community leaders felt that the one-dimensional portrayal of Korean American merchants as rude and money-hungry entrepreneurs who economically preyed on inner-city communities went unchallenged in the media.

The vitriol that remained after the 1992 Los Angeles riots between African Americans and Korean Americans was captured the following year in a 1993 *Los Angeles Times* race relations poll of Southern California residents (P. D. McClain and Stewart 2006). The poll asked respondents from a cross section of all the major racial groups to name which racial group they perceived to be the most discriminatory to their racial group and which racial group they perceived as gaining too much economic power. The findings among African American respondents were: 65 percent felt that whites were the most prejudiced group; 45 percent (an increase of 19 percent from a 1989 survey) felt that Asians were the most prejudiced group, compared to 11 percent who felt that Latinos were the most prejudiced group; 39 percent felt Asians were gaining "economic power that is not good for Southern California," compared to 29 percent who felt whites were gaining "economic power that is not good for Southern California"; and 25 percent felt Asians were the source of their social problems, with 19 percent specifically identifying Korean Americans (P. D. McClain and Stewart 2006, 184–185). While these social and economic frustrations and perceptions of African Americans are legitimate, both communities have common vested interests in the economic development of these inner cities where they work and live. Rather than viewing petite entrepreneurs as the cause of the inner-city problems, the focus should be on corporations that historically devalue investment in the inner city (Marable 1994).

The ability to form multiracial coalitions in local and statewide politics is a political puzzle that has yet to be solved in California and other multiracial states. However, one certainty is that three necessary components (common interests, common ideology, and strong leadership) will remain integral to any such coalition. Therefore, whether these multiracial coalitions form in the future will likely hinge on whether community leaders and other political loci can articulate and frame the issues across racial lines to construct and maintain them.

The multiracial and ethnic suburbs that I examined in this book offer important insights on constructing cross-racial coalitions by transcending traditional racial fault lines around the common interests that drew many of these racial groups to the suburbs in the first place. The resonating issues where common interests can be found across racial lines include public schools, reduced crime, and a sense of community, which is often associated with the suburbs and urban flight. Economic stratification is less likely in the suburbs than in larger cities, which facilitates the potential of common interests around salient issues. Leadership must therefore identify and articulate the issues within the respective communities to develop the common bonds across racial lines in racially diverse suburbs.

Despite these common interests around salient issues, the issue of race can still be a threat to forming multiracial coalitions by reinforcing zero-sum-game politics, as seen with the emergence of tipping point politics. It is therefore imperative for Asian American community leaders and candidates to reinforce consistently and proactively that these demographic and political shifts are not an attempt at racial group aggrandizement of political power, but an attempt to reflect and to incorporate the changing face of each suburb's constituencies so that all may be included in its democratic processes. Due to these complex dynamics, the Asian American–influenced suburb may likely provide the answer to one of the most pressing political questions of the twenty-first century: what racial groups will work together and on which issues?

Epilogue: And the Beat Goes On

Suburban transformations and political action in Asian-influenced suburbs are a national phenomenon, taking shape at different stages throughout major regions of the continental United States. Over the past decade, each passing election cycle has brought new examples of the suburbanization of Asian American politics as Asian American candidates emerge to break the glass ceiling of political representation while confronting the many challenges of addressing racial diversity. A vivid example is the medium-sized suburb of Edison, New Jersey. The township of Edison is nicknamed "The Birthplace of the Technological Revolution," after the city's namesake, Thomas Edison, who perfected the incandescent lightbulb in his local laboratory. Over the past five election cycles, the city has undergone another form of revolution, one that is political and reflects the city's changing demographics.

According to the suburban typologies in this book, Edison would be classified as an Emergent I suburb. It has over 100,000 total residents and is located in Middlesex County, approximately thirty minutes from New York City. The 2000 US Census found that whites made up 55 percent of the population, followed by Asian Indians at 17 percent, African Americans at 7 percent, Latinos and Chinese Americans at 6 percent each, and Korean Americans at approximately 2 percent (City-Data.com 2009). With these demographic shifts have come political shifts. According to the Middlesex County Board of Elections, the registered voters of Edison include 6,321 Asian Indians, 3,029 Chinese Americans, 3,190 Hispanics, and 592 Korean Americans. With a developing voter base, heightened mobilization efforts have followed, the end result being sustained elected representation over the past decade as three Asian Americans have been elected to its local government. Among these three Asian American elected officials are two Asian Indians: Parag Patel, who became the first Asian Indian elected to the Edison City Council in 2001 and subsequently its first president, and Sudhanshu Prasad, who was elected to the city council in 2008. The third Asian American elected official in Edison is Jun Choi, who at the age of thirty-three became the first Korean American mayor of any continental United States city, in 2005.

Jun Choi's pathway to the mayor's office in Edison was not planned. Growing up in Edison after his family immigrated from South Korea when he was three years old, Choi dreamed of becoming an astronaut and nearly followed this dream after studying aeronautical engineering at the Massachusetts Institute of Technology. But he changed his career goals after deciding that politics could bring about more direct improvements in society. He eventually earned a master's degree in public policy and administration at Columbia University. Choi then served in the New Jersey Department of Education and worked in the White House Budget Office in the capacity of a management consultant. His decision to run for the mayor's office was galvanized in 2003 when the incumbent Democratic mayor, George A. Spadoro, who was targeted with corruption investigations, announced that he was running for reelection in 2005. When no candidates from the Democratic Party emerged to challenge the embattled Spadoro, Choi decided to run by focusing on a progressive new Democrat platform that emphasized good government, labor interests, anticronyism, and incorporating Edison's emerging Asian immigrant population.

Jun Choi's 2005 mayoral campaign was propelled into the public limelight as a result of being the target of racial attacks in the local radio media. In April 2005, the two hosts, Craig Carton and Ray Rossi, of a 101.5 FM radio program, *Jersey Guys,* made racially derogatory comments about Choi's campaign specifically, and the Asian American community generally. According to a transcript of one broadcast, Carton referred to Asian Americans as "fringe people," "Orientals," and mocked them with a stereotypical "Ching, chong, ching, chong" comment. Carton then stated: "No specific minority or foreign group should ever dictate the outcome of the election. I don't care if the Chinese population in Edison has quadrupled in the last year, Chinese should never dictate the outcome of an American election, Americans should" (L. Lin 2005, 1). These comments are symptomatic of a general perception that goes back to the first stage of Asian American politics in the early twentieth century, as discussed in Chapter 3, in which Asian Americans, immigrant and US born, perceived as permanent aliens who are less than "American" when compared to whites, and their recent political mobilization efforts are guided only by racial or ethnic self-interests, not community-wide interests. This perception has underlay the tipping point politics that I discussed throughout this book and one that I dispel. If Asian Americans are becoming a significant part of these suburbs, then arguably they should be incorporated into all aspects of the local decisionmaking process for a true pluralistic democracy.

The fallout from the *Jersey Guys* program mobilized New York City Asian American civil rights groups, the Asian ethnic media, and new Asian American voters in Edison around Choi's inaugural mayoral campaign. Choi's reaction to the anti-Asian remarks was the following: "I can't be distracted by it. [The incident] is another reason why Asian Americans need to continue to be politically active" (L. Lin 2005, 1). The campaign emphasis of Asian American political incorporation is clearly articulated by Choi:

> The administration of the township is not open, inclusive and not responsive to Asian American residents. We need to empower the Asian American community by working closely with all the residents. . . . I do not represent merely Asian Americans but I do present a face of [the city's] changing face. (Swami 2005, 1)

Choi's emphasis on a two-tiered campaign strategy focused on building a panethnic coalition, with a guiding ideology of Asian American group incorporation, while simultaneously building a cross-racial alliance with white voters who wanted reform of the Democratic political machine.

Jun Choi won the June 2005 primary by a 56 to 44 percent vote, due to no single issue, but by focusing on reforming the Democratic Party and incorporating Edison's new Asian immigrants into the political process. With regard to the latter issue, Choi's campaign strategy to target the emerging Asian ethnic media by buying campaign advertisements in different languages paid great dividends. For example, Choi reached out to the emerging Asian Indian immigrant population by distributing "Choi for Mayor" flyers written in Gujarati, Hindi, and Punjab (Swami 2005).

According to exit poll data from the Asian American Legal Defense and Education Fund (AALDEF), which monitored the election precincts during the 2005 mayoral election because of the above-mentioned anti-Asian remarks, nearly 10 percent of the respondents were first-time Asian voters. These new Asian voters likely played a key role in Choi's 12 percent margin of victory during the primary election (AALDEF 2006).

In 2009, Jun Choi's reelection bid succumbed to the power struggle between Edison's political reformers and the established Democratic political machine. In the June Democratic primary, Choi faced Edison City Council member Antonia Ricigliano, who was endorsed by the Edison and Middlesex County Democratic committees. Ricigliano received 6,582 votes to Choi's 6,204, a narrow 378-vote victory. Many political observers felt that the city's struggling economy was the primary reason for Choi's unsuccessful reelection campaign.

While Choi's defeat in 2009 may be seen as a setback for Asian American political incorporation efforts in Edison, his candidacy symbolizes emerging Asian-influenced suburbs today with regard to the political optimism and opportunities that they provide for their newest residents. The size of their population is not as important as the continued development of key loci such as community-based organizations and the ethnic media. Win or lose, the electoral process is what all racial groups must go through to attain political incorporation at any level. Indeed, for the first time in American politics in the continental United States, Asian American candidates find themselves at the center of local political mobilization efforts. And multiracial coalitions around their respective campaigns have captured the hopes and optimism of Asian Americans, immigrant and US born, in reinforcing the importance of the participation of multiracial voices to reflect a true pluralistic democracy. This challenge is captured in an eloquent essay by then-mayor Choi for the New Jersey State League of Municipalities, entitled "Managing a Community's Diversity." Choi writes:

> As municipal leaders, we have a responsibility to serve all our residents and to look out for the safety and welfare of an increasingly diverse constituency. Our ability to bring together diverse coalitions and delicately navigate the multi-ethnic and multi-cultural makeup of our communities is critically important. A diverse community presents challenges, but it also presents unique opportunities that bring energy, dynamism and hope to a community. We are essentially the same. How we express ourselves may be different across cultures; however, people of all backgrounds basically want the same things. We want a better life for ourselves and our families. We want to be treated with respect and fairness. We want safe streets, good schools, lower property taxes, clean neighborhoods and we want to receive effective and efficient government services. . . . The changing demographic of America is inevitable. We hope through constant effort and equipped with the best practices available, we can find ways to not only live peacefully, but to enjoy each other's company and fulfill the promise of America that, indeed, all men and women are created equal. (Choi 2008, 1)

The incorporation of all immigrants is indeed a part of the American Dream and its democratic norms. A key component in the suburbs, as I have described it in this book, is whether the existing community members will be open to these groups or whether group resentment will spill over into the elections in the form of tipping point politics, as seen in Cupertino, California, and Sugar Land, Texas. Henry Cisneros, the first Latino mayor of a major US city, captures this dynamic when he writes:

> While this process has positive dimensions both for the nation and for the immigrants, for many communities as well as for many immigrant families, these dynamics pose serious difficulties. Long-established residents may not be willing or capable of accepting newcomers. . . . But despite the hardships and controversies, the importance of integrating immigrants into our future makes it a paramount national interest to understand the new geography of immigration, to make integration as painless as possible, and to generate positive results for all involved. (Cisneros 2008, ix)

Many Asian American candidates running for local elected positions in emerging gateway suburbs are seeking the same positive results for all constituents involved, not just those in their respective ethnic communities. In doing so, they seek to serve the evolving constituency in these transforming suburbs through public service in their respective local governments, as witnessed by those immigrants who came before them and, most likely, as will be witnessed by those who come after. By seeking greater representation for all those who define and make up their respective communities, a common and public good is served through the democratic incorporation of immigrants into local government. This was the impetus and the central goal of immigrant politics in large US cities during the twentieth century, and it is now rapidly taking shape in Asian American–influenced suburbs across the nation. Indeed, the beat goes on.

Note

1. This belief is clearly demonstrated in the 2005 San Jose City Council, District 7, election, in which Madison Nguyen was able to win the seat despite the presence of another Vietnamese American candidate, Linda Nguyen, running in the primary election. Both of them made it to the runoff election, ensuring the city's first Vietnamese American representative.

Acronyms

AAGEN	Asian American Government Executives Network
AALDEF	Asian American Legal Defense and Education Fund
ACE	Asian Coalition for Equality
APACA	Asian Pacific American Community Action
APALI	Asian Pacific American Leadership Institute
APASVDC	Asian Pacific American Silicon Valley Democratic Club
CAPAD	Coalition of Asian Pacific American Democrats
CARe	Cupertino Against Rezoning
CCBA	Chinese Consolidated Benevolent Association
CCC	Concerned Citizens of Cupertino
CISC	Chinese Information Service Center
ECAHMAA	Eau Claire Area Hmong Mutual Assistance Association
ESL	English as a second language
FLU	Filipino Labor Union
GAO	General Accounting Office
GOTV	Get Out the Vote
GVJCI	Gardena Valley Japanese Cultural Institute
LEAD	Leadership Empowerment and Development
MEDC	Minority Executive Directors Commission
NAACP	National Association for the Advancement of Colored People
NASA	National Aeronautics and Space Administration
NCAPA	Northwest Coalition of Asian Pacific Americans
OCA	Organization for Chinese Americans
OSU	Oriental Student Union
PAC	political action committee
PNAAPS	Pilot National Asian American Political Survey

PRWORA	Personal Responsibility Work Opportunity Reconciliation Act
SEIU	Service Employees International Union
SES	Senior Executive Service

References

AALDEF. 2006, June 1. "AALDEF Exit Poll Reveals Trends in Growing NJ Asian American Electorate." Available at http://aaldef.org/cgi-bin/mt/mt-search.cgi? IncludeBlogs=1&search=jun+choi&x=22&y=5 (accessed July 24, 2009).

American Community Survey. 2006. "Bellevue City, Washington." Available at http://factfinder.census.gov/servlet/ACSSAFFFacts?_event=&ActiveGeoDiv=ge oSelect&pctxt=fph&_lang=en&_sse=on&geo_id=16000US5305210&_state=04 000US53 (accessed August 5, 2010).

American FactFinder. 2000. "King County, Washington—Profile of General Demographic Characteristics: 2000." Available at http://factfinder.census.gov/servlet/ QTTable?_bm=n&_lang=en&qr_name=DEC_2000_SF1_U_DP1&ds_name=DE C_2000_SF1_U&geo_id=05000US53033 (accessed August 5, 2010).

Asian American Government Executives Network Website. 2009. "About Us." Available at http://www.aagen.org/Home/AboutUs/tabid/113/Default.aspx (accessed May 15, 2009).

Asian American Health Initiative. 2008. *Asian American Health Priorities: A Study of Montgomery County, MD*. Rockville, MD: Asian American Health Initiative.

Asian and Pacific Islander Community Directory: Los Angeles and Orange Counties, 10th ed. 2008. Los Angeles: UCLA Asian American Studies Center Press.

Bach, Ashley. 2006, August 19. "Bellevue Diversity Outpaces Seattle, County." *Seattle Times*. Available at http://seattletimes.nwsource.com/html/localnews/2003209866_ diversity19e.htm (accessed April 12, 2008).

Bagley, Clarence B. 1929. *History of King County*. Chicago: S. J. Clarke.

Barnes, Jessica S., and Claudette E. Bennett. 2002. "The Asian Population 2000: Census 2000 Brief." US Census Bureau. Available at http://www.census.gov/prod 2002pubs/c2kbr01-16.pdf (accessed August 4, 2010).

Barreto, Matt. 2007. "Si Se Puede! Latino Candidates and the Mobilization of Latino Voters." *American Political Science Review* 102 (3): 425–441.

Biggar, Hugh. 2006, July 26. "Changing Character: Chinese Language Speakers Are Leading the Way to Make Cupertino a Multilingual City." *Cupertino Courier,* 10.

Bolt, Kristen M., and John Cook. 2005, April 6. "A New Bellevue Rising: Big-Thinking Kemper Freeman Jr. Thinking Even Bigger." *Seattle Post-Intelligencer.* Available at http://seattlepi.nwsource.com/business/218982_kemper06.html (accessed May 1, 2008).

"Bonincontri Is a Boon for Bellevue." 2008, April 5. Editorial. *Northwest Asian Weekly.* Available at http://nwasianweekly.com/old/2008270015/editor20082715.htm (accessed April 13, 2008).

Broom, Jack. 2008, May 19. "A Walk Through Time: Early 1900s Hub for Immigrants Provides Glimpse into Vibrant History." *Seattle Times,* A1, A6.

Brown, P. L. 2004, January 3. "In One Suburb, Asian-Americans Gain a Firm Political Hold." *New York Times,* 1A.

Browning, Rufus P., Dale R. Marshall, and David H. Tabb. 1984. *Protest Is Not Enough: The Struggle of Blacks and Hispanics for Equality in City Politics.* Berkeley: University of California Press.

———. 2000. "Taken In or Just Taken? Political Incorporation of African Americans in Cities." In Richard A. Keiser and Katherine Underwood, eds., *Minority Politics at the Millennium.* New York: Garland, 131–156.

———. 2003. *Racial Politics in American Cities,* 3rd ed. New York: Longman Press.

Carter, Beverly K. 2008, May 7. "Bev's Burner: Some's Hot, Some's Not." *Fort Bend Star.* Available at http://www.fortbendstar.com/Archives/2008_2q/050708/burner 050708.htm (accessed May 10, 2008).

"CCC Gathers Signatures to Get Initiative on the City Ballot." 2004, July 27. *Cupertino Courier,* 19.

Chan, Sucheng. 1991. *Asian Americans: An Interpretive History.* Philadelphia, PA: Temple University Press.

Chang, Edward T. 2003. "America's First Multi-Ethnic Riots." In Don T. Nakanishi and James Lai, eds., *Asian American Politics: Law, Participation, and Policy.* Lanham, MD: Rowman & Littlefield, 431–440.

Che, I-Chun. 2003, August 13. "Bridging Cultural Barriers a Neighborhood at a Time." *Cupertino Courier.* Available at http://www.community-newspapers.com/archives/ cupertinocourier/20030813/cu-community1.shtml (accessed July 15, 2008).

Chen, Edward C. M., and Fred R. Von Der Mehden. 2009. "History of Houston's Chinatown." Available at http://www.chinatownconnection.com/houston_chinatown_ history.htm (accessed February 15, 2008).

Cho, Mindy. 1993, March 24. "Woo Says Liquor Stores Should Convert to Laundromats." *Korea Times,* 1.

Choi, Jun. 2008. "Managing Community Diversity." Available at http://www.njslom .org/magart_1008_pg32.html (accessed February 24, 2010).

Cisneros, Henry. 2008. "Foreword." In Audrey Singer, Susan Hardwick, and Caroline B. Brettell, eds., *Twenty-First Century Gateways.* Washington, DC: Brookings Institution, vii–x.

City of Cupertino Commissions. Available at http://www.cupertino.org/index.aspx? page=50 (accessed May 1, 2009).

City of Daly City. 2006. "Economic and Community Development." Available at http://www.dalycity.org/City_Hall/Departments/ECD.htm (accessed January 20, 2006).

City of Fitchburg. 2008. "About Fitchburg." Available at http://www.city.fitchburg.wi .us/home_pages/about_fitchburg.php (accessed August 13, 2008).

City of Sugar Land. 2008. "Sugar Land Boards and Commissions." Available at http:// www.sugarlandtx.gov/city_hall/boards_commission/index.asp (accessed April 2, 2008).

City-Data.com. 2009. "Edison, New Jersey." Available at http://www.city-data.com/ city/Edison-New-Jersey.html (accessed July 24, 2009).

CityLab. 2010. "Cupertino, CA." Available at http://citylab.news21.com/cities/11/ (accessed August 4, 2010).

Collet, Christian. 2005. "Bloc Voting, Polarization and the Panethnic Hypothesis: The Case of Little Saigon." *Journal of Politics* 67 (3): 907–933.

———. 2008. "Minority Candidates, Alternative Media, and Multiethnic America: Deracialization or Toggling?" *Perspectives on Politics* 6 (4): 707–728.

Concerned Citizens for Cupertino. 2008. "CCC Endorses Kris Wang."

"Conrad Lee: The New Face of Bellevue." 2007, December 22. Editorial. *Northwest Asian Weekly.* Available at http://nwasianweekly.com/old/200726052/editorial 2007252.htm (accessed April 12, 2008).

Corcoran, Katherine. 2004, January 25. "Valley Political Group Sets Sights Higher: Asian American Club Turns to State Race After Local Success." *San Jose Mercury News,* 1B, 4B.

County of Los Angeles Public Library. 2010. "Gardena: Frequently Asked Questions." Available at http://www.colapublib.org/history/gardena/faq.html (accessed August 4, 2010).

"Cupertino City Council Election: Kris Wang Establishes Web Site, Emphasizes That in the Future She Will Represent All Residents." 2003, August 7. *World Journal.*

Cupertino Courier. 2007. "Letters & Opinions." Available at http://mytown.mercurynews .com/archives/cupertinocourier/20080116/letters_opinions1.shtml (accessed March 20, 2008).

———. 2008. "Letters & Opinions." Available at http://mytown.mercurynews.com/ archives/cupertinocourier/20080116/letters_opinions1.shtml (accessed July 12, 2009).

Daniels, Roger. 1971. *Concentration Campus USA: Japanese Americans and World War II.* New York: Holt, Rinehart & Winston.

"Daphne Chou." 2010. Available at http://www.daphnechou.com (accessed August 5, 2010).

Davis, Jessica, and Oscar Gandy. 1999. "Racial Identity and Media Orientations: Exploring the Nature of Constraint." *Journal of Black Studies* 29: 367–397.

Dawson, Michael. 1994. *Behind the Mule: Race and Class in African American Politics.* Princeton, NJ: Princeton University Press.

Do, Julian. 2004, February 13. "Little Saigon TV." New American Media. Available at http://news.newamericamedia.org/news/view_article.html?article_id=d12f6b721 0c64c13f6160b8ac3acbd8d (accessed February 11, 2010).

Doherty, Steven. 2007. "Political Behavior and Candidate Emergence in the Hmong-American Community." *Hmong Studies Journal* 8: 1–35.

Douglass, Enid H. 1989. "Oral History Interview with Paul T. Bannai." Sacramento: California State Archives State Government Oral History Program.

Eau Claire Hmong Mutual Assistance Association and Partnership for Strong Hmong Families. 2006. "Hmong Leaders for Eau Claire Report." Eau Claire, WI: Eau Claire Hmong Mutual Assistance Association.

"Election 2006." 2006, November 5. *Washington Post.* Available at http://www .washingtonpost.com/wpsrv/metro/elections/2006/results/general_montgomery .html.

Espiritu, Yen Le. 1992. *Asian American Panethnicity.* Philadelphia, PA: Temple University Press.

Espiritu, Yen Le, and Paul M. Ong. 1994. Class Constraints on Racial Solidarity Among Asian Americans. In Paul M. Ong, Edna Bonacich, and Lucie Cheng, eds., *The New Asian Immigration in Los Angeles and Global Restructuring.* Philadelphia, PA: Temple University Press, 395–422.

Estrella, Cicero. 2003, December 20. "Daly City Among Top 5 in Nation for Foreign-Born." *San Francisco Chronicle*, A17.

Flanigan, William H., and Nancy Zingale. 1998. *Political Behavior of the American Electorate*. Washington, DC: CQ Press.

Fong, Joe Chung. 2003. *Complementary Education and Culture in the Global/Local Chinese Community*. San Francisco, CA: China Books and Periodicals.

Fong, Timothy. 1994. *The First Suburban Chinatown: The Remaking of Monterey Park, California*. Philadelphia, PA: Temple University Press.

———. 2002. *The Contemporary Asian American Experience: Beyond the Model Minority*. Upper Saddle River, NJ: Prentice Hall.

Frasure, Lorrie. 2007. "Beyond the Myth of the White Middle-Class: Immigrant and Ethnic Minority Settlement in Suburban America." *National Political Science Review* 11: 65–86.

Fuchs, Lawrence. 1990. *The American Kaleidoscope: Race, Ethnicity and Civic Culture*. Hanover, NH: University Press of New England.

Fujiwara, Lynn H. 2005. "Mothers Without Citizenship: Asian Immigrants and Refugees Negotiate Poverty and Hunger After Welfare Reform." *Race, Gender, and Class* 12 (2): 120–140.

Gibson, Campbell. 1998. "Population of the 100 Largest Cities and Other Urban Places in the United States: 1790–1990." Population Division Working Paper No. 27. Washington, DC: US Census Bureau.

Goodman, Alison. 1989, August 27. "Gardena Law Wins Praise, Campaign Financing Rules Among Best in the U.S., Panel Says." *Los Angeles Times*, 6.

Guerra, Fernando. 1991. "The Emergence of Ethnic Officeholders in California." In Byran O. Jackson and Michael B. Preston, eds., *Racial and Ethnic Politics in California*. Berkeley, CA: Institute of Governmental Studies, 117–132.

———. 2004. "Center for the Study of Los Angeles Handout." Presented at the American Political Science Association meeting in Chicago, IL, September 2–5.

Henry, Charles P. 1994. "Urban Politics and Incorporation: The Case of Blacks, Latinos, and Asians in Three Cities." In James Jennings, ed., *Blacks, Latinos, and Asians in Urban America: Status and Prospects for Politics and Activism*. Westport, CT: Praeger, 17–28.

Hipple, Annaka. 2003. "Finding a Voice: Latinos on Seattle's Eastside Find Strength in Numbers." *Colors NW Magazine*. Available at http://www.annikahipple.com/resources/Colors+NW.doc (accessed June 21, 2008).

Hochschild, Jennifer L., and Reuel R. Rogers. 2001. "Race Relations in a Diversifying Nation." In James Jackson, ed., *New Directions: African Americans in a Diversifying Nation*. Washington, DC: National Policy Association, 45–85.

Hosley Stewart, D. J. 2003, May 27. "Some See Cupertino Official's Remarks on Naming City Race-Based." *San Jose Mercury News*, A1.

Hua, Vanessa, and Mathew B. Stannard. 2007, December 2. "Asian Americans Flex Political Muscle in Wider Bay Area." *San Francisco Chronicle*. Available at http://www.sfgate.com/cgi-bin/article.cgi?f=/c/a/2007/12/02/mnustckrf.dtl (accessed March 12, 2008).

Hwang, Suein. 2005, November 19. "The New White Flight." *Wall Street Journal*, A1.

Jackson, Byran O. 1991. "Racial and Ethnic Voting Cleavages in Los Angeles Politics." In Byran O. Jackson and Michael B. Preston, eds., *Racial and Ethnic Politics in California*, vol. 1. Berkeley, CA: Institute of Governmental Studies Press, 193–220.

Jones-Correa, Michael. 2004. "Racial and Ethnic Diversity and the Politics of Education in Suburbia." Paper presented at the American Political Science Association meeting in Chicago, IL, September 2. Available at http://www.allacademic.com/ meta/p60553_index.html (accessed May 26, 2009).

Kang, K. Connie. 2000, October 30. "Indo-Americans Begin to Flex Political Muscle." *Los Angeles Times,* A3, A30.

Kelly, Kimiko. 2010. "Demographic Overview: Diverse, Growing, and Ever-Changing." In Edith Wen-Chu Chen and Grace Y. Yoo, eds., *Encyclopedia of Asian American Issues Today,* vol. 1. Santa Barbara, CA: ABC-CLIO, 3–15.

Kilpatrick, Doris. 1975. *Around the World in Fitchburg,* vol. 2. Fitchburg, MA: Fitchburg Historical Society.

Kwong, Peter. 1996. *The New Chinatown.* New York: Hill and Wang.

Lai, James S. 2000a. "Asian Americans and the Panethnic Question." In Richard A. Keiser and Katherine Underwood, eds., *Minority Politics at the Millennium.* New York: Garland, 157–178.

———. 2000b. "Beyond Voting: The Recruitment of Asian Pacific Americans and Their Impact on Group Electoral Mobilization." PhD dissertation, University of Southern California.

Lai, James S., and Kim Geron. 2006. "When Asian Americans Run: The Suburban and Urban Dimensions of Asian American Candidates in California Local Politics." *California Politics and Policy* 10 (1): 62–88.

Lai, James S. and Don T. Nakanishi, eds. 2007. *National Asian Pacific American Political Almanac.* Los Angeles, CA: UCLA Asian American Studies Press.

Lang, Robert E., and Thomas W. Sanchez. 2006. "The New Metro Politics: Interpreting Recent Presidential Elections Using a County-Based Regional Typology." Metropolitan Institute 2006 Election Brief. Blacksburg: Virginia Polytechnic Institute and State University.

"Lawyer Tran Thai Van to Travel to New York—Visits with Vietnamese Community, Stirs up Support." 2004, July 8. *Viet Bao Daily,* 1.

"Lawyer Van Tran Wins Primary, One Step Closer to Making History." 2004, March 3. *Viet Bao Daily,* 1.

Lee, Eleanor. 2008, March 31. "Asian American Female Wins Bellevue City Council Seat." *Northwest Asian Weekly.* Available at http://www.nwasianweekly.com/ 2008270014/council20082714.htm (accessed June 2008).

Lee, Rose H. 1949. "The Decline of Chinatowns in the United States." *American Journal of Sociology* 54 (March): 422–432.

Lewis, Paul, and Karthick Ramakrishnan. 2004. "Open Arms? The Receptivity of Cities and Local Officials to Immigrants and Their Concerns." Paper presented at the American Political Science Association meeting in Chicago, IL, September 3.

Li, Wei. 1998a. "Anatomy of a New Ethnic Settlement: The Chinese Ethnoburb in Los Angeles." *Urban Studies* 35 (3): 479–501.

———. 1998b. "Ethnoburb Versus Chinatown: Two Types of Urban Ethnic Communities in Los Angeles." Cybergeo No. 7. Available at www.cybergeo.presse.fr/ culture/weili/wili.htm (accessed March 23, 2008).

Li, Wei, and Emily Skop. 2004. "Enclaves, Ethnoburbs, and New Patterns of Settlement Among Asian Immigrants." In Min Zhou and James V. Gatewood, eds., *Contemporary Asian America: A Multidisciplinary Reader,* 2nd ed. New York: NYU Press, 222–236.

Lien, Pei-te. 1997. *The Political Participation of Asian Americans: Voting Behavior in Southern California.* New York: Garland.

———. 2002. "Public Resistance Toward Electing Asian Americans in Southern California." *Journal of Asian American Studies* 5 (1): 51–72.

Lien, Pei-te, Margaret Conway, Taeku Lee, and Janelle Wong. 2001. "The Pilot Asian American Political Survey: Summary Report." In James S. Lai and Don T. Nakanishi, eds., *The National Asian Pacific American Political Almanac*. Los Angeles, CA: Asian American Studies Center Press, 80–95.

Lien, Pei-te, Margaret Conway, and Janelle Wong. 2004. *The Politics of Asian Americans: Diversity and Community*. New York: Routledge Press.

Lin, Lynda. 2005. "N.J. Radio Station Hosts Accused of Hate, Anti-Asian Sentiment." *Pacific Citizen*. Available at http://www.imdiversity.com/Villages/Asian/arts_culture_media/pc_jersey_boys_0505.asp (accessed February 3, 2010).

Lin, Sam Chu, and Bob Galbraith. 1998, June 4–10. "Fong Wins First Round: What His Victory Means for Boxer, for Asian Americans, for GOP." *AsianWeek*, p. 1.

Liu, Michael, Thao Tran, and Paul Watanabe. 2007. "Far from the Commonwealth: A Report on Low-Income Asian Americans in Massachusetts." Boston: Institute for Asian American Studies, University of Massachusetts at Boston.

Locke, Gary. 1997, January 15. "A Hundred Year Journey: From Houseboy to the Governor's Mansion." Available at http://www.digitalarchives.wa.gov/governorlocke/speeches/speech-view.asp?SpeechSeq=107 (accessed May 1, 2008).

Long, Katherine. 2010, June 14. "5 Bellevue High Schools on *Newsweek's* Top 100 List." *Seattle Times*. Available at http://seattletimes.nwsource.com/html/localnews/2012115066_newsweeklist15m.html (accessed August 5, 2010).

Louie, Steve, and Glenn Omatsu. 2001. *Asian Americans: The Movement and the Moment*. Los Angeles: UCLA American Studies Center Press.

Lu, Crystal. 2008, January 30. "Housing and Race Issues Are Discussed at Forum." *Cupertino Courier*. Available at http://www.community-newspapers.com/archives/cupertinocourier/20080130/news5.shmtl (accessed June 10, 2008).

Lyman, Stanford. 1970. *The Asian in the West*. Reno: University of Nevada Press.

Maki, Mitch, and Harry Kitano. 1999. *Achieving the Impossible Dream: How Japanese Americans Obtained Redress*. Urbana: University of Illinois Press.

Mangaliman, Jessie. 2006, December 28. "Asian Americans Leapfrog into Politics: Success Shows Immigrants Blending into American Life Faster, Experts Say." *San Jose Mercury News*, A1.

Mansbridge, Jane. 1999. "Should Blacks Represent Blacks and Women Represent Women? A Contingent 'Yes.'" *Journal of Politics* 61 (3): 628–657.

Marable, Manning. 1994. "Building Coalitions Among Communities of Color: Beyond Racial Identity Politics." In James Jennings, ed., *Blacks, Latinos, and Asians in Urban America*. Westport, CT: Praeger, 29–44.

Massey, Douglas S. 2008. *New Faces in New Places: The Changing Geography of American Immigration*. New York: Russell Sage Foundation.

Mazza, Sandy. 2009, February 27. "Gardena Mayor Pulls in $130,000 for Uncontested Race." *Daily Breeze*. Available at http://www.dailybreeze.com/ci_11805709 (accessed February 25, 2010).

McClain, Charles J. 1994. *In Search of Equality: The Chinese Struggle Against Discrimination in Nineteenth-Century America*. Berkeley: University of California Press.

McClain, Paula D., and John A. Garcia. 1993. "Expanding Disciplinary Boundaries: Black, Latino, and Racial Minority Group Politics in Political Science." In Ada W. Finifter, ed., *Political Science: The State of the Discipline*, vol. II. Washington, DC: American Political Science Association.

McClain, Paula D., and Joseph Stewart Jr. 2006. *Can We All Get Along? Racial and Ethnic Minorities in American Politics*, 4th ed. Boulder, CO: Westview Press.

McCormick, Joseph, and Chuck E. Jones. 1993. "The Conceptualization of Deracialization: Thinking Through the Dilemma." In Georgia A. Parsons, ed., *Dilemmas of Black Politics*. New York: HarperCollins, 66–84.

McLeod, Ramon G., and Maria Alicia Gaura. 1998, June 5. "Prop. 227 Got Few Latino Votes." *San Francisco Chronicle.* Available at http://www.sfgate.com/cgi-bin/ article.cgi?file=/chronicle/archive/1998/06/05/mn101615.dtl (accessed May 12, 2009).

Metz, David Haywood, and Katherine Tate. 1995. "The Color of Urban Campaigns." In Paul E. Petterson, ed., *Classifying by Race.* Princeton, NJ: Princeton University Press, 262–277.

Miller, Arthur H., Patricia Gurin, Gerald Gurin, and Oksana Malanchuk. 1981. "Group Consciousness and Political Participation." *American Journal of Political Science* 25 (3): 495–511.

Miller, Vincent. 2004. "Mobile Chinatowns: The Future of Community in a Global Space of Flows." *Journal of Social Issues* 2 (1). Available at http://www.whb.co.uk/ socialissues/vol2vm.htm (accessed July 1, 2008).

Minority Executive Directors Coalition. 2009. "Our History." Available at http://www .medcofkc.org/about_history.html (accessed May 21, 2009).

Molina, Joshua. 2008a, March 3. "2,500 Voices Call for 'Little Saigon.'" *San Jose Mercury News,* 1A, 5A.

———. 2008b, March 4. "San Jose City Council Again Shoots Down 'Little Saigon.'" *San Jose Mercury News.* Available at http://origin.mercurynews.com/valley/ci_ 8459305 (accessed July 29, 2008).

———. 2008c, March 31. "Naming Debate Casts Shadow." *San Jose Mercury News,* 1B, 2B.

Montgomery County, Maryland. 2009. "About Montgomery County." Available at http:// www.montgomerycountymd.gov/mcgtmpl.asp?url=/content/MCGinfo/county/ AboutCnty.asp (accessed May 2, 2009).

Montgomery County Democratic Central Committee. 2009. "CAPAD-MD." Available at http://www.mcdcc.org/ht/d/sp/i/705834/pid/705834 (accessed May 10, 2009).

Montgomery County Department of Parks and Planning. 2000. *Southeastern Area and Montgomery County, Maryland 2000 Population, Race, and Housing Highlights.* Available at http://www.montgomeryplanning.org/viewer.shtm#http://www .montgomeryplanning.org/research/data_library/census2000/special_reports/ SEmapbullets.pdf (accessed August 5, 2010).

Montgomery County Historical Society. 1999. *Montgomery County, Maryland: Our History and Government.* Rockville, MD: Montgomery County Government Office of Public Information. Available at http://www.montgomerycountymd.gov/ Content/culture/images/history.pdf (accessed August 6, 2010).

Moore, Joan, and Henry Pachon. 1985. *Hispanics in the United States.* Englewood Cliffs, NJ: Prentice Hall.

Moskowitz, Eric, and Maria Sacchetti. 2007, November 7. "Wong Romps for Mayor in Fitchburg: Minority Hopefuls Defeated Elsewhere." *Boston Globe.* Available at http://www.boston.com/news/local/articles/2007/11/07/wong_romps_for_ mayor_in_fitchburg/ (accessed September 21, 2008).

Moua, Wameng. 2007, November 27. "Votes Don't Add Up for Pakou Hang." *Twin Cities Daily Planet.* Available at http://www.tcdailyplanet.net/article/2007/11/27/ votes-dont-add-pakou-hang.html (accessed September 29, 2008).

Moxley, R. Scott. 2010. "Quang Pham Leaves Race to Unseat Rep. Loretta Sanchez." *OC Weekly.* Available at http://blogs.ocweekly.com/navelgazing/breaking-news/ if-congresswoman-loretta-sanch/ (accessed August 4, 2010).

Nakanishi, Don T. 1991. "The Next Swing Vote? Asian Pacific Americans and California Politics." In Byran O. Jackson and Michael B. Preston, eds., *Racial and Ethnic Politics in California,* vol. 1. Berkeley, CA: Institute of Governmental Studies Press, 25–54.

―――. 1998. "When the Numbers Do Not Add Up: Asian Pacific Americans in California Politics." In M. B. Preston, B. E. Cain, and S. Bass, eds., *Racial and Ethnic Politics in California.* Berkeley, CA: Institute of Governmental Studies Press, 3–44.

Ng, Assunta. 2005, October 22. "What Do Eastside Asians Say About Conrad Lee?" *Northwest Asian Weekly,* 1.

"Ngoc Quang Chu 1st APA Elected to the Maryland Democratic Party." 2007, October 28. *Asian Fortune News.* Available at http://www.asianfortunenews.com/site/article_1107.php?article_id=74 (accessed August 20, 2008).

Nguonly, Esther. 2007, April 20. "Immigrant Populations Scatter into Outer Suburbs." *Capital News Service.* Available at http://www.journalism.umd.edu/cns/wire/2007-editions/04-April-editions/070420-Friday/ImmigrantMigration_CNS-UMCP.html (accessed March 20, 2008).

"North Potomac Maryland." 2009. Available at http://www.city-data.com/city/North-Potomac-Maryland.html (accessed June 10, 2009).

Oden, R. S. 1999. "Power Shift: A Sociological Study of the Political Incorporation of People of Color in Oakland, California, 1966–1996." PhD dissertation, University of California, Santa Cruz.

Office of the California Secretary of State. 2004. Van Tran for Assembly Campaign Finance Disclosure Forms.

Okamoto, Philip M. 1991. "Evolution of a Japanese American Enclave: Gardena California—A Case Study of Ethnic Community Change and Continuity." Master's thesis, UCLA Asian American Studies Center, Los Angeles.

Olive, B. 1982. "A Report on the Gardena Buddhist Church." Report submitted to the Los Angeles County Board of Supervisors. Los Angeles, CA: Los Angeles County Commission on Human Relations.

Oliver, J. Eric. 2001. *Democracy in Suburbia.* Princeton, NJ: Princeton University Press.

Oliver, J. Eric, and Shang E. Ha. 2007. "Vote Choice in Suburban Elections." *American Political Science Review* 101 (3): 373–391.

Olson, David. 2001, August 17. "Bellevue's Latinos Shaken out of Silence into Action." *Seattle Times.* Available at http://community.seattletimes.nwsource.com/archive/?date=20010817&slug=hispanic17m (accessed May 21, 2008).

Omatsu, Glenn. 2003. "The Four Prisons and the Movements of Liberation: Asian American Activism from the 1960s to the 1990s." In Don T. Nakanishi and James S. Lai, eds., *Asian American Politics: Law, Participation, and Policy.* Lanham, MD: Rowman and Littlefield, 135–162.

Omi, Michael, and Howard Winant. 1994. *Racial Formation Theory in the United States: From the 1960s to the 1990s.* New York: Routledge.

"1,000 Register to Vote for Lawyer Tran Thai Van." 2004, January 10. *Viet Bao Daily,* 1.

Ong, Nhu-Ngoc T., and David S. Meyer. 2008. "Vietnamese-American Protests in Orange County: 1975–2001." *Journal of Vietnamese Studies* 3 (1): 78–107.

Parenti, Michael. 1967. "Ethnic Politics and the Persistence of Ethnic Voting." *American Political Science Review* 61 (3): 717–726.

Park, Edward. 1996. "Asians Matter: Asian American Entrepreneurs in the High Technology Industry in Silicon Valley." In Bill Ong Hing and Ronald Lee, eds., *Reframing the Immigration Debate.* Los Angeles, CA: Leadership Education for Asian Pacifics and UCLA Asian American Studies Center Press, 155–178.

Pascual, F. D., Jr. 2004, October 19. "Electable FilAms." *Manila Mail.* Available at http://www.manilamail.com/archive/october2004/04oct19.htm (accessed January 2005).

"Patty Chi Can Do Nothing About the Suit Against the City of Cupertino Referenda. The Issue Is Not That She Opposes Vallco Mall Development but There Needs to Be an Overall Plan." 2006, June 20. *World Journal*, 1.

Pelissero, John P., David B. Holian, and Laura A. Tomaka. 2000. "Does Political Incorporation Matter? The Impact of Minority Mayors over Time." *Urban Affairs Review* 36 (1): 84–92.

Pfeifer, Mark E. 2003. "Hmong Americans." *Asian-Nation: The Landscape of Asian America*. Available at http://www.asian-nation.org/hmong.shtml (accessed May 23, 2008).

Pfeifer, Mark E., and Serge Lee. 2004. "Hmong Population, Demographic, Socioeconomic, and Educational Trends in the 2000 Census." In *Hmong Census Publication: Data and Analysis*. St. Paul, MN, and Washington, DC: Hmong Cultural and Resource Center and Hmong National Development, 3–11.

Pham, Quang X. 2005. *A Sense of Duty: My Father, My American Journey*. New York: Ballantine Books.

Pitkin, Hanna. 1967. *The Concept of Representation*. Berkeley: University of California Press.

"Residents Give Input on Proposed Eastside Light Rail." 2007, September 14. City of Bellevue, WA. Available at http://www.ci.bellevue.wa.us/5096.htm (accessed August 6, 2010).

Roberts, Sam. 2007, October 17. "In Shift, 40% of Immigrants Move Directly to Suburbs." *New York Times*. Available at http://www.nytimes.com/2007/10/17/us/17census.html (accessed July 20, 2008).

Rodriguez, Gregory. 1998, October 19. "Minority Leader: Matt Fong and the Asian American Voter." *New Republic*, 21–24.

Saito, Leland T. 1998. *Race and Politics: Asian Americans, Latinos, and Whites in a Los Angeles Suburb*. Urbana: University of Illinois Press.

San Juan, E., Jr. 1994. "The Predicament of Filipinos in the United States: Where Are You From? When Are You Going Back?" In Karin Aguilar-San Juan, ed., *The State of Asian America: Activism and Resistance in the 1990s*. Boston, MA: South End Press, 205–217.

Santa Clara County Registrar of Voters. 2008. "November 4, 2008 Primary Elections." Available at http://www.sccgov.org/elections/results/nov2008/#12 (accessed August 4, 2010).

Santana, Norberto, Jr. 2006, October 21. "Nguyen's Campaign Office Raided." *Orange County Register*. Available at http://www.ocregister.com/ocregister/homepage/abox/article_1326599.php (accessed January 21, 2008).

Seattle Civil Rights and Labor History Project. 2009. "Seattle's Asian American Movement." University of Washington. Available at http://depts.washington.edu/civilr/aa_intro.htm (accessed June 19, 2009).

Sethe, Harlan. 2005, September 28. "Cupertino Schools' Reputation Hit the International Scene in the 1980s." *Cupertino Courier*. Available at http://www.community-newspapers.com/archives/cupertinocourier/20050928/cu-cover1.shtml (accessed March 10, 2006).

"700 People from the North Fundraise for Tran Thai Van." 2004, August 30. *Viet Bao Daily*, 1.

Shinagawa, Larry H. 2008. *A Portrait of Chinese Americans*. College Park: Asian American Studies Program, University of Maryland. Available at http://www.aast.umd.edu/ocaportrait.html (accessed June 16, 2009).

Singer, Audrey, Susan W. Hardwick, and Caroline B. Brettell. 2008. *Twenty-First Century Gateways: Immigrant Incorporation in Suburban America*. Washington, DC: Brookings Institution.

Smartvoter. 2007. "Councilmember; City of Cupertino Election Information; November 6, 2007." Available at http://www.smartvoter.org/2007/11/06/ca/scl/race/5030/ (accessed August 1, 2010).

———. 2009. "Measure: Recall Election in San Jose." Available at http://www.smartvoter .org/2009/03/03/ca/scl/meas/_/ (accessed August 4, 2010).

Smith, Robert C. 1996. *Why We Have No Leaders: African Americans in the Post–Civil Rights Era.* Albany, NY: SUNY Press.

Solomon, Cara. 2003, July 31. "Changes to ESL Program Protested in Bellevue." *Seattle Times.* Available at http://community.seattletimes.nwsource.com/archive/?date=20030731&slug=esl31e (accessed June 12, 2008).

Sonenshein, Raphael. 1993. *Politics in Black and White: Race and Power in Los Angeles.* Princeton, NJ: Princeton University Press.

———. 1997. "Post Incorporation Politics in Los Angeles." In Rufus P. Browning, Dale R. Marshall, and David H. Tabb, eds., *Racial Politics in American Cities.* New York: Longman Press, 41–64.

———. 2005, February 28. "Do Asian Americans Count in L.A.?" *Los Angeles Times,* B9.

Sonenshein, Raphael J., and Mark Drayse. 2005. "Urban Electoral Coalitions in an Age of Immigration: A Spatial Analysis of Voting for the Latino Candidate in Two Los Angeles Mayoral Elections." Paper presented at the American Political Science Association meeting in Washington, DC. Available at http://www.allacademic .com/meta/p41229_index.html (accessed January 14, 2009).

Starks, Robert T., and Michael B. Preston. 1990. "Harold Washington and the Politics of Reform in Chicago, 1983–1987." In Rufus P. Browning, Dale R. Marshall, and David H. Tabb, eds., *Racial Politics in American Cities.* New York: Longman Press, 88–107.

Stinebaker, Joe, and Lori Rodriguez. 2004, November 6. "Minority Tackles Political Mainstream: Asian-Americans Are Changing Face of Area Elections." *Houston Chronicle.* Available at http://www.chron.com/disp/story.mpl/metropolitan/2886724.html (accessed August 6, 2010).

Stone, Clarence. 1989. *Regime Politics: Governing Atlanta, 1946–1988.* Lawrence: University Press of Kansas.

"Sugar Land Annual Report." 2007. City Hall of Sugar Land, Texas. Available at http://www.sugarlandtx.gov/sugarland/publications/documents/Annual_07.pdf (accessed March 3, 2007).

Sugar Land City Secretary's Office. 2008a. "2008 Sugar Land Mayoral General Election Results."

———. 2008b. "2008 Sugar Land Mayoral Primary Election Results."

Swami, Prakaash M. 2005. "Hindi-Chini Bhai Bhai in New Jersey." UrbanIndian.com. Available at http://74.125.155.132/search?q=cache:WJYGN3nx3PYJ:www.the urbanindian.com/ur/default2.asp%3Factive_page_id%3D93+hindi-chini+bhai+bhai+in+New+Jersey&cd=1&hl=en&ct=clnk&gl=us (accessed February 24, 2010).

Swift, Mike. 2007, March 3. "Other Tongues Overtaking English as Language Spoken in Majority of Santa Clara County Homes." *San Jose Mercury News.* Available at http://www.mercurynews.com/valley/ci_7666999 (accessed May 20, 2007).

———. 2008, December 9. "Census Shows Cupertino, Milpitas Have Asian-Majority Populations," *San Jose Mercury.* Available at http://www.mercurynews.com/ci_11173026 (accessed August 10, 2008).

Tabafunda, James, and Eleanor Lee. 2008. January 12. "Cindy Ryu Elected as Mayor of Shoreline." *Northwest Asian Weekly.* Available at www.nwasianweekly.com/2008270019/asian20082719.htm (accessed May 23, 2008).

Tachibana, Judy. 1986. "California's Asians: Power from a Growing Population." *California Journal* (November): 534–543.

Takaki, Ronald. 1989. *Strangers from a Different Shore: A History of Asian Americans.* Boston, MA: Little, Brown.

Takash, Paula Cruz. 1999, July. "Remedying Racial and Ethnic Inequality in California Politics." California Policy Research Center Brief Series. Berkeley: University of California, Office of the President.

Tam-Cho, Wendy. 2002. "Tapping Motives and Dynamics Behind Campaign Contributions: Insights from the Asian American Case." *American Politics Research* 30 (4): 347–383.

Teixeira, Ruy. 2006, October. "The New Frontier: A New Study of Exurbia." Washington, DC: New Politics Institute.

Tran, My-Thuan. 2008, December 7. "Orange County's Vietnamese American Political Scene Comes of Age." *Los Angles Times.* Available at http://www.latimes.com/news/local/la-me-vietnamese7-2008dec07,0,2788416,print.story (accessed February 2, 2009).

Tran, My-Thuan, and Christian Berthelsen. 2008, December 7. "From Refugees to Political Players." *Los Angeles Times.* Available at http://articles.latimes.com/2008/dec/07/local/me-vietnamese7 (accessed March 1, 2008).

"Transcript: Illinois State Senate Candidate Barack Obama." 2004, July 27. *Washington Post.* Available at http://www.washingtonpost.com/wp-dyn/articles/A19751-2004Jul27.html (accessed July 28, 2009).

UCLA Asian American Studies Center. 1997. *Asian and Pacific Islander Community Directory: Los Angeles and Orange County.* Los Angeles: UCLA Asian American Studies Center Press.

———. 2006. "Statistical Portrait of Asian Americans." Available at http://www.aasc.ucla.edu/archives/2006censusportal.asp (accessed April 15, 2009).

———. 2008. *Asian and Pacific Islander Community Directory: Los Angeles and Orange County.* Los Angeles: UCLA Asian American Studies Center Press.

Uhlaner, Carole J., Bruce E. Cain, and D. Roderick Kiewiet. 1989. "Political Participation of Ethnic Minorities in the 1980s." *Political Behavior* 11 (3): 195–232.

University of Maryland, Baltimore County, National Center for the Study of Elections Campaign Finance Database. "Friends of Susan C. Lee Contributions Dataset."

University of Washington Library. 2010. "King County Snapshots." Available at http://content.lib.washington.edu/imls/kcsnapshots/sets/timeline-text.html (accessed August 5, 2010).

US Census. 2004. "2004 American Community Survey." Detailed tables, BO2001 and BO4006D. Washington, DC: US Census Bureau.

———. 2006a. "State and County Quick Facts: Monterey Park (city), California." Available at http://quickfacts.census.gov/qfd/states/06/0648914.html (accessed August 4, 2010).

———. 2006b. "State and County Quick Facts: Los Angeles (city), California." Available at http://quickfacts.census.gov/qfd/states/06/0644000.html (accessed August 4, 2010).

———. 2006c. "State and County Quick Facts: Cupertino (city), California." Available at http://quickfacts.census.gov/qfd/states/06/0617610.html (accessed August 4, 2010).

———. 2006d. "State and County Quick Facts: Orange County, California." Available at http://quickfacts.census.gov/qfd/states/06/06059.html (accessed August 4, 2010).

———. 2006e. "State and County Quick Facts: Westminster (city), California." Available at http://quickfacts.census.gov/qfd/states/06/0684550.html (accessed August 4, 2010).

————. 2006f. "State and County Quick Facts: Garden Grove (city), California." Available at http://quickfacts.census.gov/qfd/states/06/0629000.html (accessed August 4, 2010).

————. 2006g. "State and County Quick Facts: Gardena (city), California." Available at http://quickfacts.census.gov/qfd/states/06/0628168.html (accessed August 4, 2010).

————. 2006h. "State and County Quick Facts: Montgomery County, Maryland." Available at http://quickfacts.census.gov/qfd/states/24/24031.html (accessed August 4, 2010).

————. 2006i. "State and County Quick Facts: Sugar Land (city), Texas." Available at http://quickfacts.census.gov/qfd/states/48/4870808.html (accessed August 4, 2010).

————. 2006j. "State and County Quick Facts: Bellevue (city), Washington." Available at http://quickfacts.census.gov/qfd/states/53/5305210.html (accessed August 5, 2010).

————. 2006k. "State and County Quick Facts: Daly City (city), California." Available at http://quickfacts.census.gov/qfd/states/06/0617918.html (accessed August 5, 2010).

————. 2008. "Asian and Pacific Islander Populations." Available at http://www.census.gov/population/www/socdemo/race/api.html (accessed August 3, 2010).

US General Accounting Office. 2003. "Senior Executive Service: Enhanced Agency Efforts Needed to Improve Diversity as the Senior Corps Turns Over." Washington, DC: US General Accounting Office.

Ustinova, Anistasia. 2008, January 28. "Community Splits over San Jose District Name." *San Francisco Chronicle.* Available at http://www.sfgate.com/cgi-bin/article.cgi?f=/c/a/2008/01/28/BALJUL7B1.DTL&feed=rss.crime (accessed February 1, 2008).

Vergara, Benito. 2008. *Pinoy Capital: The Filipino Nation in Daly City.* Philadelphia, PA: Temple University Press.

Vo, Linda, and Mary Y. Danico. 2004. "The Formation of Post-Suburban Communities: Koreatown and Little Saigon, Orange County." *International Journal of Sociology and Social Policy* 24 (7–8): 15–45.

Wei, William. 1993. *The Asian American Movement.* Philadelphia, PA: Temple University Press.

Wolfinger, Raymond E., and Steven J. Rosenstone. 1980. *Who Votes?* New Haven, CT: Yale University Press.

Wong, Cecil. 2008, May 21. "Letter to Beverly Carter." *Fort Bend* (Texas) *Star.*

Wong, Janelle. 2006. *Democracy's Promise: Immigrants and American Civic Institutions.* Ann Arbor: University of Michigan Press.

Wu, Frank H. 2002. *Yellow: Race in America Beyond Black and White.* New York: Basic Books.

Yang, Kuo. 2001. "The Hmong in America: Twenty-Five Years After the U.S. Secret War in Laos." *Journal of Asian American Studies* 4 (2): 165–174.

Yu, Judy, and Grace T. Yuan. 2001. "Lessons Learned from the 'Locke for Governor' Campaign." In Gordon Chang, ed., *Asian Americans and Politics: Perspectives, Experiences, and Prospects.* Stanford, CA: Stanford University Press, 354–381.

Index